Palgrave Texts in Counselling and Psychotherapy

Series Editors
Arlene Vetere
Family Therapy and Systemic Practice
VID Specialized University
Oslo, UK

Rudi Dallos
Clinical Psychology
Plymouth University
Plymouth, UK

This series introduces readers to the theory and practice of counselling and psychotherapy across a wide range of topical issues. Ideal for both trainees and practitioners, the books will appeal to anyone wishing to use counselling and psychotherapeutic skills and will be particularly relevant to workers in health, education, social work and related settings. The books in this series emphasise an integrative orientation weaving together a variety of models including, psychodynamic, attachment, trauma, narrative and systemic ideas. The books are written in an accessible and readable style with a focus on practice. Each text offers theoretical background and guidance for practice, with creative use of clinical examples.

Arlene Vetere, Professor of Family Therapy and Systemic Practice at VID Specialized University, Oslo, Norway.

Rudi Dallos, Emeritus Professor, Dept. of Clinical Psychology, University of Plymouth, UK.

David Pocock

Expanding the Limits of Individual and Family Therapies

A Critical Realist Approach

palgrave
macmillan

David Pocock
Psychoanalytic Psychotherapist
and Systemic Family Therapist
Calne, Wiltshire, UK

ISSN 2662-9127 ISSN 2662-9135 (electronic)
Palgrave Texts in Counselling and Psychotherapy
ISBN 978-3-031-76308-3 ISBN 978-3-031-76309-0 (eBook)
https://doi.org/10.1007/978-3-031-76309-0

Cover credit: Jonathan Knowles

This Palgrave Macmillan imprint is published by the registered company Springer Nature Switzerland AG.
The registered company address is: Gewerbestrasse 11, 6330 Cham, Switzerland

To my family

Foreword

In this wonderful book, David Pocock provides an erudite in-depth consideration of the philosophical foundations of current methods of individual and systemic family therapy practice and how these permeate and influence psychotherapies. This book both takes the reader back to the rich discussions of the early years of family therapies, when some of the most significant writing focused on ontology and epistemology. Yet, it does so while incorporating the developments within psychotherapy and philosophy over the 75 years of clinical practice of relational psychotherapies.

As in the author's initial tale of the elephant, it is both understandable and tragic that we can be so limited in our views of psychotherapy. That 75 years of theorising, writing, and engaging in practice have produced so many brilliant formulations about family systems and individual functioning and strategies for enacting change, yet in so many approaches the scope narrows to focus on a very few aspects of human experience. Further, schools of psychotherapy have the tendency to rediscover and rename the same therapy ingredients, leaving not only real differences in how therapists think and what they do but also artificial ones that are a by-product of language. For example, reframing, working with cognitive distortions, and narrative externalizing all involve essentially the same concept, but the vocabulary separates. As Pocock points out, some training centres can be next door to each other but not influence one another.

Endless studies of psychotherapy and of systemic therapy have yet to show one bone fide therapy is better than another (Barkham et al., 2021; Wampold & Imel, 2015).[1] What we have are alternative ways of approaching human lives and human problems. Across those therapies, some aspects, such as those qualities referred to as "common factors" including therapist empathy and therapist-client alliance have universal importance (Sprenkle et al., 2009). This underlying common ground across therapies, coupled with the benefits of incorporating multiple lenses and methods, has led to the development of several integrative therapies (Lebow, 2014), which incorporate aspects of different schools of psychotherapy, as well as a frequent tendency for therapists as they become more experienced to become more integrative and pluralistic in their practice (Orlinsky & Ronnestad, 2005). This emerging pluralism and movement of psychotherapists towards their own personal integrations, consisting of what fits them and their clients best, represent positive developments.

Yet, therapies also need to be grounded in a coherent philosophical point of view. This now has become too often a lost aspect in the practice of psychotherapy as training emphasizes pragmatics and learning approaches to intervention. Pocock offers us the critical realist frame as the underpinning for a world which can allow for the differences in emphasis that come from different perspectives. This scaffolding can serve as the foundation for the work of most therapists. Pocock's discussion also can be a launch point for a thoughtful consideration of their position for those who look to a more radical stance as their anchor. What is essential here is to move therapists into such a dialogue about their work. Therapy is more than just a set of concepts and techniques, and Pocock provides a convincing argument for why critical realism

[1] Though it should be added in certain highly specialized situations a few therapies of choice do emerge.

should underlie today's practice. This is a book that stimulates thinking about our field and its underpinnings. It stimulated many conversations within myself and with others, and I certainly will refer to this book often.

Family Institute at Northwestern
and Northwestern University
Evanston, IL, USA

Jay Lebow

References

Barkham, M., Lutz, W., & Castonguay, L. G. (2021). *Bergin and Garfield's handbook of psychotherapy and behaviour change: 50th Anniversary Edition* (7th Ed.). Wiley.

Lebow, J. (2014). *Couple and family therapy: An integrative map of the territory.* American Psychological Association. https://doi.org/10.1037/14255-000

Orlinsky, D., & Ronnestad, M. (2005). *How psychotherapists develop: A study of therapeutic work and professional growth.* American Psychological Association. https://psycnet.apa.org/doi/10.1037/11157-000

Sprenkle, D., Davis, S., & Lebow, J. (2009). *Common factors in couple and family therapy: The overlooked foundation for effective practice.* Guilford Press.

Wampold, B., & Imel, Z. (2015). *The great psychotherapy debate: The evidence for what makes psychotherapy work* (2nd ed.). Routledge.

Acknowledgements

I had no intention of writing this book. So unlikely did that prospect seem that, five years ago, with some domestic encouragement, I recycled my lifetime collection of articles that (apparently) was taking up too much space. As we are about to discuss, events like writing a book are generated by combinations of influences; one such, being a tiny virus that swept the world leaving me as one of 400 million with a condition that has come to be known as Long Covid. All plans for retirement, and much else, were put on hold but, after a while, I found it was possible to read, and then write. With the encouragement of my old friend and collaborator, Jeremy Woodcock, I picked up a previously declined invitation from Arlene Vetere and Rudi Dallos, Series Editors, to write for Palgrave Macmillan's Counselling and Psychotherapy Series and, nine months later, here we are.

Along the way, many people have helped me, and I would like to thank them here. First, my wife, Gail Jenkins, who supported me throughout, closely read everything, and challenged my tendency to long multi-clause sentences and idiosyncratic punctuation. Second, to Series Editors, Arlene and Rudi; Commissioning Editor, Liam Inscoe-Jones; and Production Editor, Tikoji Rao Mega Rao for great support and wise suggestions. Third, to Jeremy Woodcock, Sebastian Kraemer, Arlene, and Rudi who closely read and commented on every chapter. Fourth, to

Carmel Flaskas, Anna-Clare Hillier, David Pilgrim, Heather Redington, Glenn Larner, Maggie Usher, Guy Baring, and Pat Crittenden for thoughtful comments on the proposal and / or some specific chapters. Fifth, to members of the UK Association for Family Therapy discussion forum, for allowing me a conversational space to rehearse and debate some of the main arguments in this book, and to help track down key papers. In no particular order, David Steare, Percy Aggett, Elizabeth Courtney, Charlotte Burke, Rory Worthington, Angela Shanly, Chris Burroughs, Lorraine Davies-Smith, Mark Hayward, John Hills, Hugh Palmer, Richard Clarke, Joe Cottrell-Boyce, Maria Nichterlein, Ged Smith, Bebe Speed, and Nick Drury. Sixth, to Sezer Fahri and Julie Berenstein, hosts of the wonderful *The Systemic Way* podcast series, for inviting me on to flesh-out some of the preliminary ideas for the book. Seventh, to respected colleagues Jay Lebow for the foreword, and Peter Rober and Susan Lord for the generous endorsements. Finally, to all individual clients, families, supervisees, and other teachers, supervisors, therapists, and authors who, knowingly or otherwise, have helped me develop this approach.

Note: I am happy to acknowledge *Context* as the first place of publication of an earlier version of Chap. 12.

Praise for *Expanding the Limits of Individual and Family Therapies*

"David Pocock has always been one of the most original thinkers in the field of family therapy. It may be hard to say if David Pocock is psychoanalytic or systemic. As he writes in the introduction, he is both and more.

In his new book, he wants to address both systemic therapists working with families, and psychoanalytic therapists working with individuals. Within the philosophical frame of critical realism, he invites us to entertain different ways of seeing in the service of the process of therapeutic change. He encourages us to think about our thinking and question the often-unspoken foundations of our models.

The book bridges philosophical reflection, theories about psychological development and family dynamics, and therapy in practice. Deeply grounded in a critical realist philosophy, Pocock considers therapeutic work with aggression, self-harm, and suicidality. He reflects on emotions and the therapeutic alliance. He considers triangles within a psychoanalytic frame, as well as in a systemic frame. And so on.

Although I am a family therapist, and I have never been trained in psychoanalysis, I feel strangely at home in Pocock's rich world of ideas. This is a book that can refine your thinking and inspire your practice. I warmly recommend it."

—Peter Rober, Professor in Clinical Psychology at the *Institute for Family and Sexuality Studies, Faculty of Medicine, University of Leuven, Belgium, and Director of the Centre of Marital and Family Therapy at UPC KU Leuven*

"David Pocock has created a masterful and comprehensive book that is a must-read for psychoanalysts, humanistic psychotherapists, and systemic therapists interested in expanding their collection of ideas and experiences in ways that might widen possibilities and enhance their thinking and their work. Using the frame of a critical realist philosophy, he artfully offers multiple theories and practices from which to draw in any given circumstance. He purports that rather than operating from defined disciplines and schools of thought, it is useful to entertain many different ideas and methods in our work. His language is easily accessible, as he travels back and forward in time, describing the evolution of theory and practice while artfully weaving together rich personal as well as clinical examples to illustrate his points.

Operating with the premise that all of life is systemic he spins out a kaleidoscope of theoretical viewpoints that capture many useful frames and methods helping us to be "well-enough resourced" to collaborate flexibly with our clients as we work with them towards their goals. He points out that all of human development occurs within the context of relationships and all therapies are relational therapies. Family systems are interpsychically peopled, and people's intrapsychic worlds are made up of the dynamics of their family systems. All fit together seamlessly; each intertwines with and informs the others as client(s) and clinician fully and intimately participate in the therapeutic process.

As Pocock says, "life is bigger than even the most systemically inclusive psychotherapy" and it is critically important to have access to complex theories and modalities in order to meet the infinite complexities of the lives of clients that we have the privilege to work with. Pocock's clarity, insight, scholarship, and the wisdom he has garnered over a long, joyful, and fulfilling career will be invaluable for psychoanalytic, humanistic, and systemic clinicians and, indeed, for all readers."

—Susan Lord, Ph.D., LICSW Clinical Associate Professor Emerita at the *University of New Hampshire, Taos Institute Associate, private practice in York, Maine, USA*

Contents

List of Figures

1

Introduction

It was six men of Indostan
To learning much inclined,
Who went to see the Elephant
(Though all of them were blind),
That each by observation
Might satisfy his mind.

This, by John Godfrey Saxe (1872), is the first verse of my favourite Victorian poem. It is a durable parable with origins in the Indian sub-continent; one version going back to the time of the Buddha around 500 BC. The poem gives us readers a super-human vantage point—a God's-eye view—since we know about elephants and, for the duration of the poem, we are not blind and can watch from our superior position and think about the errors.

The First approached the Elephant,
And happening to fall
Against his broad and sturdy side,
At once began to bawl:
"God bless me!—but the Elephant
Is very like a wall!"

D. Pocock, *Expanding the Limits of Individual and Family Therapies*, Palgrave Texts in Counselling and Psychotherapy, https://doi.org/10.1007/978-3-031-76309-0_1

How is the mind "satisfied" as Saxe puts it in verse one? Sense data from touching the "broad and sturdy side" is processed through the lens of prior experience stored in memory, delivering the answer "… very like a wall!". There is as yet, as Gregory Bateson (1972) describes, no "news of a difference"; the wall-like nature of the 'elephant' is already nearly known; nothing new to see here! But at this stage there is still a sliver of not-knowing; the elephant is not *yet* a wall but "very like" one. The conclusion is still provisional rather than certain.

The scene is now set for blind men two to six.

> The Second, feeling of the tusk,
> Cried: "Ho!—what have we here
> So very round and smooth and sharp?
> To me 'tis mighty clear
> This wonder of an Elephant
> Is very like a spear!"

The tusk evokes a mental spear for blind man number two; for the third, the trunk becomes a snake; a leg summons a tree to mind for the fourth; an ear represents a fan for the fifth man; and the sixth, grasping the swinging tail, naturally finds it "very like a rope". As with the first, they all find their external object "very like" their pre-conception but, by the penultimate verse, hopes for enduring uncertainty are gone as competition for the correct opinion sets in.

> And so these men of Indostan
> Disputed loud and long,
> Each in his own opinion
> Exceeding stiff and strong,
> Though each was partly in the right,
> And all were in the wrong!

Finally, us gods who have truly seen the holistic elephant are invited to join with Saxe and shake our heads wearily at these foolish religious zealots.

> So, oft in theologic wars
> The disputants, I ween,
> Rail on in utter ignorance

Of what each other mean,
And prate about an Elephant
Not one of them has seen!

The poem ends, and sadly we are returned to mortal status. Our eyes close again and we too have to grope around trying to make sense of a world beyond our ideas of it. We may or may not be religious, but we all know how to extract information to satisfy what is already in our minds and then take, hold, and defend that position.

I find it an instructive but gloomy piece so let's run a more hopeful counterfactual. What might have happened if each man had taken all six of the positions around the elephant? With two perspectives the likelihood of jumping to conclusions based on prior knowledge diminishes. The internal mental map is less easily conflated with the external unknown territory unless we force ourselves to select just one. And if we do choose one, we are at least aware that there *is* a choice. *So, with a double-description (*Bateson, 1979*) doubt and not-knowing become easier, allowing the return of curiosity and a loosening of grip on the correctness of our position.* With three perspectives other things become possible: an increasing appreciation of complexity, depth, and holism. And why stop at three?

This is a book about the value, for individual, couple, and family therapists, of taking multiple perspectives to expand the pool of thinking-resources that the therapist can bring to therapy in order to map more of the multi-causal, holistic nature of the encounter. It draws widely on systemic, psychoanalytic, and humanistic/integrative traditions as well as my experience gained during forty-five years as, first, a probation and divorce court welfare officer then—mostly in parallel—a systemic family therapist in a child and adolescent mental health service, and a psychoanalytic psychotherapist in independent practice with adults.

The approach here is pluralistic and layered. It makes no attempt at a grand integration since such attempts seem often to require some bending of dissimilar ideas to make them join together, much as an impatient jigsaw puzzler might force a fit between pieces where none naturally exists. The danger of a pluralistic approach becoming a rag-bag of eclectic fragments is countered by the containment and scaffolding offered by a relatively new philosophy of science—critical realism. Along the way I will argue that all therapists have both an epistemology (theory of knowledge) and ontology (theory of what there is to know) whether they are aware of them or not. I argue that it is better to have these foundational assumptions upfront and out in the open where they are more accountable and can be reflected upon and challenged (Willig, 2019), so critical realism comes in the next chapter.

If this widely drawn pluralism is already beginning to sound a bit strange, consider how we might naturally behave when encountering an interesting unfamiliar object. I well remember a decade or more ago seeing Michelangelo's statue of David in the *Galleria Accademia* on a family trip to Florence, Italy. Like everyone else we slowly circled the statue, taking multiple viewing positions, moving closer to focus on texture and detail, then back again to take in the whole, then the surroundings. Most read the historical blurb. Associations sprang to mind: the enormous feet amusingly reminded me of an old friend; the great height of the statue was disquieting, conflicting with my Christian Sunday school internal representation of David as a slight adolescent about to take down a giant. If this is David, how big is Goliath? And of course the name 'David' has a complex personal resonance. My point is that not a single visitor was content to place themselves square in front of the statue, look, and then leave.

Institutional Barriers

Given this everyday ordinariness of taking multiple perspectives, why might a holistic trans-disciplinary approach feel strange? I think it is because our resources for thinking—our theoretical vantage points—are encultured and institutionalised, separating out the ideas that might enable a wider systemic appreciation. In London, UK, the Institute for Family Therapy is within relatively easy walking distance of the Institute for Psychoanalysis, but I don't think many make the trip either way. Geographical distance is rarely the problem. I started my family therapy training in the same month that I began personal therapy with a Jungian analyst. The direct experience as a patient helped me to develop some immunity to the following kind of routine messaging from influential texts in systemic family therapy:

> [P]sychoanalysts who question the foundations of psychoanalytic theory are placed in professional peril. Under these conditions the client confronts a relatively closed system of understanding. It is not only that the client's own reality will eventually give way to the therapist's, but all other interpretations will also be excluded. To the extent that the therapist's narrative becomes the client's reality, and his or her options are guided accordingly, life options for the client are severely truncated. (Gergen & Kaye, 1992, p. 172)

Not all attacks are so direct but, whenever family therapy develops a new interest, psychoanalysis tends to be brought out of the shadows to take on the role of the denigrated other. With the early family therapy discovery of circularity, psychoanalysis was linear; an emphasis on relationships needed a psychoanalysis of isolated minds (ignoring all of object relations theory and relational psychoanalysis); the family systemic turn to meaning rather than structure required that psychoanalytic thinking be dogmatic truth; and an interest in strengths inevitably became paired to a psychoanalytic emphasis on deficit and pathology (Pocock, 1997). This is not to say that these criticisms never apply—I list several concerns of my own in Chap. 5 and throughout—but it is the wholesale othering of psychoanalysis that seems significant. These attacks tend to crop up as asides, making them harder to counter, and act as gentle reminders not to ever stray to the dark side. This is part of what Robert Pirsig (1991) refers to as the 'cultural immune system', defining the outer boundaries and discouraging people from straying. Ironically, the resources that could shed light on this defensive splitting and projective identification are to be found only in the very ideas and practices that are being reduced to straw men and rejected.

I'm speaking of the mainstream developments in family therapy. Fortunately during the period of my training in the late 80 s, some of my teachers—most notably Arnon Bentovim and Sebastian Kraemer—had brought across psychoanalytic traditions without undergoing a systemic Damascene conversion. The work of John Byng-Hall (e.g. 1995), bridging systems and attachment theory was a particular inspiration. Friends, colleagues, and writing buddies Jeremy Woodcock and Carmel Flaskas have been an enduring support and there have been others around the world who are willing to cross the borders of psychoanalysis and systems—all of whom derive their knowledge of psychoanalysis primarily from their experience as patients, not from propaganda (Flaskas & Pocock, 2009).

My adult psychoanalytic training began six years after I qualified as a family therapist. The only practical possibility for me was my local training which I knew to be rigorous but traditional and did not include the emerging tradition of relational psychoanalysis in which I was beginning to take an interest, although it did, at that point, include a small amount of teaching on Bowlby. I was undecided for a while whether but, having read *Emotional Understanding: Studies in Psychoanalytic Epistemology* by Donna Orange (1995), I felt that were enough points of connection available through private reading to make a reasonable bridge across to my development as a child and adolescent family therapist. I had a great stroke of luck in finding a training analyst (another London Jungian) who, despite never having read any relational texts, seemed to me entirely relational in her approach and who helped me enormously both personally and professionally.

The psychoanalytic world is bigger and more securely established and, while there continue to be internal tensions between its various traditions, there were no equivalent attacks on the systemic psychotherapy world. Cognitive behavioural therapy was the main threat in the UK, largely because, being briefer, more evidence-based, and cheaper, it was commanding Government interest and funding, hastening the retreat of psychoanalytic therapists and psychoanalytic thinking from the NHS.

Fast-forward several years to a time when I both chaired the psychoanalytic training committee of my local membership organisation and taught the Independents section of the curriculum. I included several Relational Psychoanalysis papers under a section entitled Contemporary Independents. These seem to be valued by trainees, but after a few years I was no longer asked to teach that part of the curriculum, and all but one of the relational papers were quietly dropped. A term on the contributions of science to psychoanalysis that I also taught was removed. Around the same time my professional accreditation organisation ruled that the practice of relational and attachment versions of psychoanalytic therapy would—along with Lacanian therapy—not be accredited although these ideas could be introduced as theory. To my knowledge that situation remains unchanged.

The place of John Bowlby in systemic family therapy and psychoanalytic therapy is, I think, instructive. Attachment theory, research, and therapies have grown enormously. It is one of the most researched models of self-in-relationship. I'm particularly impressed by the Dynamic Maturational Model of Attachment and Adaptation (DMM) of Pat Crittenden and colleagues (e.g. 2008) of which more throughout the book. On the basis of this, one would think that Bowlby's work would be honoured in both worlds. Nothing could be further from the truth.

Bowlby, a member of the British Psychoanalytic Society, had loyalties to observation and science only and none at all to the existing cannon of psychoanalytic thinking. Indeed, he could be blunt and critical, especially towards Klein. In contrast, according to Adam Phillips (1988), Donald Winnicott—also a radical—played the game and hid the extent of his radicalism by modifying existing psychoanalytic language. Bowlby was never fully accepted and even Winnicott tried to block his membership of the British Psychoanalytic Society. This closing of psychoanalytic ranks against Bowlby has been described by James Grotstein (1981, p. 26) "as one of the most dreadful, shameful, and regrettable chapters in the history of psychoanalysis". We are fortunate that this institutional rejection of Bowlby has not prevented the successful use of attachment theory in psychoanalytic work by some (e.g. Holmes, 2014; Fonagy, 2001) and a renewed appreciation within the emerging tradition of Relational Psychoanalysis (Mitchell, 2000; Kuchuck, 2021).

Bowlby wrote one of the earliest papers on family therapy (Bowlby, 1949) which, through word of mouth, inspired John Bell—one of the very earliest North American pioneers—to begin seeing whole families (Byng-Hall, 1991). He introduced Ronald Laing to Bateson's double-bind theory of schizophrenia leading to an intensive study of 100 families with a diagnosed schizophrenic member and Laing and Esterson's (1964) book, *Sanity, Madness, and the Family*. Bowlby's legacy in systemic family therapy endures, found notably in the work of John Byng-Hall (1995), Arlene Vetere and Rudi Dallos (Dallos & Vetere, 2022), Sue Johnson (2019), and Pat Crittenden and colleagues (Crittenden et al., 2014). However, these ideas are outside of the mainstream of family therapy developments, at least in the UK and Europe, which is still highly influenced by the turn to postmodernism in the late 80 s onwards bringing a highly relativist version of social constructionism in which, in its strongest form, all realist theories of individual and family functioning are under suspicion as the oppressive search for 'essences'. The assumption is that the therapist will rigidly wield this expert knowledge, thereby exercising unilateral power and control in the manner described in the Gergen and Kaye quote, above. These assumptions will be examined in the next chapter but suffice to say here that this book is written partly to counter this strong version of social constructionism in family therapy, while welcoming more moderate versions as necessary, but not sufficient on their own to give a holistic account of the world and the possibilities of knowledge.

All that said, I need to add that I benefitted greatly from both my systemic family therapy and psychoanalytic psychotherapy trainings. I have some sympathy for the argument that training institutions can't teach everything otherwise trainees would never graduate. My point is that the institutional inclusion and exclusion of ideas is not just based on potential clinical value but also on tribalism and ideology.

A reasonable reader might ask "Why bother with multiple vantage points? My tradition already has a rich variety". *My argument is that much individual therapy under-theorises the system of multiple influences on a patient or client and that much family systems therapy, through a need to establish a distinct identity away from psychoanalysis, has a limited or—in the case of strong constructionism—absent idea of the individual self as part of the system* (Nicols, 1988). Regardless of which psychotherapy country we belong to, over the borders our neighbours also have rich resources. Fortunately ideas don't need passports, they only need an invitation to travel.

Assembling the Elephant

As I near the end of my career I'm no longer much concerned about where my set of ideas, theories, experiences, ways of putting things, and ways of using myself originally came from, only whether I have some things in my collection that may help whoever I'm working with. I suspect this weakening of original loyalties is true for many psychotherapists regardless of their tradition of origin. Ideas and experiences tend to soak-in to the mind over the years, becoming part of the furniture, and are often in dialogue with each other depending on what is happening in the therapeutic process. The following observable moment of therapeutic change may help to illustrate.

I've written previously about Emma aged ten and her white British family (Pocock, 2013). She had given up playing, laughing, or any kind of spontaneity around one year prior to the referral. Her deeply worried parents attended for a first session at the child and family consultation service with her and her brother Ian, aged six. Ian was lively and engaging, chatting to everyone, and happily using the toys and drawing equipment. Although I had given my usual general invitation to both children to use the play materials, Emma sat quietly, and replied conscientiously and seriously when I spoke to her. A number of facts emerged: the couple had struggled in their relationship and the father had been seriously depressed over the preceding two years. His depression (described to me by the parents in a quiet tone with the hope that Emma would not hear) was referred to in the family as "tiredness".

At one point, shortly before Emma stopped playing, the father was taken by ambulance to hospital following a suicide attempt. Emma had observed this. I asked Emma if she remembered the time he was taken to hospital. She said simply "yes". I then asked, "Did you think you had made Daddy tired?" "Yes" she said, "I thought I had worn Daddy out". Both parents, who were kind and responsive, were horrified. "How awful" they said "for you to have to feel that! And no one knew!" They reassured and comforted her. In that moment Emma became a recipient of parental care rather than an anxious provider of it. After a few minutes Emma asked, "Can I play now?"

Change—often for the better, occasionally for the worse—happens all the time in therapy, but mostly it is out of sight (of which more in the next chapter) so observable moments like this are rare. I worked with the parents on their relationship for a year, but I never saw Emma again as she was doing well. When asked by her parents if she wanted to see me again she replied "No, I only needed to go for that bit about not wearing Daddy out".

As I listened to their story, I was half-aware of thoughts gathering to form a pattern. This became the context for the question "Did you think you had made Daddy tired?" which came into my mind fairly spontaneously. This process took place, partly out of awareness, combining a variety of perspectives taken from the well-worn collection in my mind. Only in retrospect was it possible to elaborate consciously the layers of ideas somewhere in my head that may have combined to contextualise the question.

- A first child can turn more to the father after the birth of a younger sibling.
- Introjective identification with a parent's distress can reduce a child's anxiety by the child omnipotently taking the distress inside herself to try to solve it (Eekhoff, 2016).
- The father may have experienced relief from his depression by focusing on that of his daughter: a process known as projective identification (Klein, 1946).
- In Fairbairn's 'moral defence' (1952) a child can avoid anger with a parent when her needs are not met by making the parent good in her mind and herself bad.
- The term 'tiredness' was a benignly motivated framing of father's depression, but as an idea, lent itself to some actionable anxiety-reducing strategy for Emma—keeping herself subdued.
- Emma was using a hypothesised A3/A4 strategy on the Dynamic Maturational Model of Attachment and Adaptation (DMM): inhibiting negative affect, distorting cognitive understanding through self-blame, and adopting compulsive caregiving and compulsive compliant strategies (Crittenden, 2008). (See Chaps. 5, 6, 11, and 12 for more details on the DMM.)
- In 'parentification' as described by Ivan Boszormenyi-Nagy and Barbara Krasner (Boszormenyi-Nagy & Krasner, 1986) the caregiver-child relationship is reversed to reduce the child's anxiety.
- As with many cultures, white British culture encourages a caregiving role for girls more strongly than for boys.
- In sibling de-identification the personalities of children in the same family tend to diverge to create as much of a non-competitive domain

as possible. This may be part of the non-shared environment which has been shown through extensive research to be more influential on development than the shared environment (Pocock, 1992; Plomin, 2011).

- In Minuchin et al.'s (1978) concept of triadic detouring concern, a child may discover through trial and error that parents in conflict may unite in concern when she is in distress. (See Chap. 10.)
- The above may establish a mutually reinforcing circular pattern in which Emma's worrying lack of spontaneity may increase concern if parental tension rises, thereby establishing a homeostatic negative-feedback loop.
- Finally, similar experiences in working with other families.

These, if you will, were my blind men in dialogue with each other to assemble (formulate) a pattern. As will be evident, some perspectives are from systemic family therapy, some from psychoanalysis, the DMM is from attachment research and therapy. Some are quite different to each other but are complementary; some, such as parentification and the A4 DMM strategy, are saying nearly the same thing in different languages. Some, such as the DMM and non-shared environment, are research-based. Some are experiences learned along the way with other families.

Note that perspectives such as introjective identification by Emma and projective identification by the father are lineal (cause-and-effect) descriptions but, when joined together, suggest a circular relational process of mutual adaptation. Similarly parentification, the DMM strategy, and moral defence are all descriptions of the self adapting in the context of a relationship to reduce anxiety. Maybe one or two of the perspectives on their own might have been sufficient—I can't say—but in combination there was more chance of assembling a good-enough picture of this 'elephant' to facilitate change.

Bateson uses the term 'abduction' to refer to constructing patterns from the accumulation of information derived from different perspectives (Harries-Jones, 1995). Roy Bhaskar, the originator of critical realism, uses a similar process of working backwards from observable phenomena to track the combinations of deeper causes that must very likely be present to make the phenomena possible. Bhaskar (2016) calls this process 'retroduction'. This stands in contrast, first, with *deductive* reasoning which starts with a theoretically derived hypothesis which is then tested, and second, with *inductive* reasoning which begins with observations which may then be organised into general theory.

This begs some questions. First, what is the status of these ideas as knowledge; are they the objective truth? We examine this in the next chapter. Suffice to say here that they are all fallible, human-made social constructions derived from various knowledge communities. Second, do these perspectives map the whole system? Clearly not. The ontological world beyond all our ideas about it comprises every potential influence all at once. Not just minds and human family relationships but, for example, genes, tissues, organs, the material world, culture, economics, peer relationships, illness, TV programmes, books, neighbours, race, gender, sexuality educational opportunity, politics, hobbies, and on and on. Literally everything. Fortunately not every potential influence becomes active as we will come to later. But what if the father's depression meant he had lost his job and the economic strain and perhaps the couple's fear of losing their home had not got onto my conceptual map? Or if this was a black family and the causal power of racism remained under the radar? A transdisciplinary approach can't map it all, but it does at least give more places to look, and a systemic transdisciplinary approach reminds us that there are *always* more places. The best we can hope for is that our map-making is sufficient for us to have something to offer up to the collaborative process of therapeutic change.

Two final points. First, none of the above ideas had transformative value alone, nor indeed the question "Did you think you had made Daddy tired?" Emma might have denied it, or changed the subject, remained silent, or given a flat and compliant agreement. Instead she picked up the idea and invested it with her own experience and replied in a manner that conveyed more emotion that my question invited "Yes", she said, "I think *I wore Daddy out*". The moment was more than the sum of its parts. We will discuss the transformational phenomenon of emergence later. Second, the *lasting* systemic change came about not through my understanding of Emma but through the *parents'* new understanding of Emma, enabling them to provide emotional comfort, reassurance, and a better explanation of her father's 'tiredness' using their good parental resources.

Choices

An ambition of the book is to map the self in the system and the system in the self. One fundamental assumption is that, since all human development takes place in the context of relationships, all psychotherapy, regardless of the intention, is relational therapy. What is in the mind of the therapist as participant-observer—as far as it is possible to know—also needs to be on the systemic map.

Those choosing to step across the boundary of their psychotherapy tradition of origin are likely to come under the influence of certain prejudices about their neighbours. These biases are straw-men guardians of the outer limits of acceptability, discouraging free passage. It will help to become aware of these feelings of transgression but, for the moment, just to park them and keep curiosity alive. Many of my systemic family therapy colleagues might struggle to get even this far given the numerous distorting tropes about psychoanalytic thinking which abound in systemic writing but, rest assured, I'm not interested in furthering the cause of any therapy tradition. I do care about therapists being well-enough resourced to have enough to offer to those who seek our help. Equally, my psychoanalytic colleagues may struggle with the suggestion that psychoanalytic individual therapy, regardless of intention, is inevitably systemic (since that is simply the way the world is) and that therapists would therefore benefit from developing a foundational systemic sensibility to underpin psychoanalytic theorising.

It has always interested me why psychotherapists choose a particular orientation. Chance must play a large part—the geographical availability of particular trainings being one—but there are deeper reasons. I've recently retired from long-term psychoanalytic work in which it helps if the patient knows very little about the therapist (enabling the patient to fill in the gaps with their non-conscious presuppositions making these available for thinking) so I'm now relatively free to share. I can think of several experiences which influenced my psychotherapy choices. Here, I'll list four key ones.

First, as a child there was often tension and distance between my parents, so managing to live simultaneously in two different worlds and to facilitate a relationship between domains has been something of a lifelong repetition compulsion. That might sound 'pathological', but it has enabled me to explore some rich borderlands and has given me a deeply rewarding career.

Second, from age 11 to 17 years I became caught up in a religious youth group run by the Baptist Church. Football and table tennis soon turned to bible study and multiple trips to chapel on a Sunday and, eventually, pressure for a public baptism—a very big deal in that church. At the same time my childhood love of nature was turning into a specific interest in biology, and the kind of lives that my non-religious friends were living became increasingly attractive. There was no one neutral I could talk to, so I realised I had to work it out for myself. Doubts were the work of the Devil, so this was no trivial matter. After some weeks I realised there was no way of conforming to religion that I could live with: faith needed to give way to evidence, or in this case, lack of evidence. With considerable trepidation I took a major detour from my paper-round and put a note through the door of the youth group leader stating that I no longer believed in God. I still recall vividly the relief I felt when the letter finally dropped through the letter box and there was no turning back. I cycled back home through the leafy lanes singing *Won't Get Fooled Again* by the Who at the top of my voice. I've been wary of closed systems of belief ever since.

Third, my first degree was in biology which gave me an understanding of the possibilities and limitations of science. Evolution showed how everything living is historically connected, and ecology revealed the connections between everything in the present—nothing living can be fully understood outside of the multiple influences of its environment. It would take several more blind men collaborating to overcome the false impression of the elephant as an isolated creature. I would powerfully encounter these ideas again in Gregory Bateson's (1972) *Steps to an Ecology of Mind*.

And fourth, in my mid-thirties as a patient in psychoanalytic psychotherapy for the first time, I was not only deeply relieved but astonished to find that it was possible to feel emotionally understood and to discover, with my therapist, the various experiential contexts in which I could be made sense of, and make sense of myself. Contextual understanding and feeling emotionally understood have remained central to my practice as both an adult psychoanalytic psychotherapist and a systemic family therapist (Pocock, 1997, 2018).

The Book

Although I have both psychoanalytic and systemic family therapy trainings, the focus of this book is not especially about integrating the two—the critical realist scaffold supports many different models of understanding. The book does however present at least an implicit argument for *not* excluding psychoanalytic ideas since it challenges the wholesale rejection of psychoanalysis on unscientific grounds. These are arguments derived from positivism. I argue instead that, while science is valuable, *the positivist philosophy of science is unfit for understanding open systems*. But this, for the moment, is a side issue. Mainly, the book welcomes many ways of seeing in order to attempt to understand multiple systemic causal tendencies, thereby expanding the range of thinking resources available to serve the therapeutic encounter. Using the seventeenth century philosopher John Locke's phrase, critical realism acts as an 'under labourer' for this pluralistic project: clearing the ground of some old flimsy philosophical foundations on which psychotherapy has been based, to provide more secure footings.

I haven't attempted anything other than a brief introduction to some key ideas in what has become known as 'basic critical realism'—just sufficient, I hope, to make sense of how I use the framework throughout the book. Much of Bhaskar's writing is difficult for those, like me, without a background in philosophy so I have often relied on secondary sources. (Any errors in understanding are, however, my own.) For anyone wishing to dive deeper I recommend starting with Hubert Buch-Hansen and Peter Nielsen's (2020) *Critical Realism: Basics and Beyond*, and/or

Christian Smith's (2010) *What is a Person?*, and/or David Pilgrim's (2020) *Critical Realism for Psychologists* which has a particularly useful glossary, and/or Andrew Collier's (1994) *Introduction to Critical Realism* which covers basic critical realism, or for a short read, Phillip Gorski's (2013) paper—available open access at ResearchGate—*What is Critical Realism? And Why Should You Care?* An overview of the complete arc of Bhaskar's thinking over many years, and generally acknowledged to be the most readable of his books, is his last before his death in 2014—*Enlightened Common Sense: The Philosophy of Critical Realism* (Bhaskar, 2016).

The direction of travel in this book is from the foundational level of philosophical assumptions up through several theoretical and strategic considerations to practice. We start in the next chapter with the often hidden role that philosophical assumptions play in how we use theory. It sketches the meeting point and considerable overlap between Bateson's systemic ontology (what the world is like beyond our ideas of it) and that of the originator of critical realism, Roy Bhaskar (1977, 1979, 1986, 1989, 2012, 2016). This may well be the most unfamiliar and perhaps challenging part of the book, especially for the reader unfamiliar with systems theory, but this is the essential scaffold for everything that follows. The value of making these philosophical assumptions explicit is that they are then available for thinking and for challenge.

The core of Chap. 3: *Pluralism* is an examination of the life of a historical figure, Catherine of Siena, a fourteenth century religious mystic. This allows a more detailed look at one person from multiple perspectives of self and system without risking the confidentiality of anyone I have worked with. The added benefit of looking back seven centuries is that it allows the causal power of cultural influences to stand out starkly as difference.

The possibilities and limitations of different kinds of knowing, the varieties of not-knowing, and the relationship between power and knowledge are the subject of Chap. 4: *Knowing and Not-Knowing.* Chapter 5: *Theory Choice* considers how we select theory. Science is endorsed as a secure base for theory while stopping short of scientism. Other ways that theory may be judged reliable are explored. The critical realist alternative to a positivist understanding of science is outlined and illustrated with

Crittenden's Dynamic Maturational Model of Attachment and Adaptation (Crittenden, 2008, Crittenden et al., 2014).

Despite Bateson's anthropological work in *Naven* (Bateson, 1958), a systemic consideration of emotion was a relative late-comer to mainstream developments in family therapy and, accordingly, family therapy has tended to have a cognitive bias. Chapter 6: *Emotion in the System* discusses emotional experience as both *given* (brute reality) and socially *made* (Orange, 1995). The importance of meeting those we seek to help emotionally and using emotional resonance as a guide throughout therapy is underlined. Three contemporary theories are reviewed: Beatrice Beebe and Frank Lachmann's (2002) system of self and interactive emotional regulation; Peter Fonagy et al.'s (2002) concept of mentalising; and Jessica Benjamin's (1999) version of intersubjectivity.

The need for collaboration to be both a cognitive *and* emotional endeavour is further emphasised in Chap. 7: *Collaboration and Change.* Fourteen guidelines for collaborative work are offered. The challenges of working with others who seem the same or different to us is the subject of Chap. 8: *Sameness and Otherness* with, I will argue, assumptions of sameness being the more hidden problem. Models of culture are briefly examined, and some challenge is made to the notion of intra-cultural therapy.

Chapter 9: *Who to See, and Other Choices,* draws distinctions between the need for consistency in individual therapy and the much wider range of choices of who to see in shorter-term systemic family therapy. The need for adaptability is underlined in both modalities and illustrated with a challenging individual therapy case of serious self-harm.

In Chap. 10: *Triangles,* the dynamics of three-person relationships are described, with the following versions reviewed and briefly illustrated: oedipal, caregiver-sibling pair, cross-generational coalition, detouring attacking (scapegoating), detouring concern, distance regulation, and divided-loyalty conflict. More space is given to a specific triad that, to my knowledge, has not yet been described in psychoanalytic or systemic writing, that of a coalition (and hidden primary attachment) between child and grandparent but where the child is cared for by the mother.

Chapter 11: *Aggressive, Out-of-Control Behaviour* and Chap. 12: *Self-harm and Suicidality* focus on clinical presentations that have been particular interests of mine, bringing the various elements of the book together. The mentalisation of aggression, rather than its enactment, is a common theme across the two chapters.

Concluding arguments for critical realism and summaries of my position are brought together in Chap. 13.

Who Is the Book For?

I would naturally like the book to be read widely but I have two principal readers in mind: one a systemic family therapist who has perhaps become a little uneasy about where the strong postmodern turn has taken the field and is willing to rethink some of the assumptions behind this; and the second, an individual psychoanalytic or humanistic psychotherapist who is curious about what a systems approach might add to their work. Neither will be asked to give up much; the book is about expanding the range of ideas.

A further ambition is that, by elaborating critical realist ontological and epistemological assumptions for individual and family therapy, new dialogue may be opened with other psychotherapy traditions which hitherto have appeared separate. Katherina Sternek (2010), for example, views gestalt therapy as underpinned by critical realism, Holt Hauser (2023) argues for critical realism in person-centred psychotherapy, as does David Pilgrim (2020) for psychology and Andrew Collier (1981), David Will (1986) and Alan Norrie (2020) for psychoanalysis. Critical realism can also provide a more coherent foundation for more moderate social constructionist approaches in family therapy as well as for the many integrative approaches in individual, couple, and family psychotherapy which, disparate as they sometimes appear, may in fact be the largest emergent 'grouping' of real-world practices in the last twenty-five years (Lebow, 1997, 2019).

At many stages in the writing I have found myself reflecting on my own training experiences, now several decades in the past, but still powerful in my mind. So I think the other reader I am trying to help is my trainee self. This is the book I would like to have read. One of my biggest hopes is that contemporary trainees, struggling with the same issues, will find something of value in it.

Many theories will be covered; some will be familiar to each reader and simultaneously unfamiliar—even strange—to others. It would be an impossible task to cover every idea in the detail that it deserves, but I will try to be careful with my explanations of the main arguments. In many cases, however, I can only point to the potential value of a concept and leave it to my readers to follow up if curiosity has been raised.

Readers may already have noticed that the book includes more autobiographical details than might usually be expected in a psychotherapy text, especially one that incorporates psychoanalytic thinking. I think we need to acknowledge that psychotherapy is not solely about working with the objective world 'out there' but, instead that the self of the therapist is always an irreducible part of the system under observation. This, as we discuss in the next chapter, is the second-order or reflexive position. I have therefore chosen not to stand back but to include myself, where relevant—as far as I am able to understand me, that is.

Terms

Finally, some notes on nomenclature. I hope this book will be of interest to counsellors and psychotherapists of all persuasions and none, but rather than repeatedly use the laborious terms 'psychotherapists and counsellors' I will use 'psychotherapist' or simply 'therapist' to refer to both. When I refer generically to a therapist I will roughly alternate between the genders she/her, or he/him. I will use 'psychoanalysis' in a more general sense to refer to the body of psychoanalytic or psychodynamic thinking, and 'psychoanalytic psychotherapy' to refer to the practice of those ideas unless the therapist is specifically a trained psychoanalyst. (I appreciate that in the US psychoanalytic psychotherapists are referred to as psychoanalysts, but I will use the UK context.)

I have mixed feelings about the term 'systemic family therapy' simply because, in my view (as discussed in the next chapter), there are rational grounds for concluding that the world simply is ontologically an open system regardless of how we think of it, so everything has systemic implications. Nevertheless I will use the term as it conveys an openness to *systems thinking* which is not so reliably found in other modalities. To ring the changes I will also use the term 'systemic psychotherapy' and the reductive, but more recognisable term, 'family therapy' as synonyms.

The name 'critical realism' does not start with Bhaskar. There are prior uses of the term, principally by two 'schools' of philosophy: American Critical Realism and a group of British philosopher-theologians (Bhaskar, 2016). All references to critical realism in this book are solely to Bhaskar's work and those who have developed his ideas.

The term 'social construction of reality' is, from a critical realist perspective, somewhat misleading since it is *knowledge* that is constructed not external reality itself. 'Social *construal* of reality' is more accurate (Bhaskar, 2016) as it more obviously implies an ontology external to the construction. Nevertheless, since it is the more familiar term (at least in family therapy) I will use 'social construction' throughout. The term '*moderate* social construction' (also known as weak social constructionism) may, however, be read as a synonym for social construal. 'Postmodernism' is used as a general term in the book to include poststructuralism.

I have found that the psychoanalytic term 'unconscious' tends to be unpalatable to the systemic family therapy tradition despite the fact that Bateson uses it frequently. I think this relates to a concern that only an expert (psychoanalyst) can pronounce on its contents so is linked—properly in my view—to concerns about therapist power. It is also quite a vague term even in psychoanalytic circles, so I will use it simply to refer to anything in the mind that is, at least in the present moment, out of awareness. To ring the changes I will use 'non-conscious' as a synonym.

There is no entirely satisfactory general word for those individuals who seek our help: the terms 'client' and 'patient' or 'family members' will have to do. ('Family' being a particularly slippery concept with many different culturally determined meanings.) I will generally use 'patient' when referring to a psychoanalytic context of individual work and 'client' when discussing systemic family therapy since those are the terms commonly used in those therapeutic domains. However, as the reader may already appreciate, it is no longer clear to me when I am systemic and when psychoanalytic. I hope I am always both and more.

References

Bateson, G. (1958). *Naven: A survey of the problems suggested by a composite picture of the culture of a New Guinea tribe drawn from three points of view.* Stanford University Press.

Bateson, G. (1972). *Steps to an ecology of mind.* Balantine.

Bateson, G. (1979). *Mind and nature: A necessary unity.* Dutton.

Beebe, B., & Lachmann, F. (2002). *Infant research and adult treatment: Co-constructing interactions.* The Analytic Press.

Benjamin, J. (1999) Recognition and destruction: An outline of intersubjectivity. In S. Mitchell and L. Aron (Eds.). (1999). *Relational Psychoanalysis: The Emergence of a Tradition* (pp. 181–210). Analytic Press.

Bhaskar, R. (1977). *A realist philosophy of science.* Harvester.

Bhaskar, R. (1979). *The possibility of naturalism.* Harvester.

Bhaskar, R. (1986). *Scientific realism and human emancipation.* Verso.

Bhaskar, R. (1989). *Reclaiming reality.* Verso.

Bhaskar, R. (2012). *The philosophy of metaReality: Creativity, love, and freedom.* Routledge.

Bhaskar, R. (2016). *Enlightened common sense: The philosophy of critical realism.* Routledge.

Boszormenyi-Nagy, I., & Krasner, B. (1986). *Between give and take: A clinical guide to contextual therapy: Conversations in theory and practice.* Basic Books.

Bowlby, J. (1949). The study and reduction of group tensions in the family. *Human Relations, 2*, 123.

Buch-Hansen, H., & Nielsen, P. (2020). *Critical realism: Basics and beyond.* Red Globe Press.

Byng-Hall, J. (1991). An appreciation of John Bowlby: His significance for family therapy. *Journal of Family Therapy, 13*, 5–16.

Byng-Hall, J. (1995). *Rewriting family scripts: Improvisation and systems change.* Guilford.

Collier, A. (1981). Scientific realism and the human world: The case for psychoanalysis. *Radical Philosophy, 29*, 8–18.

Collier, A. (1994). *Critical realism: An introduction to Roy Bhaskar's philosophy.* Verso Books.

Crittenden, P. (2008). *Raising parents: Attachment representation, and treatment.* Routledge.

Crittenden, P., Dallos, R., Landini, A., & Kozlowska, K. (2014). *Attachment and family therapy.* Open University Press.

Dallos, R., & Vetere, A. (2022). *Systemic therapy and attachment narratives: Applications in a range of clinical settings*. Routledge.

Eekhoff, J. (2016). Introjective identification: The analytic work of evocation. *American Journal of Psychoanalysis, 76*, 354–361.

Fairbairn, R. (1952). *Psychoanalytic studies of the personality*. Tavistock and Routledge.

Flaskas, C., & Pocock, D. (Eds.) (2009). *Systems and psychoanalysis: Contemporary integrations in family therapy* (pp. 39–55). Karnac.

Fonagy, P. (2001). *Attachment theory and psychoanalysis*. Routledge.

Fonagy, P., Gergeley, G., Jurist, E., & Target, M. (2002). *Affect regulation, mentalization, and the development of the self*. Other Press.

Gergen, K., & Kaye, J. (1992). Beyond narrative in the negotiation of therapeutic meaning. In S. McNamee & K. Gergen (Eds.), *Therapy as social construction* (pp. 166–185). Sage.

Gorski, P. (2013). What is critical realism? And why should you care? *Contemporary Sociology: A Journal of Reviews, 42*, 658–670.

Grotstein, J. (1981). *Splitting and projective identification*. Aaronson.

Harries-Jones. (1995). *A recursive vision: Ecological understanding and Gregory Bateson*. Toronto Press.

Hauser, H. (2023) More than *my* experience: An argument for critical realism in person-centred psychotherapy. Person-Centred and Experiential Psychotherapies, December, 1–18.

Holmes, J. (2014). *Attachment, psychiatry, psychotherapy, psychoanalysis: Selected papers of Jeremy Holmes*. Routledge.

Johnson, S. (2019). *Attachment theory in practice: Emotionally focused therapy (EFT) with individuals, couples, and families*. Guilford Press.

Klein, M. (1946). Notes on some schizoid mechanisms. In *The writings of Melanie Klein* (Vol. 3, pp. 1–24). Free Press.

Kuchuck, S. (2021). *The relational revolution in psychoanalysis and psychotherapy*. Confer Books.

Laing, R., & Esterson, A. (1964). *Sanity, madness, and the family*. Routledge.

Lebow, J. (1997). The integrative revolution in couple and family therapy. *Family Process, 36*, 1–17.

Lebow, J. (2019). Current issues in the practice of integrative couple and family therapy. *Family Process, 58*, 610–628.

Minuchin, S., Rosman, B., & Baker, L. (1978). *Psychosomatic families: Anorexia nervosa in context*. Harvard.

Mitchell, S. (2000). *Relationality: From attachment to intersubjectivity*. Routledge.

Nicols, M. (1988). *The self in the system: Expanding the limits of family therapy*. Routledge.

Norrie, A. (2020). The flesh made word: Critical realism, psychoanalysis, and the ontology of love. *Journal of Critical Realism, 19*, 341–361.

Orange, D. (1995). *Emotional understanding: Studies in psychoanalytic epistemology*. Guilford.

Phillips, A. (1988). *Winnicott*. Fontana.

Pilgrim, D. (2020). *Critical realism for psychologists*. Routledge.

Pirsig, R. (1991). *Lila: An inquiry into morals*. Black Swan Books.

Plomin, R. (2011). Commentary: Why are children in the same family so different? Non-shared environment three decades later. *International Journal of Epidemiology, 40*, 582–592.

Pocock, D. (1992). Parental perceptions of sibling differences: Towards a theory of sibling differentiation. *Journal of Family Therapy, 14*, 123–144.

Pocock, D. (1997). Feeling understood in family therapy. *Journal of Family Therapy, 19*, 283–302.

Pocock, D. (2013). A philosophy of practice for systemic psychotherapy: The case for critical realism. *Journal of Family Therapy, 37*, 167–183.

Pocock, D. (2018). You, me, and us. In S. Lord (Ed.), *Moments of meeting in psychotherapy* (pp. 199–208). Routledge.

Smith, C. (2010). *What is a person? Rethinking humanity, social life, and the moral good from the person up*. University of Chicago Press.

Sternek, K. (2010). Critical realism, the epistemic position of gestalt theoretical psychotherapy. *Gestalt Theory, 43*, 13–28.

Will, D. (1986). Psychoanalysis and the new philosophy of science. *The International Review of Psycho-Analysis, 13*, 163–173.

Willig, C. (2019). Ontological and epistemological reflexivity: A core skill for therapists. *Counselling and Psychotherapy Research, 19*, 186–194.

2

What Is Real? What Is Knowledge?

> There is not a separate world for philosophy and another world for everything else: there is only one world. … What differentiates the discourse of philosophy is that it talks about the most abstract or general features of that world, which are not normally discussed in—but are tacitly presupposed by—our practices. Roy Bhaskar (2016, p. 3)

The subject of this chapter is how we acquire knowledge of the world that exists outside of our minds but which we can only know through our minds. Inevitably—some might say "regrettably"—this takes us to the philosophy of knowledge, known as *epistemology*, and to the philosophy of what is there—and what might become known—which is called *ontology*. I imagine my family therapy reader thinking, "But isn't that discussion all in the past? Do we *really* need to go back over all that *again*?" I think it is the case that fewer family therapists now consciously identify with what I call strong constructionism, but many such assumptions still operate *implicitly* in our practices: a point made by Bhaskar in the above quote. Similarly, I can't imagine there are any individual therapists who would proudly proclaim themselves to be naïve realists, but nevertheless we can all slide into that error-prone epistemological position if we lose touch with our part in perception.

D. Pocock, *Expanding the Limits of Individual and Family Therapies*, Palgrave Texts in Counselling and Psychotherapy, https://doi.org/10.1007/978-3-031-76309-0_2

Epistemology and ontology are ancient and complex concerns in human thought. Broadly, and at the risk of simplifying, since the following terms are used in many different ways, there are two main epistemological contenders—realism and idealism. There are strong, moderate, and weak versions of each of these, but the difference is easiest to comprehend in their strongest versions.

Strong realism—also known as naïve realism, objectivism, or the correspondence theory of truth—assumes that we can know the world directly, unmediated by our perceptual processes: that knowledge *corresponds* to how the world actually is. I prefer the term *'naïve realism'* since it captures the everyday experience of simply not bothering too much about perceptual processes when going about one's daily business. If I see a dog in the street it doesn't occur to me that I am processing my visual sense data into an existing dog template in my mind, itself embedded in language, depending on everything that is non-dog, and that it is completely possible (but unlikely) that what is out there is a convincing dog-shaped cardboard cut-out, or a stuffed dog, or that I'm dreaming, hallucinating, or delusional.

Bhaskar (2016) refers to this as the *natural attitude*. Day to day we don't differentiate what we know from what is there, and it is not immediately obvious why we should bother to do so. Naïve realism works pretty well much of the time ... right up to the moment when it doesn't, which is why optical illusions—like the famous rabbit-duck illusion (Fig. 2.1)—surprise us and literally catch us in two minds, compelling us to realise that we process visual sense data through pre-existing templates. In this case we struggle to decide whether our internal duck or internal rabbit fits best with the new data. If you had never seen a duck, or a picture of one, only the rabbit would present itself.

Saxe's poem *The Blind Men and the Elephant* is, among other things, a warning of the limitations of a naïve realist position. Of course, being naïve, the blind men don't know they are taking a position at all, *they think they see the world just as it is*. They are each receiving sense data from their bit of the external world, but don't realise that they are filtering this data through the lenses of the knowledge and experience that they already have in mind (a long pointy thing becomes "very like a spear") to reach a pre-programmed conclusion. Psychologists call this 'observer bias'. It's

Fig. 2.1 The rabbit-duck illusion

worth recalling that, initially, each blind man found their particular object only "very like" their preconception, rather than a complete correspondence. This uncertainty was soon lost once the arguments for the correct definition of an elephant began—a regular occurrence in human affairs, one from which psychotherapy is not immune.

Strong or naïve idealism is the polar opposite. While an external reality may or may not be said to exist (depending on which version), knowledge is understood to be an entirely mental phenomenon. Even if the existence of a real world is conceded—a position sometimes referred to as 'empty realism' (Buch-Hansen & Nielsen, 2020)—our knowledge of it is said to be entirely organised through mental processes so all kinds of knowledge are ultimately self-knowledge. Subjectivism, interpretivism, and strong constructionism are examples of strong idealism. We will return to the strengths and limitations of strong social constructionism later but, for the moment, *I strongly recommend to my systemic reader that you set aside the deep assumption in contemporary family therapy that social construction and realism are incompatible.* In critical realism, knowledge is assumed to be socially made *and* able to reference the world as it is. Not only that, critical realism also assumes that some social constructions are more adequate descriptions of the shape of the world than others. In Chap. 6 we will explore the deeper, embodied, and intuitive forms of the knowledge of how to be human which are also essential for therapy, but this chapter will focus on theoretical knowledge—our 'know that' as John Shotter (1993) puts it.

Most psychotherapies that concern themselves with these issues explore some kind of middle ground between the extremes. Freud is said to have been indifferent or even hostile to philosophy but, as is often pointed out, there are several versions of Freud. He certainly knew of—and was influenced by—Schopenhauer, Spinoza, Feuerbach, Fechner, Brentano, and Kant, but was anxious that psychoanalysis should be accepted as a science, not another contested set of philosophical ideas (W. Kraemer, personal communication). However, from early on, Freud took the contemporary-sounding view that neither psychic nor external reality could be known with certainty.

> The unconscious is the true psychical reality; in its innermost nature it is as much unknown to us as the reality of the external world, and it is as incompletely presented by the data of consciousness as is the external world by the communications by our sense organs. (Freud, 1900, p. 613)

While questions of epistemology and ontology continue to be debated periodically in psychoanalysis (see Hanly, 2009, for a review), I don't recall these terms being mentioned once during my psychoanalytic training. However, perhaps to the surprise of my systemic reader, the importance of not-knowing was strongly emphasised throughout. The influential post-Kleinian, Wilfred Bion (Green, 1973) endorsed the poet John Keats' (1899, p. 277) term 'negative capability'—"when man is capable of being in uncertainties, mysteries, doubts, without any irritable reaching after fact and reason". This is not at all an easy state of mind to maintain, especially for us trainees, eager to know. However the main lessons in not-knowing are not academic but gained experientially in the training therapy where uncertainty abounds (or should), and trainee and training therapist have to slowly work things out together. That is not to say that naïve realism and its associated omniscience never creep back in. We will come back to that in Chap. 4.

First and Second Order

Turning now to systemic family therapy, it is time to introduce two key terms—first-order and second-order systems—that will be very familiar to my systemic reader, although not perhaps in the way that I believe they should be used.

Saxe's blind men take a first-order position, although of course, as said, they don't realise they are taking any position at all but assume they are in touch with the simple unvarnished truth. Naïve realism is first-order: systems are simply assumed to be available to be objectively observed. What you see is what you get.

In contrast, a second-order position comes about if the men are able to come to an awareness that what they see at least partly depends on what they already have in mind: the particular lens they are using to filter and organise information about the external world. An internal dialogue in which one can reflect in a second-order manner "this *reminds* me of a spear" includes oneself in the act of observation and is wholly different in consequence to the naïve, first-order, objective assumption "this *is* a spear". The former recognises that more information is required and extends curiosity; the latter has already arrived at a firm conclusion, curiosity is no longer needed, and the bigger-picture elephant can never be perceived. *In summary, the second-order position requires an understanding of the role that the observer plays in the observation—a condition also known as reflexivity.*

In 1969, straight after what was no doubt an excellent lunch at a conference of psychiatrists in Hawaii, Gregory Bateson (1972) set out to grab the attention of his audience and asked for a show of hands from anyone who thought they saw him. "I see a number of hands, so I guess insanity loves company!" A good joke for an audience of psychiatrists. "Of course you don't really see me. What you 'see' is a bunch of pieces of information about me which you synthesise into a picture image of me. You make that image. It's that simple" (Bateson, 1972, p. 478), This, in a nutshell, is Bateson's constructivism: our image of the world is what we construct from information extracted from our sense data. Bateson's second-order systemic epistemology was applied across his many areas of interest—biology, ecology, anthropology, semiotics and linguistics, social science, and cybernetics. New developments in family therapy often pay homage to him and then frequently depart sharply from his vision.

It is often assumed that family therapy begins with Bateson but there was a founding decade (1952–1961) in which there was a considerable development in psychoanalytic thinking; from individuals to relationships and then to families (Broderick & Schrader, 1991). But *systemic* family therapy—and the need for a systemic epistemology—starts with Bateson. He didn't use the word ontology or develop the ontological (externally real) aspects of his worldview since he found it awkward to continuously refer to epistemology and ontology as if they could be separated (Dell, 1985). Instead, he used the single term 'epistemology' to idiosyncratically cover both, but it is clear that his whole point in thinking systemically is that the world itself is an infinitely connected open system of which we are a part.

Ecology is a systemic epistemology, but it can *only* work as a set of ideas *because the world beyond all our ideas of it must ontologically be an open system of multiple causality*. Bateson frequently quoted Alfred Korzybski (1933) "a map is not the territory" and was passionate that an eco-systemic territory needs eco-systemic maps and solutions. In the Hawaii talk he goes on to develop his ideas on information as difference, homeostasis, the myth of power, and delivers a strong plea to end the dangerous idea of considering humankind as separate from ecological systems, leading to epistemological errors—simplistic short-term and context-free solutions.

> These [catastrophic dangers] range from insecticides to pollution, to atomic fallout, to the possibility of melting the Antarctic ice cap. … I believe that this massive aggregation of threats to man and his ecological systems arises out of our habits of thought at deep and partly unconscious levels. (Bateson, 1972, p. 487)

My point is that Bateson passionately argued for a systemic epistemology *because the world is ontologically systemic.*

Note, in passing, that Bateson was entirely comfortable with the psychoanalytic use of the term 'unconscious' and used it frequently: a word that is almost never spoken by the majority of systemic family therapists given the rather anti-psychoanalytic culture of post-Batesonian family therapy. However, my main reason for me dwelling on his hidden systemic ontology is to demonstrate, as I will do shortly, how far contemporary systemic therapy, under the influence of postmodernism, has departed from Bateson. I believe that his focus on epistemology, and relative neglect of an ontology which anchors the epistemology, made it easier for systemic family therapy to slide further towards the strong-idealism end of the realism-idealism continuum. Indeed the theories of knowledge brought by postmodernism are described by Bhaskar (1977) as 'super-idealism', where knowledge is reduced entirely to the social means by which it is said to be produced. *In strong constructionism there is almost no territory left, only competing maps.* Or more accurately (if somewhat confusingly) maps become the sole territory to be mapped! As we will see, critical realism recognises the causal power of ideas, beliefs, and theories but says this is only part of the ontological whole.

While much systemic family therapy (apparently) venerated Bateson, the feelings were not reciprocated. According to Peter Harries-Jones (1995) he felt betrayed when members of his schizophrenia research team, Paul Watzlawick et al., brought out *Pragmatics of Human Communication* in 1967, ahead of a book on schizophrenia he had been preparing. It probably didn't help that they dedicated it to him! Bateson had always been against the idea of communication as some kind of pragmatic tool. While he felt many of his ideas were included, but insufficiently attributed to him, he was also angered that culture and emotional ethos from his anthropological work had been stripped out (Bateson, 1958; Harries-Jones, 1995; Krause, 2012). He quarrelled with another member of the team, Jay Haley, over the metaphor of power which Bateson argued consistently against. When members of the original Milan Group wrote to Bateson asking if he thought their interventions (outlined in their book *Paradox and Counterparadox*, Palazzoli et al. 1979) were systemic, he replied curtly that it was impossible to tell because he couldn't read the emotional tone (Paulo Bertrando & Carlos Sluzki, personal communications).

Nevertheless, systemic family therapy flourished with Salvador Minuchin's Structural Family Therapy, Jay Haley's Strategic Family Therapy, and the aforementioned Milan Group becoming particularly influential. But, looking back, this was a period of epistemological inconsistency. For Haley and the Milan Group, families were committing—using Bateson's term—'epistemological errors' in, for example, seeing the wider systemic problems as located in the identified patient. The notion of objective truth was seen as so problematic that, for some—especially the Milan Group—it became legitimate to make up fictional accounts to push the system into change; for example, pretending that the women in the team behind the screen had taken one view, and the men another. (Note, that without a real external world to anchor knowledge there are no lies, only stories in competition with each other.) The constructivist impossibility of objective knowledge that Bateson understood somehow didn't quite apply to therapists, some of whom assumed for themselves the God's-eye view that Saxe offers to the readers of his poem. Therapists, for the most part charismatic men, developed powerful techniques, expertly delivered, which excited much interest but, with the parallel growth of feminism, some mounting disquiet.

Near the end of his life, when asked who was carrying forward his epistemological studies, Bateson nominated a Chilean biologist, Humberto Maturana who was very much in the second-order camp since objectivity is, along with Bateson, seen as impossible in Maturana's worldview. I won't spend long on Maturana's ideas and those of his collaborator Francisco Varela, since the mainstream of systemic family therapy, having first embraced the new strange-sounding concepts of structural determinism, structural coupling, co-evolution, and the impossibility of instructional interaction, was soon happy to give them up when the postmodern turn to language swept through family therapy in the late 1980s.

A brief example may illustrate some of the key aspects of Maturana and Varela's (1980) work. The relationship between me and my cat is based on us co-ordinating certain behaviours He approaches, I prepare my lap and say, "Come on then!" He jumps up and arranges himself; I stroke him under the chin and on the cheeks in just the way that he likes, and he purrs. We come to an arrangement about how he uses his claws on my knees, and we settle down and relax. This is a good relationship which has co-evolved between us over several years. However, when I attempt a conversation with him that uses human verbal language it is disappointingly one-sided. His capacity to respond—and indeed mine—is entirely determined, according to Maturana, by our internal structures. This is structural determinism: he just isn't built for a good chat. Conversely, I wouldn't be of much use accompanying him on his nocturnal mouse hunts; I lack the necessary stealth and night vision. His behaviour, such as jumping up on my lap, is not based on my input of information (for example, me signalling the lap is clear, by patting it) but by what his internally organised (autopoietic) system does with that information. Our relationship works as a system because his internally organised structure and mine have become co-ordinated, in a process referred to a structural coupling, to form a predictable pattern.

Maturana's and Varela's concepts sound rather abstract, but I imagine most therapists have had the experience of a client coming to a session and saying something like "I tried that thing you suggested last week" when the therapist has suggested no such idea. The client has built the suggestion out of something the therapist has said but in a manner entirely determined by their internal organisation. The analytic psychotherapist who delivers a full transference interpretation only to find it falls flat may assume the patient is resistant. There may, instead, simply have been insufficient structural coupling—no shared carefully defined language—and therefore limited co-evolution of thinking around the particular issue for the interpretation to have any chance of fitting. We will return to this in Chap. 4, but the basic message is that we can never be sure what people will do with what we say, or what we might do with what they say, especially because both participants process ideas non-consciously as well as consciously. It is one important part of our not-knowing.

With the growing influence of Maturana's constructivism and a mounting feminist critique of what was perceived as unacceptable power and control inherent in Structural, Strategic, and Early-Milan models, the terms first and second order developed a new prominence, defining these early powerful models as first-order and the more collaborative, non-expert, not-knowing stance of constructivism as second-order. While these terms have a certain logic when used that way, the effect of this distinction was to *create a split with, I argue, 'first-order' coming to stand as a context marker for the unacceptable use of 'expert' knowledge, and 'second-order' a reassurance that one is on the side of the angels* (Pocock, 1999).

Splits are totalising and do not allow exceptions—no third positions—so which side of the first and second order divide does this statement belong?

> But therapists who have been trained in interpersonal channels of communication know that the act of observation influences the material observed, so that they are always dealing with approximates and probable realities. (p. 80)

This is by those so-called 'first-order' structural family therapists Salvador Minuchin and Charles Fishman (1981) who look like they have been given a second-order script by mistake. It is not unusual to find narrative therapists who only see narratives, or social constructionists who privilege only beliefs. These contemporary approaches are usually located as second-order, but *if you only see what is already in your mind then, using the original definition of observed* versus *observing systems, is this not first-order?* And let me own my part in this. I can get caught up in a single mind too, forget to hold my ideas lightly (Orange, 1995), and lose reflexivity; it is one of the daily hazards of the work. This is why I greatly regret the slippage of meaning of first- and second-order to refer to historical periods of family therapy development.

I prefer the original meaning: for 'second-order' to refer to the therapist's capacity to include themselves in the system under observation; to hold onto the precarious position of reflexivity; to maintain uncertainty, curiosity, and openness to other ways of thinking including everything that the client or family members need us to hear. If we think adhering to a contemporary model of practice makes us second-order and project our everyday tendency to slip into naïve realism back into pre-1990s family therapy under the rubric 'first-order' then we settle for complacency.

Not only this, I also see theories themselves being labelled as first-order or second-order (e.g. Simon, 1992) whereas *it is our epistemology that determines whether we use a theory in a state of mind of naïve realism or of reflexivity*. The theory itself—for example, Minuchin's theory of triadic detouring concern, mentioned in relation to Emma—makes no contribution at all as to whether it is held and used as first-order objective truth or reflexively as a second-order viewpoint owned by the therapist.

Postmodernism

Maturana's ideas reached the UK during my systemic family therapy training and were enthusiastically embraced by some. One group of trainees in the year above made themselves frog badges to celebrate his pre-eminence. (His conclusions were drawn from work on the frog's nervous system.) I am not the first to note that, while the psychoanalytic world is inherently conservative, systemic family therapy has a penchant for making radical leaps (Pocock, 1995a), none greater than the widespread adoption of social constructionism within the mainstream of systemic family therapy under the juggernaut paradigm of postmodernism.

Postmodernism had been growing in influence across many fields of study since the 1960s. A key paper in 1988—*Human Systems as Linguistic Systems*—by Harlene Anderson and Harry Goolishian marked the radical 'linguistic turn' in systemic family therapy. This assumes that 'realities' by which people live their lives are formed in language and conversation. Problems are said not so much to be solved as 'dissolved' when new 'realities' are co-constructed in the conversation of therapy. However, I believe the tipping-point for mainstream family systems therapy was 1990 with the publication of Lynn Hoffman's paper *Constructing Realities: An Art of Lenses.* Both papers were recently recognised jointly by the *Journal of Family Therapy* and *Family Process* as among the most influential two dozen in the last twenty years.

Hoffman is, for my money, among the most stylish writers in systemic family therapy, humanising, personalising, and making accessible complex ideas. She was a trusted figure, and, after the difficult intellectual challenges of constructivism, the mainstream seemed ready to follow her complete break from Bateson, cybernetics, constructivism and indeed any search for underlying 'patterns that connect' (Bateson, 1979) into what she called "Family Therapy Part 2" and a strong version of social constructionism. By her own admission she had simply fallen out of love with everything that had gone before. Family Therapy Part 1 became further marked down as a first-order domain where the therapist always knew first and knew best: knowledge being a synonym for power and therapist control of the process.

Strong constructionism is a philosophical shift away from the assumption that language can adequately represent our world and fully into the assumption that all we can experience of the world are socially created 'realities' made together in language and conversation. Most systemic family therapists are unaware of the critiques of strong constructionist assumptions about language, which are mostly found outside of systemic literature, or of the distinction from moderate versions of constructionism of which critical realism is, I think, the most helpful example (e.g. Bhaskar, 1977; Elder-Vass, 2012; Searle, 1995; Smith, 2010). I make some mention of these critiques in an earlier paper (Pocock, 2013). Space prohibits a full discussion here, but I strongly recommend *Part 3: Language* of Dave Elder-Vass's (2012) *The Reality of Social Construction* for a full and coherent exploration of the issues. As an example, much of the linguistic turn hinges on post-structuralist interpretations of Ferdinand de Saussure's work, one of the founders of linguistics, who is assumed to demonstrate the 'linguistic arbitrariness' of language: that words only gain meaning from their relationship to other words, not to the world itself. But, as the critical realist Andrew Collier puts it:

> [P]eople think that Saussure has shown that words get meaning from their relation to other words, not by referring to reality. But what he has in fact shown is that *words refer to reality by virtue of their relationship with other words*. (1999, p. 48. [My emphasis])

Strong social constructionism appears to take us straight to the strong idealism end of the realism-idealism continuum, but is that really the whole story? Let us apply what Bhaskar (2016) refers to as an 'immanent critique' to the argument that language and discourse make up our world. An immanent critique starts within the proposal but looks to reveal any hidden weaknesses or blind spots.

I will begin with the strengths of strong constructionism. It assumes that the habitual way in which we think about particular issues is linguistically, culturally, and—since culture is passed down the generations—historically determined. In Doris Lessing's (1994) autobiographical account of growing up in white Southern Rhodesia (now Zimbabwe), the white narrative—she calls it 'the monologue'—included the routine discourse that the black population had smaller brains than whites. There was simply no question about it. Science shows us this is wrong, but the distorting discourse had causal power in supporting the injustice. (Explanations that show how false discourses support injustice are described in critical realism as 'explanatory critiques'.) Similarly, in Freud's early theorising on sexuality he considered it to be an essential difference between men and women that men were active and women passive. Grafted onto that was the notion that homosexuality was also passivity. The passage of time and the shifts in culture allow us the perspective of difference revealing that what Freud took to be essential about sexuality were gender roles socially constructed in culture and language.

Big ideas like the white Southern Rhodesian 'monologue' and Freud's views on sexuality can dominate and subjugate other meanings which for Derrida become deferred—or cast into shadow. Knowledge here is indeed power especially if we become 'docile bodies' as Foucault (1977) puts it, unable to resist being colonised with these assumptions. The power of big ideas like these—or metanarratives using Lyotard's (1984) term—are the target for the postmodern critique. Note that Lyotard's definition of postmodernism as 'incredulity towards metanarratives' is not based on whether one idea gives a more adequate account of the real world than another It is purely an analysis of the power of big ideas to dominate and exclude other more locally determined accounts. People can come to use big ideas like 'personality disorder' to define themselves in a manner that Michael White and David Epston (1990) describe as 'problem-saturated'. In my early child and adolescent mental health work I would occasionally come across children defined in their family as evil. This was difficult enough to work with, but it changed markedly once ADHD and autism became more widely known. Referrals then frequently closed down the area of legitimate enquiry to that of diagnosis, making open exploration of other relational issues even more difficult.

I find these postmodern accounts of the power of knowledge, and the ability of language to help make up our world-views, to be compelling for one very good reason: they say something about the world as it is. Now for the weakness: in other words, they provide a *realistic* account (Held, 1995). *Strong social constructionism relies on this concealed realist assumption.* Indeed, what other good basis is there for choosing to invest in an idea other than it seems to give a reasonable account of the way things are in the world? This is strong constructionism's Achilles' heel. It creates a paradox since strong constructionism is assumed to be entirely incompatible with realism (Shotter, 1993; Gergen, 2001). It is, as said, the new metanarrative for many, providing a place of belonging and an appealing identification with a radical movement. But *the unacknowledged and forbidden realism of strong constructionism creates in my view a classic Batesonian double-bind* (Bateson, 1972). To notice and speak of the reality of strong social constructionism is to disqualify oneself as a member of the strong social constructionist club; the incongruity cannot be commented on thereby completing the double-bind.

Furthermore, if strong constructionism is actually correct there would be no reason to take it seriously. It would merely be only "one of many culturally relative constructions of knowledge about 'reality', the merits of which we have no reliable independent standard by which to judge" (Smith, 2010, p. 136).

While there have been warnings of the dangers of postmodernism becoming the new big knowledge (metanarrative), these have all come from those at least partially from outside the postmodern tent (Golann, 1988; Goldner, 1991; Frosh, 1991; Held, 1995; Kraemer, 2009; Luepnitz, 1992; Minuchin, 1991; Pilgrim, 2000; Pocock, 1995a, 1995b; Speed, 1991). To be inside requires the continuing idea that realism provides only 'first-order' knowledge and the consequent unacceptable exercise of therapeutic power and control, imposing the therapist's 'reality' on family members. And, by the way, the increasing tendency, post 1990, to describe all systemic family therapy that came before as 'first-order' is another excellent example of the power of language to seduce and lead us away from its original meaning to create instead a context-marker for unacceptable practices. If you are a systemic therapist, do you, for example, know of anyone who is happy to describe their work as 'first-order'? I've never met anyone who does. It is a political term masquerading as a neutral description.

As I have written previously (Pocock, 2013), the paradox at the heart of strong social constructionism means that all attempts at such practice inevitably contain, embedded within them, forms of covert realism. At a conference workshop, about a decade ago, I invited a group of mostly experienced systemic family therapists to vote on whether they generally accepted all views of family members as equally valid accounts or whether they chose which to support on the basis of their likely truth. Every vote was for accepting all views equally rather than choosing between them. Only then did I introduce specific practice in the form of three statements made to me by family members over the years: "My grandson was born evil", "If I don't arrange all the items on my desk in the correct order, someone close to me will die", and "I've no doubt my daughter wanted us to have sex just as much as I did". In a second vote, no one felt able to support these comments other than as "true for that person".

Another strong constructionist or post-structural therapy called narrative therapy (White & Epston, 1990) offers attractive democratic possibilities in strengthening hidden or subjugated narratives which define the person in more benign terms, but the model is silent on *the inescapable fact that the therapist still has to choose* (Burr, 1999). Clitorectomy, holocaust denial, and overt racism are all (thankfully) subjugated narratives in Euro-American culture; I don't imagine any therapist would choose to strengthen these. Other forms of covert realism can be found in Hoffman's (2001) acknowledgement that the therapist will have favourite theories but without explaining what makes one idea more favoured than another. Anderson (1997) speaks of therapists 'using discourse' which might include realist theoretical ideas but without any (apparent) commitment to their truth status. So on what grounds are they chosen? During a live therapy session led by Michael White, as part of a workshop on narrative approaches, he asked the family members if they would like to hear what another family had done in a similar circumstance which had helped, but quickly added "but this isn't therapy" (M. Hayward, personal communication). I can't imagine the final comment made any difference to the family members but might have reassured him and the audience that he hadn't strayed into overt realism.

I agree with Carla Willig (2019) that being able to give a coherent account of one's ontological and epistemological position is a key aspect of therapist reflexivity. Is this really possible in strong constructionism without some level of self-deception? I should add that I am reassured whenever I see examples of covert realism in practice since it means that therapists are putting the needs of their clients ahead of the powerful influence of their metanarrative. But *wouldn't it be more accountable—more in line with second-order reflexivity—to have one's realism-based choices out in the open where they can be scrutinised and held accountable?* If we take seriously that knowledge and power are the same, as Foucault says, isn't covert realism a dangerous denial of therapist power?

Not all social constructionist therapies are as strong. For example, I am fully in agreement when Sheila McNamee (2004) calls (positively) for "promiscuity" in practice: using multiple positions rather than being tied to single approaches. Her recognition that therapy, in collaboratively constructing new meaning, is a social process seems to me to be necessary and unarguable. But, in my view, it leaves unanswered the question of how and why we choose particular positions. What are the limits? Would we include those early Freudian views of sexuality—that men are essentially active and women passive? I'm sure not. Our grounds for rejecting such ideas is not just that they are unpalatable to the modern taste, they have simply proved to be incorrect. Where we can, we surely need to judge how well our fallible ideas help us navigate the world and this takes us to realism. This moderate version of constructionism is necessary and welcome but not, I argue, sufficient to give a holistic account of practice.

A recent book, *Psychotherapeutic Competencies: Techniques, Relationships, and Epistemology*, by Laura Fruggeri et al. (2023) is, in my view, a further example of moderate constructionism. The authors describe their approach as social constructionist but make room for many theories of family functioning from the earlier decades of family therapy together with some attachment theory. They use these in constructing deductive functional hypotheses. But, again, realism as a basis for choice is obscured. Hypotheses are described as being confirmed or disconfirmed, however, that realist notion is translated into pragmatic language—more or less useful, rather than more or less true. (See Chap. 4 for further commentary on pragmatism as anti-realist.)

What happens when we fully acknowledge the realism inherent in social constructionism? This brings us finally to Bhaskar's critical realism.

The Reality of Social Construction

When Bateson talked about errors of thinking (epistemological errors), he did not simply mean that such non-systemic ideas were at variance with his own, he meant that *they are at odds with how the world actually is* (Dell, 1985). He particularly disliked the kind of scientific endeavour which chops up the world, separating things from their context. My point is that Bateson was, covertly, *a systemic realist ontologist.* As said, he concealed this by conflating epistemology and ontology into the single term 'epistemology' which he used idiosyncratically (Held & Pols, 1985). Later, within the systemic family therapy world Bebe Speed's (1991) co-constructivism and the interactive constructivism of William Pinsof (1994) were among the first to conceive explicitly—as Bateson did only implicitly—of a *realist ontology together with a constructivist/social constructionist epistemology.* It is reasonable to consider both Speed and Pinsof as proto-critical realists. I include some early papers of my own (Pocock, 1995a, 1995b, 1998) in the same proto-critical realist category, since at that time I had yet to hear of Bhaskar.

Bateson and Bhaskar appear to have been unaware of each other's work despite some striking overlaps and complementarities (Mingers, 2011; Dalton, 2014). Both Bateson and Bhaskar conceive of the ontological world as a holistic open system of multiple and simultaneous influences. Whereas Bateson speaks of systems, Bhaskar conceives of multiple interacting causal powers (or mechanisms or tendencies), operating in an open system, which may or may not become activated to produce an event. Note that, while this present discussion of what we can know about the world external to ourselves sounds like the misleading subject-object dualism of Descartes, as the critical realist Dave Elder-Vass (2012) puts it:

> ...we are ourselves material beings who are not dualistically separated from the world 'out there' but rather are part of the same material world as the things and events of which we have empirical experience. We obtain (fallible) knowledge of these things and events through a material process of perception. This process is itself influenced—but not simply *determined*—by the concepts we have, and those concepts are themselves shaped by our social interactions. (p. 251)

Bateson derived his world view from his multiple areas of study but, as said, was wary of fleshing out his ontological position lest this be perceived as separate from mind—a dualist error of thinking that he opposed throughout his working life. Bhaskar has a different starting point. He asks this deceptively simple question: given that science has a good record of developing reliable knowledge about the world, what *must the world necessarily be like in order for scientific knowledge to be possible.* (Fans of philosophy may recognise this as a 'transcendental argument'.) His answer, detailed in his first book *A Realist Philosophy of Science* (Bhaskar, 1977), is that the world *must* be an ordered, structured, stratified, and open system of interacting causal powers or mechanisms (the Real) that may or may not interact to generate an event (the Actual) which, itself, may or may not be available to observation (the Empirical).

However, while the world remains just as it is—the *intransitive* dimension in Bhaskar's terminology—our knowledge of the world is the *transitive* dimension: socially constructed and therefore fallible, subject to change, bias, and all the other concerns that the postmodern critique brought to bear. Note that I am in favour of postmodernism as a *critique* of the ideals of value-free objective knowledge and certainty. My complaint is when postmodernism *becomes* the new knowledge and certainty, as in strong constructionism. It then fails to critique itself (Pocock, 1995a, 1995b), or in the lyrics of Pete Townsend of *The Who,* "Meet the new boss, same as the old boss".

With the world as it is allowed to contribute to our knowledge of it, then rational choices between constructions become possible. *Either / or* choices come back on the agenda alongside postmodernism's *both / and* assumptions. As John Searle (1995, p. 26) puts it "The world acts back on us to constrain the points of view that are possible". Both quantitative and qualitative research are ways in which ideas are tested against those constraints. But every human being makes similar tests all the time. If we did not do so we would not be successful in even the most basic of our daily activities: the soup that needs more salt; locating the light switch by feeling in the dark; seeing how long we can hold our breath. No matter what ideas guide our actions reality usually has a say, and sometimes—for example in the case of the Breatharians who believe that it is possible to live without food—it is the final word.

The testing of ideas through all means, including science, allows a Darwinian selection. Ideas can become more 'object adequate' (Elias, 1971) through survival of these encounters with the constraints of the world (Glasersfeld, 1984). Of course in situations of complexity, research or day-to-day testing is not so easy—or in the case of religion, impossible—but that does not mean that all ideas are true, or none are true (Collier, 1999). However, as we will discuss, ideas—whether true or false—all have potential causal power as anyone who watched the January 6th storming of the White House will have noticed.

And where do these mental constructions come from? Beyond simple individual testing, our knowledge (our know-that) and skills (know-how) are derived from our participation in knowledge communities: in the case of psychotherapy—training, reading, supervision, etc. It is, in other words, socially constructed. Additionally, our more unconscious intuitive ways of being in the world—our knowing-within (Shotter, 1993)—are also made socially but through participation in close relationships, and acculturating norm-circles (Chap. 8): for example, family, friendships, work, culture, hobby clubs, political affiliations, and experiences in psychotherapy.

I can now explain why I am using the term 'strong social constructionism' to refer to the ideas as taken up in mainstream systemic psychotherapy rather than plain 'social constructionism' which is the commonly used term. *Critical realism is a third position between realism and idealism, incorporating the two but rejecting the extremes at both ends—naïve realism and strong constructionism. It is both moderately realist and moderately socially constructionist* (Elder-Vass, 2012). Its second-order epistemology is only moderately relativist in the sense that what we experience of the world is relative to our vantage points, themselves constructed in knowledge communities. Strong constructionism, in contrast, is *strongly* relativist since ideas are relative only to each other and do not reference the world as it is (except when it has to by way of covert realism). For strong constructionists, discourses make up the world: critical realism agrees that discourses have causal power but locates these alongside many other causal powers.

The Real, the Actual, and the Empirical

Critical realism challenges the 'epistemic fallacy' (Bhaskar, 1977) of strong constructionism: that our understanding of knowledge can be reduced solely to the social means by which it is produced. But it also critiques the positivist account of science and what Bhaskar calls the 'fallacy of actualism'—a shallow form of realism. I imagine my readers may have their head in their hands at the prospect of embracing yet another unfamiliar concept, but this is, for me, one of the most important ideas in critical realism, with major implications for understanding how patterns form and how change can occur.

Scientific experiments—for example, testing the effectiveness of a new drug—artificially close the system by controlling for all variables other than the one being studied. If the results show efficacy then it is assumed that particular mechanism has a causal effect that never varies. The positivist account of scientific laws are universal assumptions of invariant causal relationships between events. But, as Bhaskar argues, the ontological world is an *open* system of multiple causal tendencies—not at all like the closed system of an experiment—and it is *whether and how these tendencies interact that determine whether an event is actualised.*

If I grip a pencil above my desk and then decide to let go, it will fall down and hit the desk creating a small sound. This is an actualised event that I can experience (empiricism) through my eyes and ears and brain. Science tells us that one important mechanism at play is gravity. What if I repeat the experiment but this time decide not to let go of the pencil? There is no empirically observable event, so what happened to gravity—has it been switched off? Clearly not, it is present as a constant *potential* causal power. Whether or not there is a falling-pencil-hitting-the-desk event depends on how the potential power of gravity interacts with other potential powers—my decision whether to let go, my neural pathway, cell physiology, musculature, and so on. If I do let go, the quality of the sound depends on whether the pencil hits the hard wood surface or some stray papers, as well as the various mechanisms of my hearing apparatus.

Each of these *potential causal powers are themselves emergent from deeper strata of mechanisms.* In the inorganic world, hydrogen and oxygen are both explosive gasses but they can combine to form water which has entirely different emergent properties to either of them. In the organic world, cell physiology cannot be understood without the lower stratum of molecular biochemistry, but biochemistry cannot *entirely* account for cell physiology. The latter has emergent powers beyond those of the lower stratum. So higher strata cannot be understood without lower strata but cannot be reduced to the lower layer. Moving further up the layers, it is impossible to understand a relationship between two people without knowing about individuals, but a relationship cannot be reduced to the sum of those individuals; *the relationship has unique emergent properties or, as systems theory puts it, the relationship is more than the sum of its parts.* Similarly, despite the enormous advances in understanding what happens in dyadic infant-caregiver relationships, this knowledge cannot, as we will see in Chap. 10, give a complete account of triadic relationships, let alone larger groups like families (Dallos, 2014).

In the real world of open systems the Batesonian patterns that connect are, from a critical realist perspective, made up of *numerous potential causal powers interacting together and, at times, actualised to generate relatively stable systems of causality.* Bhaskar (1977) describes the process of mapping of the individual causal powers in a system as 'retrodiction', and the process by which one retrospectively maps the combination of powers necessary to generate an event as 'retroduction'.

A change in one causal mechanism may break a circuit and alter the system. Light is the emergent actualised property of a working flashlight but if you remove just one of the component mechanisms, all of which have causal tendencies—the on-switch, the battery, the bulb, or the casing—then the light goes out. *In psychotherapy the more mechanisms we understand the greater the chance of interrupting the maladaptive patterns.* In the case of Emma in Chap. 1, her response to the question "Did you think you had made Daddy tired?" was enough to begin altering the relational system.

In passing, since I develop this argument in Chap. 4, there is a crucial difference in language between Bateson and Bhaskar over the conception of power. For Bateson, lineal conceptions of power are an epistemological error—no one part of a system of circular causality is any more powerful than another. This has properly attracted much criticism from feminists (e.g. Goldner, 1993). *For Bhaskar the ontological system is entirely constituted through powers which may or may not be activated.*

So what are these ontological potential causal powers that may or may not interact to form an event? Everything all at once: the genes that may or may not get expressed depending on the environment, the old traumatic memory that may or may not be triggered by a new disturbing experience. Ideology, beliefs, norms, being loved, the implied threat of violence of a partner, the theoretical idea in a therapist's mind, a promotion at work, racism, structural poverty, a TV programme, or even absences such as the ambulance that didn't arrive in time or the unavailability of an attuned caregiver in infancy: all have causal tendencies.

Note that in critical realism, ideas, beliefs, and cultural practices all embedded in language are included as causal tendencies. The question, then, for strong constructionism is well-put by David Pilgrim (2020):

> To have faith in the words or texts requires us to have confidence in their very existence, thereby confirming ontological realism. And once that is conceded, why only isolate words as being real and nothing else? Why special plead for language, rather than other palpable and hidden forces in our lives? (p. 35)

Fortunately, when it comes to psychotherapy, not everything needs to be mapped—that would be impossible. Indeed while some events are observable, such as Emma starting to play again, others, such as the idea forming in Emma's mind that she had "worn Daddy out", are not. *In Bhaskar's ground-breaking 'holy trinity' of concepts there are potential causal powers (the real), that may or may not interact to generate an event (the actual), which itself may or may not be observable to us through our senses (the empirical).*

Two Inches of Difference

For me, this explanation of how change happens is full of hope, but it is also cause for some therapist humility. I'll end this chapter with one of the earliest case examples that I heard from one of my first family therapy teachers—Andy Treacher. Across the passage of nearly four decades I may have lost or distorted some of the details, but this is the gist. A couple sought help because of severe rows over how to manage their toddler getting out of his cot at night. The parents were exhausted and close to breaking up as the situation had gone on for months. Over a series of sessions the therapist explored the history of relationships on both sides of the family, especially the patterns of how conflict was managed across the previous two generations. Nothing seemed to help until one day the couple arrived looking rested and relieved. The therapist was getting ready to quietly congratulate herself when the couple announced that the maternal grandfather had raised the cot sides by two inches. The toddler couldn't climb out, the couple had their first good night's sleep in months and the conflict abated. It was a difference that allowed a bigger systemic change—a difference that made a difference (Bateson, 1979).

Of course, the causal powers that allowed conflictual events to emerge in this couple when triggered by physical exhaustion may remain as tendencies and these may or may not be actualised again by other triggers. However, unlike the illusion of positivism, it is impossible to predict anything for sure in an open system of multiple interacting causal tendencies. Although the couple work was not, in itself, sufficient to change the system at the time when the toddler escapes and the exhaustion were still in play, it may have built some resilience against similar future triggers. Only time can ever tell.

In an open system you can never be sure where change may come from. The system of causal powers is infinitely complex, massive, and incapable of being squeezed into the therapy room. Choices of who to see in psychotherapy allows focus on *parts* of the system (Chap. 9) but the vicissitudes of life bring alterations from out of left field. Life is bigger than even the most systemically inclusive psychotherapy.

References

Anderson, H. (1997). *Conversation, language and possibilities: A postmodern approach to therapy*. Basic Books.

Anderson, H., & Goolishian, H. (1988). Human systems as linguistic systems. *Family Process, 27*, 371–393.

Bateson, G. (1958). *Naven: A survey of the problems suggested by a composite picture of the culture of a New Guinea tribe drawn from three points of view*. Stanford University Press.

Bateson, G. (1972). *Steps to an ecology of mind*. Balantine.

Bateson, G. (1979). *Mind and nature: A necessary unity*. Dutton.

Bhaskar, R. (1977). *A realist philosophy of science*. Harvester.

Bhaskar, R. (2016). *Enlightened common sense: The philosophy of critical realism*. Routledge.

Broderick, C., & Schrader, S. (1991). The history of professional marriage and family therapy. In A. Gurman & D. Kniskern (Eds.), *The handbook of family therapy, Volume II*. Brunner/Mazel.

Buch-Hansen, H., & Nielsen, P. (2020). *Critical realism: Basics and beyond*. Red Globe Press.

Burr, V. (1999). Overview: Realism, relativism, social constructionism, and discourse. In I. Parker (Ed.), *Social constructionism, discourse and realism* (pp. 13–25). Sage.

Collier, A. (1999). Language, practice, and realism. In I. Parker (Ed.), *Social constructionism, discourse, and realism* (pp. 47–58). Sage.

Dallos, R. (2014). Assessing attachment in families: Beyond the dyads. In S. Farnfield & P. Holmes (Eds.), *The Routledge handbook of attachment: Assessment* (pp. 192–209). Routledge.

Dalton, C. (2014). Beyond description to pattern: The contribution of Batesonian epistemology to critical realist research. *Journal of Critical Realism, 13*, 163–182.

Dell, P. (1985). Understanding Bateson and Maturana: Toward a biological foundation for the social sciences. *Journal of Marital and Family Therapy, 11*, 1–20.

Elder-Vass, D. (2012). *The reality of social construction*. Cambridge University Press.

Elias, N. (1971). Sociology of knowledge: New perspectives (part two). *Sociology, 5*, 355–370.

Foucault, M. (1977). *Discipline and punish: The birth of the prison.* Pantheon Books.
Freud, S. (1900). The interpretation of dreams. In *The standard edition of the complete psychological works of Sigmund Freud Vol. 5*. Hogarth Press.
Frosh, S. (1991). The semantics of therapeutic change. *Journal of Family Therapy, 13*, 171–186.
Fruggeri, L., Balestra, F., & Venturelli, E. (2023). *Psychotherapeutic competencies: Techniques, relationships, and epistemology in systemic practice*. Routledge.
Gergen, K. (2001). *Social constructionism in context.* Sage.
Glasersfeld, E. von. (1984). An introduction to radical constructivism. In P. Watzlawick (Ed.), *The invented reality* (pp. 17–40). Norton.
Golann, S. (1988). On second-order family therapy. *Family Process, 27*, 51–65.
Goldner, V. (1991). Feminism and systemic practice: Two critical traditions in transition. *Journal of Family Therapy., 13*, 95–104.
Goldner, V. (1993). Power and hierarchy: Let's talk about it! *Family Process, 32*, 157–162.
Green, A. (1973). On negative capability: A critical review of W. R. Bion's 'attention and interpretation'. *International Journal of Psychoanalysis, 54*, 115–128.
Hanly, C. (2009). On truth and clinical psychoanalysis. *The International Journal of Psychoanalysis, 90*, 363–373.
Harries-Jones, P. (1995). *A recursive vision: Ecological understanding and Gregory Bateson*. Toronto Press.
Held, B. (1995). *Back to reality: A critique of postmodern theory in psychotherapy.* Norton.
Held, B., & Pols, E. (1985). The confusion about epistemology and 'epistemology'—And what to do about it. *Family Process, 24*, 509–517.
Hoffman, L. (1990). Constructing realities: An art of lenses. *Family Process, 29*, 1–12.
Hoffman, L. (2001). *Family therapy: An intimate history.* Norton.
Keats, J. (1899). *The complete poetical works and letters of John Keats*. Houghton, Mifflin, and Company.
Korzybski, A. (1933). *Science and sanity*. Science Press.
Kraemer, S. (2009). Is there another word for it? Countertransference in family therapy. In C. Flaskas & D. Pocock (Eds.), *Systems and psychoanalysis: Contemporary integrations in family therapy* (pp. 39–55). Karnac.
Krause, I.-B. (2012). *Culture and reflexivity in systemic psychotherapy: Mutual perspectives*. Karnac.

Lessing, D. (1994). *Under my skin: Volume one of my autobiography to 1949.* Harper Collins.

Luepnitz, D. (1992). Nothing in common but their first names: The case of Foucault and White. *Journal of Family Therapy, 14*, 281–284.

Lyotard, J. (1984). *The postmodern condition.* Manchester University Press.

Maturana, H., & Varela, F. (1980). *Autopoiesis and cognition: The realization of the living.* Reidel.

McNamee, S. (2004). Promiscuity in the practice of family therapy. *Journal of Family Therapy, 26*, 224–244.

Mingers, J. (2011). The contributions of systemic thought to critical realism. *Journal of Critical Realism, 10*, 303–330.

Minuchin, S. (1991). The seductions of constructivism. *Family Therapy Networker*, September/October, 47–50.

Minuchin, S., & Fishman, H. (1981). *Family therapy techniques.* Harvard University Press.

Orange, D. (1995). *Emotional understanding: Studies in psychoanalytic epistemology.* Guilford.

Palazzoli, M., Cecchin, G., Prata, G., & Boscolo, L. (1979). *Paradox and counterparadox.* Aronson.

Pilgrim, D. (2000). The real problem for postmodernism. *Journal of Family Therapy, 22*, 6–23.

Pilgrim, D. (2020). *Critical realism for psychologists.* Routledge.

Pinsof, W. (1994). An overview of integrative problem centred therapy: A synthesis of family and individual psychotherapies. *Journal of Family Therapy, 16*, 103–120.

Pocock, D. (1995a). Postmodern chic: Postmodern critique. *Context, 24*, 46–48.

Pocock, D. (1995b). Searching for a better story: Harnessing modern and postmodern positions in family therapy. *Journal of Family Therapy, 17*, 149–173.

Pocock, D. (1998). Stories about knowing. *Gestalt!* https://www.researchgate.net/publication/376853003_Stories_about_knowing

Pocock, D. (1999). Loose ends. *Journal of Family Therapy, 21*, 187–194.

Pocock, D. (2013). A philosophy of practice for systemic psychotherapy: The case for critical realism. *Journal of Family Therapy., 37*, 167–183.

Searle, J. (1995). *The construction of social reality.* Harmondsworth.

Shotter, J. (1993). *Conversational realities: Constructing life through language.* Sage.

Simon, G. (1992). Having a second-order mind while doing first-order therapy. *Journal of Marital and Family Therapy, 18*, 377–387.

Smith, C. (2010). *What is a person? Rethinking humanity, social life, and the moral good from the person up*. University of Chicago Press.

Speed, B. (1991). Reality exists O.K.? An argument against constructivism and social constructionism. *Journal of Family Therapy, 13*, 395–409.

Watzlawick, P., Bavelas, J., & Jackson, D. (1967). *Pragmatics of human communication: A study of interactional patterns, pathologies, and paradoxes and problem resolution*. Norton.

White, M., & Epston, D. (1990). *Narrative means to therapeutic ends*. Norton.

Willig, C. (2019). Ontological and epistemological reflexivity: A core skill for therapists. *Counselling and Psychotherapy Research, 19*, 186–194.

3

Pluralism

> The moves from a constructivist to a feminist stance, or from a systemic to a psychodynamic perspective, do not appear to require the paradigm shifts that the history of these ideas in family therapy would have led us to expect. We feel considerable freedom of movement. This is because we track the clinical process closely, and because, in whatever frame we occupy, we remain sensitive to the same set of issues: the place of language in constructing reality, the position of the observer or observing group that inevitably frames the problem and defines the terms of the problem-maintaining system, the moral limits of relativism, and the attempt to operate with the belief in an "observer-independent world-out-there" without succumbing to a naive, simple construction of "truth." We remain sceptical about essences, universals, and stable meanings, and *we believe the layering of these intellectual perspectives is necessary if we are to capture the nuanced complexity of the issues at hand.* Virginia Goldner et al. (1990, p. 346. [My emphasis])

As we discussed in Chap. 2, 1990 was a pivotal year in the history of family therapy development, with the mainstream following Lynn Hoffman and others into the strong constructionism of 'Family Therapy Part 2'. I should add that, by 'mainstream', I'm not assuming that all systemic family therapists immediately took the 'linguistic turn', but the influence was

D. Pocock, *Expanding the Limits of Individual and Family Therapies*, Palgrave Texts in Counselling and Psychotherapy, https://doi.org/10.1007/978-3-031-76309-0_3

widespread, and the ideas were cumulatively adopted by training institutes that shape each generation of systemic psychotherapists, establishing the new norms.

The above quote comes from another paper published in *Family Process* in the same year—*Love and Violence: Gender Paradoxes in Volatile Attachments*—by members of the Gender and Violence Project at the Ackerman Institute in New York: Virginia Goldner, Peggy Penn, Marcia Sheinberg, and Gillian Walker. They worked with couples in which the man had been violent to the woman, but where both wanted to stay together. This one, regrettably, does not appear in the list of the top twenty-four papers. It represents the road not taken by most family systems therapy, but for me it is *the* most important paper of the last thirty-five years since it refuses to be organised by the dualisms on offer at that time: modernism versus postmodernism, psychoanalytic versus systemic, constructionism versus realism, and Family Therapy Part 1 versus Part 2 (Hoffman, 1990). Instead, the paper starts by paying close attention to the clinical process and draws on theory and metatheory (epistemology and ontology) only as frames to assist and inform their sensitive and nuanced approach. In practice, as the authors say, their movement across these domains was *not constrained* in the way these splits would suggest. On the contrary, the authors felt "considerable freedom of movement". I remember the relief I felt on first reading this, and it has been a source of support ever since.

Pluralism—the use of multiple and layered perspectives—is the next level up from the epistemological and ontological foundations of the critical realist scaffold which completed the last chapter. As I write, I can see in my bookshelf a copy of the *Collins World Atlas*. I take it down and across the front cover is emblazoned "The world revealed through award-winning mapping!" But of course, as useful as it is, an atlas can't *reveal* the world—no book will ever be large enough to do that. Maps are, as Korzybski (1933) reminds us, not to be confused with the territory. The first forty pages provide a range of socially constructed perspectives which elaborate features only from their particular vantage point—climate, per capita income, earthquake coverage, religion, and so on. Each map on its own is reductionist but imagine these are transparencies and laid over each other. Each then becomes a context for the other. The map of personal wealth gives context to the map of mobile phone coverage; the spread of infant mortality is illuminated by the map of doctors per 100,000 people; the distribution of various kinds of vegetation makes more sense when layered with the map of climate, and so on. Multiple layers provide a depth of inter-related understandings, and the world begins to emerge in its complexity. All in a single book that I can hold with one hand. Atlases are amazing!

In psychotherapy, the more maps we have in our mind, the more resources we have available in the collaborative search for the multiple causal tendencies that make a life. It is a central argument of Chap. 6 that, when people feel understood and are able to understand themselves and others contextually, compassion for self and others increases and new choices open up. As Donna Orange (1995, p. 15) writes, understanding "emerges from the work/play of two or more people together. Understanding is a *relational way* of being and knowing". Nevertheless, the therapist can *prepare to try* to understand the moment that any information arrives about the client(s). Such preliminary thoughts, of course, have potential causal power only, unless—and until—they can serve the therapeutic process. There are, no doubt, different ways of approaching tentative formulation, but the question I ask myself when presented with new information, and indeed throughout therapy, is "where are the contexts in which this person's situation or this family dilemma may be understandable?"

Catherine of Siena

One of the tensions in writing for publication is the conflict between providing authentic and detailed clinical material while at the same time protecting confidentiality. The acts of disguising, compiling composite examples, and restricting identifying context make it impossible to even sketch a complete life of a client or family. Furthermore, as Lynne Layton (1999) discusses from a psychoanalytic perspective, conventions for the disguise of case material often remove social issues (race, gender, social class, etc.) as identifiers, thereby inadvertently concealing the very inequalities that can contribute to people seeking psychological help in the first place.

So all disguises inevitably remove a sense of overall veracity. It is a particular problem for this book which seeks to expand holistic understanding and therefore requires a lot of detail. In contrast, there is considerable freedom in writing about a historical figure and my description of Catherine of Siena's life is the fullest of those in the book although, other than a brief quotation, it cannot include her first-person voice.

Catherine of Siena interests me for reasons that are not entirely clear—although I do love medieval history. I suspect she represents an old ideal, rejected by me but still lurking within—that of the heroically committed religious life. But whereas I escaped *from* religion, Catherine, with considerably fewer choices, may have escaped into it.

How is it possible that a semi-literate daughter from a family of Italian tradesmen came in the late Middle Ages to acquire extraordinary political power becoming, before the age of thirty, able to help heal the schism in the Catholic Church through influencing the relocation of the papacy from France to Rome and, among other high-level commissions, acting as an emissary for Pope Gregory XI in peace negotiations between Florence and Rome? The story of Caterina di Jacopo di Benincasa, known as Catherine of Siena (1347–1380), is an extraordinary one by any measure but even more so to the modern ear given the enormous differences in European culture across seven centuries. It is also, at times, something of a challenge to the squeamish, so please take this as a trigger-warning if you have just had your breakfast!

In attempting a provisional understanding of Catherine within the many contexts of her life, I am indebted to the scholarship of Caroline Walker Bynum (1987) in her wonderful book *Holy Feast and Holy Fast: The Religious Significance of Food to Medieval Women.* Other information is taken from the comprehensive Wikipedia page. I approach this as an atheist, but in this account I first record the 'facts' phenomenologically—as Catherine and those around her seem to have experienced them. Note that one of the points of agreement between critical realists and postmodernists is that facts do not stand alone—they are theory-laden and value-laden (Pilgrim, 2020).

Catherine was one of twin girls: the twenty-third and twenty-fourth child (around half of whom died in childhood) of Lapa Piangeti, daughter of a local poet, and Jacopo di Benincasa who ran a cloth dyeing business together with their sons. Lapa was forty years old, and the twins were born prematurely and were in delicate health. Lapa believed that she could only nurse one child and chose Catherine. She was the only one of her children that Lapa breastfed for a lengthy period and may have done so until her next and final pregnancy. Catherine thrived, but her twin, Giovanna, was sent out to a wet-nurse and died soon afterwards. When Catherine was two years old Lapa gave birth again. As was commonly the case at that time, the new baby was also given the name Giovanna.

In her early years Catherine was a happy child, and the family pet name for her was Euphrosyne, the Greek goddess of merriment and joy. She is said to have had her first vision of Christ when she was six years old, when she and a brother were returning from visiting a married sister. In the vision the glorified Christ, wearing the papal dress, appears seated on a beautiful throne with the apostles John, Paul, and Peter. At age seven, Catherine committed her life to God and determined to remain a virgin. She became very close to her sister, Bonaventura, who was one year older.

As an adolescent, Catherine was aware that the dissolute behaviour of Bonaventura's husband was a cause of considerable distress to her sister. Bonaventura starved herself to try to force her husband to reform and this was, apparently, successful. Bonaventura was able to persuade Catherine to make herself look pretty and to dress elegantly, but shortly afterwards, at age sixteen, Bonaventura died in childbirth. Around the same time, Giovanna, the youngest child in the family and named after Catherine's dead twin, also died. According to at least one account, Catherine came under pressure to marry Bonaventura's widower.

Catherine began fasting as a child and developed an early distaste for meat. She identified with early Christian hermits, known as the Desert Fathers, whose ascetic practices of poverty, service, and self-denial formed the basis for Christian monasticism. Several sources speak of her running away to a cave as a young girl. As she moved into adolescence there was increasing conflict with her parents over her asceticism and refusal to consider marriage. During the most intense period of their disagreements

Catherine cut off her long hair to make herself look unattractive. Following a vision of St Dominic she tried to persuade her parents to allow her to join the Dominican order as a nun. Her mother instead took her on holiday to take the waters to try to improve her daughter's health. Catherine deliberately scalded herself in the hot springs and developed a pox from which she made no effort to recover. Finally, her mother compromised; she would not allow her daughter to become a nun but accepted Catherine's wish to join the Mantellate, a local Dominican lay organisation of devout women.

As the family conflict deepened, Catherine withdrew into isolation in a cell in her parents' home and practiced extreme sleep deprivation and self-starvation. From about age sixteen she subsisted on bread, water, and raw vegetables. Around twenty-three she gave up bread, surviving on the eucharist, cold water and morsels of food—mostly bitter herbs that she sucked and then spat out or swallowed and vomited-up. According to her most reliable biographer—Raymond of Capua—who was a later spiritual advisor to Catherine, Christ summoned her out of her withdrawal and commanded that she should once more eat with her family. She tried to do this but found that she could not physically comply. She described eating as the act of dealing out punishment to herself, "a miserable sinner". Several eye-witness accounts record her poking twigs down her throat to bring up food that she could not bear to rest in her stomach. However, she could immediately rouse herself to attend to spiritual matters. Raymond writes:

> … I myself saw it happen, not once, but again and again, that her emaciated body would be reduced to the last extremity, unable to take anything to restore its forces but a drink of cold water … and then suddenly she would seize … an opportunity to take on some work for the honour of God's name or the good of souls, and like a flash, without the help of any other restorative [i.e. without eating] … all her forces would revive. (Quoted in Bynum, 1987, p. 168)

She appears to have lost the ability to read bodily sensations, describing any hunger pangs as "greed" and seemed incapable of feeling cold. Her restless energy and sleeplessness increased as she ate less and less. She argued with her confessors who were urging her to moderate her fasting that, since eating caused her torture, it was the sin of suicide for her to eat; a far worse homicide of the self than starving oneself because it was homicide by greed. Nevertheless, as Bynum records, Catherine did regard her inability to eat as an infirmity, not a personal choice.

There is no sense that, at any point, did Catherine see herself as a good and holy person. As an adolescent she conceived a "holy hatred" of herself and, in addition to the fasting, she routinely wore a hair shirt and iron chains under her dress and engaged in self-flagellation. She described her body as a "dung heap". Right up to her death she was tormented by doubts about her own worthiness under assaults from the Devil. She saw her suffering as quite literally merging with Christ's agony on the cross. Several reports suggest that Catherine only agreed to keep on living because the Virgin Mary had promised her that Catherine's pain would free souls trapped and tortured in purgatory.

After ending her period of isolation and re-joining the family, she engaged in frenetic housework, doing the laundry at night. She nursed the family servant back to health and carried out all of the servant's work. She gave vast quantities of the family's food to the poor and, on one occasion, angered her father by giving away his best wine.

The exception to Catherine's relationship with food was her passion for the eucharist—God's body and blood—not symbolised by bread and wine but, in the Church's view at that time, his actual body and blood. Against the advice of her spiritual advisors she received communion every day, apparently in a state of ecstasy. Various accounts record her substituting not just the body and blood of Christ for ordinary food but also diseased flesh. She twice sucked on the breasts of dying women, drinking the pus. As she told Raymond, "Never in my life have I tasted any food and drink sweeter or more exquisite". After one such incident Christ came to her in a vision and rewarded her overcoming her bodily qualms in sucking the pus as a sacrifice to him, by gently encouraged her to suck the blood from his wounded side in order that she might be filled with its overflowing goodness. Her letters, thereafter, became filled with the images of nursing from the breast of Christ.

Catherine's rejection of earthly bridegrooms was completed with a 'mystical marriage' to Christ. The ring, that she could always see, was at times a ring of gold or silver embedded with jewels and, at other times, Christ's foreskin arising from the pain and bleeding of circumcision. Her parents eventually abandoned hopes for her marriage and were forced to accept her ascetic life. She threw herself into charitable acts in Siena, largely through a local hospital, and began to become well-known. She was referred to locally as *santa donna*—a holy woman. Interest in her grew exponentially when rumours of miracles sprang up. Raymond records:

> The whole city was in commotion. Everybody … flocked to catch sight of her. "What a woman!" they said. "One who drinks no wine herself but can, by a miracle, fill with wine an empty cask." (Bynum, 1987, p. 170)

The miracle in question was God making the wine cask flow again after she gave her father's expensive wine away. Other miracles followed: she restored the capacity to produce milk to two women whose breasts had gone dry, she cured illness, and there were miraculous multiplications of food in the same vein as Christ's feeding of the five thousand.

As her fame spread, her authority to intervene in political matters grew. She travelled through northern and central Italy advocating reform of the clergy. In Pisa, she powerfully challenged an anti-papal movement, receiving in that city the stigmata—Christ's five wounds—visible, at her request, only to herself. She wrote numerous letters to people of influence pleading for peace between the warring principalities of Italy and for the return of the papacy, from the luxury of Avignon in France, back to Rome. She corresponded regularly with Pope Gregory XI, often addressing him as Babbo (Daddy) and instructing him on how he should behave, but with the occasional display of humility. This seemed to both irritate the Pope and endear her to him. Despite his ambivalence, he found her an impressive person and, among other commissions, appointed her as his ambassador to try to forge peace between the Republic of Florence and the papal states. After the death of Gregory the new Pope, Urban VI, summoned her to Rome to try to help mend yet another schism emerging in the Church.

At the age of thirty, Catherine returned to Siena, founding a strictly observant woman's monastery. She dictated and edited the hundreds of letters and prayers which make up the *Dialogue of Divine Providence*, extending her fame beyond her death and making a significant contribution to Italian literature. Another period of intense fasting and restriction of water at the start of 1380 led to a major stroke and she died eight days later in Rome at the age of thirty-three, the same age as Christ.

Devotion to Catherine spread quickly after her death and continued to grow over the centuries. She was canonised in 1461, and declared a patron saint of Rome in 1866, and a patron saint of Italy in 1939. She was only the second woman to be made a Doctor of the Church in 1970, in recognition of her writing. In 1999 Pope John Paul II proclaimed her a patron saint of Europe. She is widely recognised as one of the outstanding figures in medieval Catholicism and in the political history of Italy.

Contexts

How are we to develop a provisional understanding of Catherine in a historical period so different to that of most contemporary Euro-American culture? The eye may first be drawn to her extreme fasting since anorexia and bulimia are familiar to our modern age. Indeed, Catherine is often cited in historical reviews of eating disorders but, although she developed a "holy hatred" of her body, there is no evidence of body dysmorphia. She never thought of herself as fat for the good reason that, in a time when starvation was a real possibility, the culture did not place a premium on thinness.

Bhaskar's retroductive approach in critical realism is to track backwards from observable phenomena to explore the deeper multiple causal tendencies that have combined to create the phenomena.

Catherine and her world are a whole, but we cannot begin to try to understand that holism all in one go since the complexity would overwhelm us. We can however walk around, taking different vantage points. *But as soon as we develop ideas, these too become part of the system under consideration, lest we fall into the naïve realism of Saxe's blind men.* Where we can (since we also have non-conscious parts of our mind) we need to both notice and take responsibility for our part in the observations. This is the second-order position. To repeat an obvious point, these speculations have no absolute therapeutic value (although, hopefully, an educative one) since a meaningful understanding of Catherine clearly cannot take place without her. There is, in fact, no evidence that she sought to understand herself: that notion, in itself, being largely an aspect of our modern age.

I will use four main vantage points: culture, family relationships, the body, and the self. Within each of these is a further variety of lenses, provided by theory, other historical knowledge, and my experiences as a therapist and an embodied person.

Culture

Religion

The late-medieval Christian world was a place of intense moral dualism: good versus evil, God versus the Devil, and the spirit separate from the flesh. Hell and the 'cleansing' fires of purgatory were as real to the general population as cars and televisions are to us. To emphasise the point, churches often displayed graphic depictions of what might be expected in hell if regular church attendance and quiet obedience were not observed. The shift in emphasis, away from the threat of damnation and towards God's love, was still some centuries off. Accordingly, churches were packed, and Catholicism had enormous power. Using the lens given by Foucault's (1977) metaphor of the panopticon (an unseen supervisor—in this case, God—in a central tower able to watch every prisoner in a circular arrangement of cells) such power is wielded, not through external sanctions, but through internalisation. It is analogous to what Freud described as the super-ego—each person first polices and disciplines *themselves* for wrong thoughts and deeds.

Culture and the Physical World

Repeated crop failures, due to bad weather, and rampant diseases in livestock resulted in the Great Famine of 1315 to 1317, which is estimated to have killed 30–60% of the European population. The Black Death reached Siena three decades later, a year after Catherine's birth, and killed around 50% of people across Europe, very likely including members of her family. Our modern understanding of these phenomena was, of course, unavailable. Overlaying a map of these historical events with a map of the religious beliefs prevalent at the time would indicate that such calamities could only be seen as God's anger with his human creation. There were no 'natural' disasters. God's use of the flood to wipe out the entire human race, excepting one holy family as depicted in Genesis, was well-established in the medieval mind. The only solution available to the majority of the frightened population in the face of these devastations was a spiritual one. The emergence in Siena of a young woman so devoted to Christ that she transcended the need for food, healed the sick, and produced miraculous multiplications of food and wine for others, was bound to be a rare cause for hope and great excitement.

Gender

In systemic family therapy literature the lens of gender is often discussed separately from that of culture, which I think reflects more the fact that preoccupations with each came at separate periods in the history of family therapy development; culture being a relative late-comer. Yet the establishment of norms for the roles of men and women is a fundamental part of every culture in every period of history. The deep patriarchy—especially that of the church—provided women with very limited areas of autonomy or personal expression and few resources that they could control. Obedience to parents, husband, and the church was expected. However, the instability caused by the Black Death, and the consequent shortage of labour and new bargaining power, began to bring with it great social change. In England, the Peasants' Revolt was the first major challenge to feudalism. Chaucer's *The Wife of Bath,* one of the *Canterbury Tales*, written during the same period, portrayed a very different motive for a woman—one who desired, above all else, sovereignty: the right to self-determination.

As we will discuss in Chap. 8, the influence of culture can be viewed in a more fine-grained manner through the theoretical layer of norm circles (Elder-Vass, 2012). There is evidence that Catherine identified with other powerful women in the history of the church. Such identifications have causal tendencies. Mary Magdalene fasted for thirty-three years, stood under the cross and was blessed to be covered with Christ's blood. Catherine was vocal about her interest in Agnes of Montepulciano who was able to survive on vegetables alone, because of her 'perfection'. Agnes had a miraculous reputation in 'multiplying loaves' (this was at the height of the Great Famine), was devoted to the eucharist, was elected to prioress in her religious community, and went on to build a church in Florence—the one area open to women to take leadership roles being within female religious groups. Catherine's namesake—the fourth century martyr, Catherine of Alexandria—was significant for her 'mystical marriage' to Christ. Bynum suggests that Catherine's identification with the Dominicans may well have been based at least partly on their doctrine that weakness can become strength, drawn from the Gospel of Matthew: "So those who are last [in this world] shall be first [in the world to come], and those who are first, last". The power differential between men and women might therefore be reversed. Holy women could, indeed, conceive of an intense union with Christ through 'marriage' that was unavailable even to priests.

Renunciation was a powerful signifier of faith but, as Bynum describes, each gender renounced what they were able to control. For men this was sex, wealth, and property; for women, as providers of sustenance to their families, it was always food.

The causal mechanisms of cultural discourse are not the sole influence in constructing the self as some postmodern theorists suggest, otherwise everyone under those influences would be the same and Catherine was certainly exceptional, even in her day. No one is shaped only by culture, nor indeed by any single influence. Much depends on how culture interacts with other causal tendencies.

Family Relationships

The prolonged breastfeeding of Catherine, and the fact of her being the youngest surviving child, may have made her particularly special to her mother. This contrasts in the extreme with the fate of her twin Giovanna and the 'second' Giovanna who also died several years later. From the perspectives given by our understanding of mourning processes (Freud, 1917), if Catherine was not helped to understand these deaths as she matured, this may have predisposed a failure to healthily resolve the losses and to fall into chronic guilt.

Catherine's first vision at age six came after a visit to a married sister followed, in subsequent months, by the decision to remain a virgin and give herself to God. Is that a coincidence or did Catherine experience something alarming about marriage or about sex during that visit? (While there is no evidence for this, I have, drawing on my experiential lens of similar contemporary clinical presentations of rejection of the body, found myself wondering if Catherine was sexually molested in childhood.)

Catherine was very aware of Bonaventura's unhappy marriage and of the use of self-starvation by Bonaventura to influence the husband, to reform his louche behaviour. This may have been a model for Catherine in her battles with her parents for autonomy. This is sometimes described as manipulation, including by Bynum. A more compassionate framing would see this as the *only* means Bonaventura had of exercising any influence over the course of her life, given the relative powerlessness of women in all other areas.

Bonaventura encouraged Catherine, now an early-adolescent, to dress fashionably and to make herself attractive. Following Bonaventura's death in labour, Catherine strongly rejected fashion and appearance. Had she made a causal link between the two in her mind? Raymond was certain that God had killed Bonaventura for tempting Catherine away from her true spiritual path. Recall that in those times there were no natural causes: God's will was the sole reason for everything.

Catherine's battles with her parents in adolescence look familiar to the modern eye, but these were exceptional for those times, when it was simply understood that girls would obey their parents and accept the duties and dangers of marriage and child-bearing. Bonaventura's unhappy marriage and her death in childbirth would have done nothing to encourage Catherine to follow that path. One might say that, from her perspective, she was both metaphorically and literally fighting with her parents for her life. How much was the attraction of a deeply committed religious life simultaneously an escape from the only alternative available to her as a young woman?

Was the question of marriage finally decided in Catherine's favour once her devotional path began to be seen as significant by others outside of the family, as her fame as a holy woman grew? From a social learning perspective this powerful community recognition would be strongly reinforcing and empowering for Catherine, providing her with choices.

The Body

The vantage point of modern medicine tells us that, at a certain point, starvation is not reversed simply by normal eating. The body then has its own say, through a variety of causal mechanisms. Metabolic processes try to protect the brain by using up fat then muscle first. Eventually, Catherine's loss of the ability to read bodily sensations (such as temperature), her hyperactivity and sleeplessness are suggestive of dysfunction of the autonomic nervous system. After God told her to eat twice-a-day, Catherine tried to comply, but her body appears to have rejected the food, evidenced by spontaneous vomiting. The dangers of refeeding after starvation, caused by dramatic electrolyte imbalance, are now understood. That said, Catherine 'ecstatically' responded to the communion throughout this period, partly because of her intense identification with the suffering body of Christ but, at a metabolic level, because of the greater ease with which her body would be able to make use of simple carbohydrates. These would be more manageable for her presumably damaged digestion than the bitter herbs that she ate at other times.

The Self

Freud (1917) gives us the viewpoint of melancholia—an irresolvable grief reaction in which guilt may predominate. As other contemporary commentators have noted, guilt at the death of her twin, Giovanna, may have grown with the subsequent death of her younger sister, the 'second' Giovanna. Catherine's ordinary hatred of her younger sibling for removing her special status and displacing her at the breast might, using Piaget's (1926) lens of the egocentric conception of young children, have translated into self-blame, adding to that already derived from her twin's death. Was this a factor in her unusually early decision to commit herself to God and, using the concept of identification, a compensatory life of self-denial of the Desert Fathers?

Devotion to Christ's blood has a long history in medieval Catholicism but it usually symbolised the washing away of sin: for Catherine blood was food. This sounds less strange when it is understood that, in the Middle Ages, breast milk was regarded as a form of blood. Some recent commentaries draw attention to the erotic nature of the fusion between holy women and Christ but, as Bynum says, the compelling image in Catherine's writing is Christ as a breastfeeding mother. For example, in lecturing the cardinals who had turned to Clement VII as Pope rather than the elected Pope Urban VI, Catherine writes:

> Where is the gratitude which you ought to have for the Bride [the true Church] who has *nourished you at her breast?* I see in [you] naught, but such ingratitude as *dries up the fountain* of pity. What shows me that you are ungrateful, coarse, and mercenary? ([My emphases.] Letters of Catherine of Siena, 1347–1380)

Lis Lind (1989) discusses, from an object relations perspective, how unbearable and irresolvable remorse can lead to a cleaving of the self—a split between body and mind. Catherine's body was "a dung heap", her ordinary pangs of hunger were "gluttony"—one of the deadly sins, especially destructive to the soul. The one person in Catherine's world who did not see her as holy was Catherine herself. As Raymond noted, she was prone to self-blame and to exaggerating in her mind the most trivial sin.

Her intense religiosity draws the eye, but I think it defends against its opposite—a profound sense of badness which she associates to her ordinary bodily need for food, given to her as an infant in plenty, but fatally denied to Giovanna.

What was Catherine's sin that may have been eased by this extreme splitting? I don't think she ever knew, so it could never be resolved. The death of her twin, denied the mother's breast by Catherine's bodily needs, as Catherine might unconsciously experience it, and the death of the second Giovanna, are neither mentioned by Raymond, nor by Catherine in her extensive writing. It seems possible *that Catherine's unconscious survivor's guilt was a causal mechanism in her extreme ambivalence about receiving rich nourishment, denied to her twin.* This may have been enacted, on the one hand, through the ecstatic feeding on the breast of Christ, thereby recreating the special feeding relationship with her mother. This is represented through her vision of feeding on Christ's wound and, literally, embodied in her devouring the eucharist. Simultaneously, on the other hand, this ecstatic nourishment might always stimulate guilt leading to a revulsion towards—and blame of—her "gluttonous" body which in her unconscious mind had denied Giovanna life.

Perhaps the closest Catherine came to self-knowledge of her unreasonable guilt was her belief that her suffering would shorten the tortures of those in purgatory. We also have the evidence of her miraculously (and reparatively on behalf of Giovanna?) restoring milk to women whose breasts had dried up. Some mitigation may have come through fusing her own suffering with that of Christ on the cross. In connecting with Christ she may unconsciously have been able to reconnect with her twin (Shackle, 2003)—all three sacrificing themselves so that others might live.

The Non-inevitability of Catherine

I need once more to underline the point that this is not an objective narrative of Catherine. It is a second-order speculative account of *my* provisional attempts to understand Catherine in her causal contexts from a multiplicity of theoretical positions and sets up a series of, now, unanswerable questions. It uses what Bateson (1979) describes as an abductive method, assembling a picture from a variety of vantage points, and what Bhaskar (1977) refers to as 'retroduction'—retrospectively mapping the interacting causal powers that, through emergence, generate the system of Catherine-in-context. My account depends greatly on who I am, and what I have in mind, using the writing of others, including statements by Catherine herself. My account is constructed, therefore fallible, subject to my biases (including non-conscious ones) and interests, likely needing revision in the light of new facts, and relative to all the vantage point is that I have used. It is a series of partial, reductive, and layered maps of the territory of Catherine and her world. As an example of bias, I note how I want to cheer her on to find means of self-expression as a woman, but this may well say more about my preoccupations, informed by my history and my contemporary culture.

[On what is probably my twentieth re-reading of this account I finally noticed another possible, hitherto unconscious, association drawing me to Catherine's story and shaping the emphasis I give to gender and guilt. As we will discuss in Chap. 8, I had the opportunity of attending Grammar School, supported by the concealed government policy of favouring averagely less-able boys through sexist entry exams: a system that twice rejected my bright sister on the flimsiest of grounds, setting us on separate paths. Hers included a religiously committed life. I have some survivor's guilt of my own.]

Others may assemble a different picture and, indeed, there are several and varied contemporary constructions. In attempting a provisional explanation of Catherine, she cannot be explained away. So much always remains unknown and that is the case, even in a long individual psychotherapy. But the critical realist assumption is that socially constructed maps can achieve some reliable object-adequacy in accounting for the world of causal tendencies, providing a rational reason for preferring some theoretical accounts to others. If that was not the case, map-making as a profession would never have caught on.

I hope it is apparent that no single context could account for Catherine. Numerous causal tendencies interact to actualise the complex system; *a change in any one of them may have altered the direction of her life.* The specific religious cultural hegemony of the time did not dictate

Catherine—she had some choices—but it would be difficult to imagine any coherent account of the path of her unresolved mourning (assuming this comes close) that did not include the internalised culture of her times as an organising backdrop. The same is true of all the contextual layers. But there is nothing inevitable about Catherine—she was not driven by these causal tendencies. She is simply less understandable without them.

Readers will probably notice that the discussion of culture has been the largest of any of the layers. It would be an error to assume that this is due to the exotic strangeness of fourteenth century Italy. Everyone has a similarly complex culture. It is just hard to perceive when you live in it, in the same way that, it is said, fish do not appreciate water. Strangeness only comes from unfamiliarity and difference. We return to this theme in Chap. 8.

References

Bateson, G. (1979). *Mind and nature: A necessary Unity*. Dutton.

Bhaskar, R. (1977). *A realist philosophy of science*. Harvester.

Bynum, C. (1987). *Holy feast and holy fast: The religious significance of food to medieval women*. University of California Press.

Elder-Vass, D. (2012). *The reality of social construction*. Cambridge University Press.

Foucault, M. (1977). *Discipline and punish: The birth of the prison*. Pantheon Books.

Freud, S. (1917). Mourning and melancholia. In *The standard edition of the complete psychological works of Sigmund Freud* (Vol. 14). Hogarth Press.

Goldner, V., Penn, P., Sheinberg, M., & Walker, G. (1990). Love and violence: Gender paradoxes in volatile attachments. *Family Process, 29*, 343–364.

Hoffman, L. (1990). Constructing realities: An art of lenses. *Family Process, 29*, 1–12.

Korzybski, A. (1933). *Science and sanity*. Science Press.

Layton, L. (1999). Social factors in the case study. *Psychoanalysis, Culture, and Society, 4*, 325–327.

Lind, L. (1989). Segregation of the ego and intra-psychic projection as a defence against super-ego anxiety. *The Scandinavian Psychoanalytic Review, 12*, 58–77.

Orange, D. (1995). *Emotional understanding: Studies in psychoanalytic epistemology*. Guilford.
Piaget, J. (1926). *The child's conception of the world*. Kegan Paul.
Pilgrim, D. (2020). *Critical realism for psychologists*. Routledge.
Shackle, E. (2003). The effect of twinship on the mysticism of Catherine of Siena (1347–1380): A Vergotean analysis. *Archive for the Psychology of Religion, 25*, 129–141.

4

Knowing and Not-Knowing

> To be not-knowing provides the container for knowing, and vice versa.
> Glenn Larner (2000, p. 79)

> If we stay on the surface we will only ever achieve a superficial account.
> David Pilgrim (2020, p. 166)

If I were to nominate a single concept that has probably caused the most confusion across systemic, analytic, and humanistic psychotherapy traditions it would be 'not-knowing'. It is, unfortunately, one of those general technical terms that means almost nothing without clarification. I have seen interpretations ranging from the therapist holding their ideas with a mild level of uncertainty, right up to recommendations to clear the memory of all assumptions about a patient (Bion, 1988). If we are not to get lost in ambiguity and paradox, 'not-knowing' needs unpacking and defining in psychotherapy, otherwise those using the term may simply talk past each other, since they may mean entirely different things by it. Glenn Larner's paradoxical-looking maxim (above) looks at first glance like part of the problem, whereas I believe it contains a solution, of which more later.

D. Pocock, *Expanding the Limits of Individual and Family Therapies*, Palgrave Texts in Counselling and Psychotherapy, https://doi.org/10.1007/978-3-031-76309-0_4

My definition of not-knowing is *the absence of certainty*. As we discussed in Chap. 2, critical realism assumes that knowledge is the transitive dimension: a human construction and therefore fallible, subject to bias and change. However the presence of a real, external, intransitive world means that there are rational reasons for preferring one account of the world over another on the grounds of object-adequacy, not just personal preference. While postmodernism emphasises multiple meanings—'both-and' rather than 'either-or'—critical realism makes space for both.

There are degrees of fallibility. I am confident that abusing children is damaging, I'm less confident about the form that damage might take in each child and about what constitutes the edge of the definition of abuse. Is shouting to be considered abuse and, if so, for how long and how loudly? We will return to the question of choosing theory on the basis of reliability in the next chapter.

As discussed in Chap. 1, pluralism helps to establish the limits of knowing. Looking at the same object through multiple lenses tends to undermine the blind-man first-order illusion that what we 'see' is straightforwardly outside ourselves. A single view can enable certainty; multiple views undermine that certainty and—as with the duck-rabbit illusion—help us to reflect that what we see depends on how we construct that information via our preconceptions. I frankly doubt that Wilfred Bion's (1988) advice to approach each session without memory is achievable, and, indeed, I don't read Bion's not-knowing as including questions regarding the reliability of theory, more that knowing should be set aside, but not interrogated. Rather than trying not to remember, I think a more achievable aim is to come to a second-order awareness of our assumptions since, only then, might they be bracketed and placed to one side for a while to allow in something new.

Not-knowing as the absence of certainty is a starting point, but there are several important themes to explore including, but not restricted to: different kinds of knowledge, the inescapability of philosophical assumptions, the relationship of knowledge to power, off-the-peg knowledge, and lineal and circular descriptions. The related themes of conscious and unconscious knowing, cognition and emotion, and experiential knowledge are taken up in Chap. 6.

Three Kinds of Knowledge

I have written briefly about Steve before (Pocock, 2005)—a middle-aged white working-class British man, married with two teenage children. He had been ill for most of his adult life with depressed feelings, anxiety, low motivation, and stomach pains for which he had received a diagnosis of irritable bowel syndrome. I always offer a choice of chair or couch to individual therapy patients, and he chose the latter. We are now a year into his psychotherapy and within a week of me taking a long summer break. He explains that he really doesn't mind the break; it is, he says, a "perfect arrangement" for him since he can spend more time with his children. Within a few minutes he draws his knees up to his chest to cope with intense pain in his abdomen. He tells me that what he would like to do to ease the pain would be to curl up on his left side which would mean turning his back to me. But he doesn't do that and continues to suffer. I gently enquire why he thinks he hasn't turned onto his side, and he says that he fears I would feel so rejected that I would never forgive him, and our relationship would be permanently damaged.

What ideas might help Steve and I to understand what is happening between us, and inside him? John Shotter (1993) talks about three kinds of knowledge: *knowing-that*—our theories, conscious ideas, and hypotheses; *knowing-how*—our skills; and a third kind which he calls *knowing-within*—a lifetime intuitively learning to be a person in relationships. I believe all three of these are needed all of the time in any form of psychotherapy. My *know-that,* which comes to mind with Steve, includes theories of somatisation. Ordinary upset and angry feelings of infants, when their needs are not being met, become, as an adaptive response, inhibited, or falsified by positive emotion or, in more extreme situations, somatised if they are unacceptable to a caregiver and provoke a dangerous retaliatory response of rejection (Crittenden, 2008; Crittenden et al., 2014).

My *know-that* also includes the idea of transference as a causal tendency. This is the use of old relational internal templates as lenses for interpreting the present but, in the manner of Saxe's blind men, without any awareness of these lenses, instead assuming the world is being perceived just as it is. Steve's assumptions that I would feel rejected and that our relationship would be damaged doesn't fit at all with what I actually feel when I check with my *knowing-within.* As far as I can tell, I would prefer him to be comfortable, even with his back turned to me; I don't like to see him in pain. That difference between how Steve thinks I will feel and my actual internal state, as I imagine him turning his back, raises curiosity. It suggests to me that I should look for other contexts in which Steve's experience of me as about to catastrophically reject him may be understandable. Another of my *know-thats* is the theory of projective identification: that the devastating rejection that Steve anticipates I will feel may be *his* disowned feeling about me leaving him, which has stirred up an implicit memory of abandonment. This feeling of rejection, I consider, is now being defensively separated and disowned by him (split off) and perceived as belonging to me.

Steve's *know-that* includes a family story that he cried so much as a baby that, as was commonly advised in the time of his infancy, his mother placed him in a pram at the end of a garden shared by the block of flats where they lived and "kept an eye on him" from the second-floor window. He reported that his mother often seemed lonely and unhappy and that the relationship between his parents was a difficult one. She was often very angry with Steve for apparently minor disobediences and did not tolerate dissent. At other times when he was compliant she "babied" him. Steve's self-narrative does not include any connection between these experiences in childhood and his presenting problems.

My *know-how* (skills) includes offering the idea of a possible link between how he seems to be experiencing me through his *knowing-within* and these old abandoning experiences (causal tendencies) of being dangerously left alone without comfort. I don't do this to blame his mother—she is also worthy of being contextually and compassionately understood. My hope is that, if Steve comes to a reflexive awareness of his propensity to always expect rejection and retaliation when he has ordinary feelings of anger, he may come to discover that these anxieties are in relation to experiences that happened in the past rather than always about to happen in every current relationship. This new self-knowledge might enable Steve to have new experiences of his ordinary protest and autonomous choices being found acceptable, rather than living a *Groundhog Day* life of repeated fearful anticipation of rejection if he asserts himself. I know about the benefit of this internal shift from my theoretical *know-that* and also from my *knowing-within,* since I made similar shifts in my personal therapy.

Seven Kinds of Not-Knowing

That sounds like a lot of different kinds of knowing, so where is the not-knowing? Well, everywhere, but tucked out of the way by the smoothed-out flow of my narrative. First, I don't know for certain if the social construction 'transference' has general validity. Indeed, I am aware that the definitions of transference and countertransference have undergone many social modifications in the psychoanalytic knowledge community: from the time of Freud, who saw countertransference as an obstacle requiring the analyst to get more analysis, via Paula Heimann's (1950) revision of the countertransference as information about the patient, and up to contemporary relational views of the therapeutic relationship being mutually organised by the co-mingling of transference of both patient and therapist (Orange, 1995).

Second, I don't know with any certainty if these theories, even if generally valid, apply to Steve *in this moment.* There are other possible bodily causal tendencies that can contribute to an irritable bowel event: problems in the microbiome caused by poor diet, genetic factors, or other gut conditions. The timing of him experiencing pain at that specific moment could just be coincidence. Third, I don't know the best way to present the idea in a manner that Steve can then think about (*know-how*). Fourth, I don't know if this is a good *time* to suggest a connection between his current pain to his story of being left alone in his pram and me leaving him for a month, or whether I should wait for another occasion. Fifth, I don't know if the idea will be any kind of fit for Steve. Sixth, if he does pick up the idea, I don't know how that perturbation will impact on him and his relationship to me and others. Bateson, drawing on evolutionary theory, calls this a stochastic process: the idea introduced by me would be a new causal tendency analogous to the role of random spontaneous mutation in evolution. What is not known in advance is whether the idea will interact with other causal tendencies to survive and generate a lasting change in the system, or simply fall on deaf ears. And seventh, I don't know whether Steve, perhaps out of a wish to not antagonise me, will *compliantly* accept my suggested link, rendering our relationship less authentic. The power of my idea—overinvested by us both—may then cast into shadow more object-adequate explanations that may come from either of us.

Case examples showing successful interventions are like shooting an arrow from fifty metres into a barn then drawing a bullseye around it and claiming accuracy, thereby editing out the multitude of times the barn was missed from having to shoot in the dark or, at best, in the half-light.

Coming back to Larner's quote at the head of this chapter, not-knowing frames the limits of knowing, *but we have to know enough epistemology to not-know*—knowing and not-knowing both rely on the other. Every session involves managing a myriad of risks of getting it wrong. I will argue that trying to escape such risks—especially the risk of therapist certainty—by therapists attempting to deny their knowledge and power, leads to just another, and possibly greater, risk. How therapists know when they are getting it wrong, and how to correct that, is one of the subjects of Chap. 7.

The Inescapability of Epistemology and Ontology

I hope it is clear that my definition of the possibilities and limitations of knowing are underpinned by my critical realist assumptions. In passing, I should add that critical realism understands that its own knowledge assumptions are socially constructed *and*, it is argued, object-adequate. Like all socially constructed knowledge it could be in error and improved: indeed critical realism continues to evolve beyond Bhaskar's death. Yet, unlike highly relativist strong constructionism, critical realism survives being applied to itself. It has an internal consistency and is not self-refuting.

But can't we just forget these tedious philosophical preoccupations and concentrate on theory and practice? As previously argued it is perfectly possible not to believe that one is taking an epistemological and ontological stance but that only conceals the real choices being made. Philosophical assumptions are everywhere. Much of the early focus on observed circularities in family therapy (Watzlawick et al., 1967) relies on the *empiricism* of surface observations of interaction. The hypothesising of the original Milan Group draws on *functionalism*—the assumption that symptoms serve a function in maintenance of the system. Salvador Minuchin borrows from Saussure's *structuralism*: that families have an underlying structure like a language. Jacques Lacan does the same in re-interpreting the Freudian unconscious. Carl Whitaker was strongly influenced by *existentialism*. Discussions of religious experience in the last chapter and of emotional experience in Chap. 6 draw on *phenomenology* (Orange, 1995). The Post-Milan Group, as well as responding to the postmodern turn, use *pragmatism* to describe their hypotheses—more or less useful rather than more or less true. And, as said, the rejection of any avowed epistemology tends to allow in first-order *naïve realism* to fill the vacuum together with its associated temptation of omniscience. There is just no escaping philosophy!

In passing, I am not a fan of pragmatism as used in much psychotherapy (not all pragmatisms are anti-realist e.g. Peirce, 1877), since it seems to serve as another form of covert realism. Pragmatism is anthropocentric; concerned only with what humans find useful, not whether ideas fit with how the world is, so it is another form of strong idealism (Collier, 1994). But as Bebe Speed (1984) says, an idea is useful *because* it provides it a good-enough representation of the world. If a friend gives me directions to help us meet at an unfamiliar pub, I may describe them as useful if they get me there, but this is by virtue of their ability to orientate me to the territory. Speed gives the full version of the quote by Korzybski (1933), only the first part of which was regularly quoted by Bateson "A map is not the territory it represents, but if correct it has a similar structure to the territory which *accounts for its usefulness*". [My emphasis.] If we hold an idea such as the location of a pub to be possibly true, but it turns out to be incorrect, then we know we should discard or modify the idea (Pocock, 2013). No such modifying feedback is possible for pragmatism which, as Collier (1999) says, through its narrow binary of useful-to-me versus not-useful-to-me, inhibits learning about the world and has, therefore, a conservative effect on practice.

Knowledge and Power

The extreme relativism of strong constructionism (ideas refer only to each other, not to the world as it is) means that each person can have their own reality. As discussed in Chap. 2, this itself is a powerful—but hidden—truth claim: an uncontested metanarrative that for some writers restricts the therapist to that of a conductor of conversation while being careful not to add any of their own thoughts. Rather than the therapist as expert, the client or clients are promoted as experts. In some of these postmodern versions, therapists may use theoretical ideas, since therapists too are "users of discourse", but without any apparent commitment to the relative truth of these ideas. As said, this begs the question of how ideas are chosen, since it is unlikely that they are drawn randomly from a hat.

I agree with Virginia Goldner (1993) that using 'conversation' as a metaphor for psychotherapy leaves something to be desired, but stay with that for a while and think back to the last time you had a 'good conversation' with a friend. If your experience is anything like mine, 'good' means that no one dominated and pushed their views on the other. (This, of course, can happen but I wouldn't count it as a *good* conversation.) Each hears something new from the other and, in doing so, this triggers new thoughts which might be offered up if they further the dialogue. Imagine that, for fear of overly influencing the course of the conversation, the other person kept all their thoughts to themselves. How might that feel and how might that influence the flow? Good conversations are like a cake: each provides some ingredients, but the finished product is not my cake or your cake but something new, baked through the interactive flow. It is *co-constructed but also emergent—more than the sum of its separate (causal tendency) ingredients.* We return to this in a discussion of Jessica Benjamin's (2017) concept of 'The Third' in Chap. 7.

If we take seriously the attempt to meet clients where they are, does it really assist to consider them experts? In my experience, individuals and families seek help when they have exhausted their resources. In a publicly funded agency like the NHS they have probably waited many months or even years for a first appointment. They often feel defeated, angry, depressed, fearful, ashamed, and disempowered. For them to be faced with an implicit assumption that they know best seems to me, to put it mildly, not the greatest of starts. Is this ideological assumption really empowering or just bewildering? The notion of the client as expert seems to be an over-correction in a zero-sum game of 'Who's the Expert?' What if no one knows for sure but it may be possible to work some things out together?

Where the conversational metaphor breaks down is that psychotherapy is not a meeting of conversational equals. While the therapist may try to conceal or deny his power, his professional status and the hopes and expectations of his clients inevitably strengthen his influence. Additionally, where power lies is not just a binary choice between therapist and client. When meeting with a family, which members get to speak, and who keeps quiet? And even if everyone speaks, who does so with authority and whose narrative is the accepted one? Is disagreement possible? How are the children to be heard when the grown-ups talk so much? We will discuss possible solutions to this in Chap. 9 when discussing who to see in family therapy. For now, I am just highlighting the problem.

One common way for the constructionist therapist to try to reduce her power is to only ask questions: the use of circular questions being first popularised in Milan therapy and becoming more central in the Post-Milan development (Cecchin, 1987). Initially, circular questions were for the purposes of exploring hypotheses but others, such as Karl Tomm (1987), saw the possibilities of using questions as interventions. Tomm, at least, is open about the strategic power of questions.

The idea that, by restricting therapist behaviour to that of asking questions, the therapist is decentred, and their power is reduced is, I would argue, a dangerous illusion. If, for example, the therapist asks a daughter whether her mother's anxiety was better or worse after the father left the family, this certainly helps gather information about the daughter's perception, but it also introduces the therapist's premise that father leaving the family could have been influential on the extent of the mother's anxiety. However, it does so indirectly rather than directly (Golann, 1988; Smith, 2023). The 'illusion of alternatives' (Haley, 1993) is a hypnotic technique. It draws attention to the alternatives of, in this case, "better" or "worse" and simultaneously shifts the eye away from the assumption embedded in the question that an event of separation can influence anxiety. Of course, the effect of separation on anxiety is an entirely reasonable assumption but, inserting it implicitly makes it difficult to disagree with or even think about further since the only answers requested are "better" or "worse". There is no invitation to explore whether that idea might help therapist and family members to understand better.

Concealed power, especially if the therapist believes she is not acting powerfully, seems to me far more powerful and problematic than the therapist simply and straightforwardly offering a possible link between the mother's anxiety and the loss of the couple relationship such that it can then be talked about. Once an idea is out in the open family members may accept, reject, or modify (play) with it as long as it is safe to disagree with the therapist (of which more in Chap. 7). As Stuart Golann puts it when discussing the emergence of second-order practices in the late 80s:

> ... one major negative consequence is the potential use of [metatheory such as constructivism] to rationalise or obscure the introduction of a disingenuous or misguided form of therapist powerlessness into practice. Power obscured eventually emerges—a therapeutic wolf clad as a second-order sheep. (Golann, 1988, p. 4)

What is a questions-led therapy like for clients? Some may appreciate it, but David Howe, in a rare study of consumer views in the late-80s soon after the introduction of 'second-order' practices, found the *great majority* of family members surveyed did not feel understood. In *Introducing User Friendly Family Therapy* (1994) Sigurd Reimers and Andy Treacher comment that families in Howe's survey wanted to understand both their problem and their experience of being in family therapy. But the stance of the therapists was to focus only on interactional behaviour and not worry at all about whether family members understood how change might take place.

> No one really understood what we lived through. They never did really understand the situation. How badly it was upsetting us all. It was all too simple for our case. Just lots of questions. You answered one and boom! onto the next one. They never got to the bottom of anything. There was so

much I wanted to say but I couldn't say it their way. ('Luke's' mother, quoted in Howe, 1989, p. 56)

Importantly, in Howe's survey, the family members often knew their therapists very well as some therapists also had long-standing roles as their social workers. The clients were baffled and often upset that their ordinarily straightforward relationship with their social worker changed dramatically when they behaved as perpetual question-generating therapists.

Practicing techniques in a spirit of purity is usually something that only trainees are expected to do. I have, more than once, observed trainees ploughing on with circular questions in an obvious state of discomfort while someone in the family is quietly sobbing without anyone offering support. The day of graduation from any psychotherapy training marks the moment when approaches and techniques can begin to be made one's own and rehumanised. Most take advantage of the transgressive opportunities as therapy practice becomes part of the self. This can take years.

The therapists in Howe's survey must surely take credit for commissioning the study but they were shocked by the findings. They assumed that not only was their work effective, but also that those they worked with were generally satisfied. We will return in Chap. 7 to the question of how therapists come to know when they are losing the therapeutic alliance.

I need to emphasise that *my critique of strong constructionism is directed, not at any therapist, but at the philosophical assumptions* which, through the overt rejection of realism as a means of knowing, can tie practitioners in some strange knots. These are then undone by allowing an unacknowledged realist choice of ideas (including strong constructionism itself) in through the back door. Fortunately, as said, therapists seem to behave differently to the way they are taught to behave, or even to how they *assume* they behave. In my experience, having supervised many individual and family therapists, most will not allow theory or ideology to stand in the way of making a response that is influenced by a different knowledge: the many years of learning to be a human being—our *knowing-within*. Nevertheless, as I show in Chap. 7, theory can sometimes get in the way.

As discussed in Chap. 2, there are more moderate versions of constructionism, which I *do* identify with. I am fully signed-up to all versions of co-construction, co-evolution, collaboration, and dialogical work that allow the therapist to participate as a fellow player, not just a facilitator of others. Barry Mason's (1993) positions of 'authoritative doubt' and 'safe uncertainty' are entirely consistent with the critical realist position in not requiring the therapist to shed their knowledge and expertise. Paulo Bertrando and Teresa Arcelloni (2006) openly share at least some of their hypothesising with family members. Larner's (2002) unusually deep understanding of theorists such as Derrida and Levinas supports his 'paramodern' position which bears a strong family resemblance to critical realism and allows a plurality of therapeutic approaches to flourish alongside each other. For Larner, it is an ethical responsibility not to allow ideological theoretical differences to stand in the way of meeting the needs of the other as best we can (Larner, 2011). Peter Rober (2005, 2024) goes beyond the role of therapist as solely a facilitator of the views of others and puts the therapist's inner reflections, and how she might use these to contribute to the therapeutic process, firmly on the map. Additionally there are many therapists whose integrative approaches appear compatible with critical realist assumptions (e.g. Dallos, 2006; Dallos & Vetere, 2022; Flaskas 2002; Goldner et al., 1990; Miller & Wrate, 2014; Lebow 2019; Woodcock 2009, 2021).

Off-the-Peg Knowledge

When thinking about knowledge and power, we need to discuss the exceptional power of diagnoses. These off-the-peg knowledges can be useful in tying down definitions so people can mean roughly the same thing when they use such terms (useful, for example, in research). However, diagnoses are groupings of empirically observed behaviours, they do not in themselves supply an explanation, although they can often reductively masquerade in that role. Psychiatric diagnoses may point to organised (often narrow) treatment pathways, and they may be linked to insurance-mandated payments, but they never take us far in understanding. Instead, they often inadvertently function to close down curiosity. If, for example, a patient says he is long-term "depressed", a first therapeutic thought should probably be "what does *he* mean by 'depression'?" A second might be "when and under what circumstances did that start?" And a third, "what are the factors (systemic causal tendencies) that maintain the 'depression'?"

From a critical realist perspective, diagnoses are empirical and event-based phenomena. In other words they are shallow forms of realism (empiricism and actualism) which can terminate thinking about the *underlying* causal powers that give rise to a set of symptoms which come to be called 'depression'. In the case of one man I worked with for long-term 'depression' and suicidal ideation, he began in one session to get in touch with anger at a friend who had betrayed him. I noticed how robust he sounded in the telling and asked him to pause and check how depressed he felt in that moment. He was surprised that he could not feel *any* depression. He assumed it was a constant companion. He was excited at the idea that 'depression' might be an alternative to healthily accepted anger (forbidden in his childhood) and decided to use a journal whenever depressed in order to safely and kindly talk to himself to track down and accept the repudiated feelings. As the work progressed we found other causal tendencies including exhaustion from work, eating poorly, lack of exercise, and spending too much time alone. 'Depression' made an appearance when several of these combined. It became de-actualised when the combinations broke down, or when new causal tendencies, such as feeling valued by others, arrived.

Diagnoses are not the sole property of clinicians, although are arguably more powerful when used by a therapist, especially a doctor. As mentioned, the drive for diagnosis of ADHD and autism increased dramatically in the 1990s onwards when I was working in a child and family consultation centre. This was often led by parents drawing on media representations of these conditions. These monolithic explanations squeeze the space for not-knowing and the exploration of additional or alternative meanings, so can serve to protect against shame and doubt and the quiet agony of not being able to name what is wrong. Diagnoses are also sticky labels: all too easy internalised for those with a profound sense that there is something wrong with them. One patient (Mary in Chap. 9) initially described herself to me as "a borderline" and after years in inpatient care this had become a central part of her identity. The diagnosis also provided some relief since naming something can be a container of anxiety. Of course, it comes with the costs of closing down curiosity about formative relational and other life experiences and accepting a restrictive 'not-normal' self-definition.

Throughout my career, starting in the early 1980s in my role as a Divorce Court Welfare Officer (probation officers at that time held that role in parallel), I have worked with divorced and separating parents and their children. In recent years I have become aware of exponential growth in a new off-the-peg knowledge—'Parental Alienation Syndrome'—which is used by professionals, including some family therapists, and parents (mostly men) to provide the main account of why children no longer wish to have contact with the non-resident parent (almost all fathers). This discourse has acquired extraordinary causal power in UK Family Court decision-making, often allowing fathers with a history of abuse (including abuse against their own children) to have contact against the child's expressed wishes. Reports in the media of serious injustices through over-reliance on the term led, in 2023, to concerns from the Family Justice Council who issued updated advice that such expert evidence should be based on a *reliable* body of knowledge and expertise and should be free of conflicts of interest. (Several 'experts' had been financially benefiting from recommendations that they should work on undoing the 'syndrome'.) Can resident parents undermine the non-resident parent in the eyes of a child? Of course. But is this the sole context in which children begin to refuse to see the non-resident parent? Not in my experience. As soon as an idea is turned into a reductive, objectified, shining syndrome, any attempt to map the complexity of the system is cast into deep shadow. Despite good intentions, this is what 'expert' misuse of power looks like.

Lineality, Circularity, and Power

Systemic family therapists, since Bateson, have long taken an interest in the concept of circularity: self-regulating (homeostatic) patterns including the beliefs that maintain those patterns. Hypothesising in Post-Milan Therapy is, for example, always linked to circularity. Based on this premise, cause-and-effect (lineal) explanations are seen as non-systemic, and this becomes a further justification for excluding other kinds of knowing from our non-systemic neighbours, especially psychoanalytic knowledge. But if we believe, as I think we should, that the world simply is systemic—in other words, if we are *realist systemic ontologists*—then it is impossible to be non-systemic. We need to avoid a logical muddle between *description* of the way things are and *prescription* of what we should do. We can't, for example, make good sense of the existence of dolphins in the world without understanding the ecosystemic laws of evolution, but there is no need for a dolphin police-force to enforce those laws! That is just the way the world is (Efran & Clarfield, 1992)—the intransitive dimension in Bhaskar's terminology. Everything we do (or don't do) has a systemic implication, whether we know it or not.

Of course, just because any therapist behaviour inevitably has potential systemic consequences, this does not mean that these will be *helpful* consequences. This is why Bateson was against the myth of power—acting as if unilateral control of aspects of the world was possible without due regard to systemic consequences; for example, using pesticides and artificial fertilisers to increase crop yield without systemic concern for the long-term effect on insect pollinators and soil-degradation. However, in my account of Emma in Chap. 1, the lineal theory of identification (a child, in this case, taking inside herself the difficulties of the father to try to solve them) seemed to be helpful as, at least, a partial understanding of the causal tendencies which generated her emergent loss of spontaneity. This seemingly cause-and-effect explanation played its part in a wider systemic understanding (itself partial—no account ever being complete). *My point is that lineal theoretical explanations can be very helpful if they are themselves part of a wider systemic sensibility.* Part of my motivation for writing the book is to encourage traditional analytic, humanistic, and cognitive therapists not necessarily to give up much, but to locate what they do within a systemic frame of multiple causal influences.

Discussions of lineality and circularity lead us to another thorny problem—how one conceptualises power in circular patterns. There is more at stake here than abstract theorising. Paul Dell (1989, p. 1), for example, writes:

> I have seen families in therapy whose prior therapists told victims of violence that their own behaviour in the mutual-causal family system had provoked the abusive behaviour that they were experiencing.

In a lineal explanation A simply leads to B. For example, in a couple relationship in which the man is dominant, the exercise of his dominance through a violent act may be seen as the cause of the wife's submission. So male violent behaviour (A) => female submissive behaviour (B). The power relationship seems clear. But let's assume the couple remain together and there are no further acts of violence. After two years an observer notices a simple, self-sustaining circularity as in Fig. 4.1.

This shallow empirical observation suggests that the behaviour of each in the circle is the sole context for the behaviour of the other even in the absence of violence. So where has the power gone? Has it truly evaporated into circularity?

Bateson was not just against the pursuit of power, he also said that it does not exist: no single part of the circle being more powerful than any other. I have never understood why both of these things can logically be true. If power is an impossibility then why is the unilateral pursuit of it a problem (which I believe it is)? It can't be just the myth of power that is

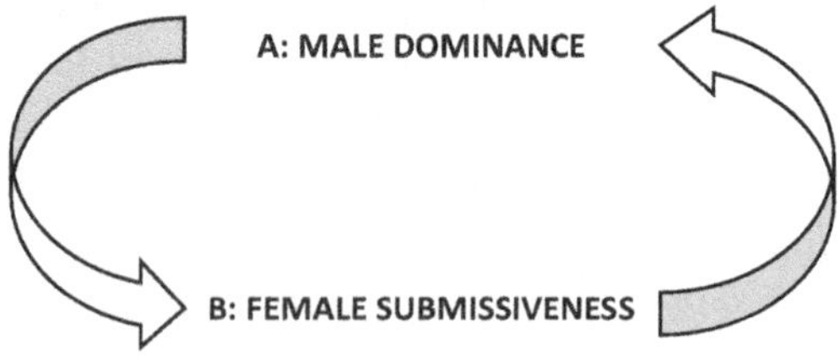

Fig. 4.1 Circular empiricism

the problem, as people can hold all kind of strange beliefs without acting on them. It must be the enactment of power that Bateson holds to be problematic, while at the same time denying its existence. There is a good reason why I don't find the malign goblins living at the bottom of our garden to be a problem, which is that they almost certainly do not exist. And even if I did believe in goblins, this would only be systemically influential if the belief ever influenced my behaviour.

Lynn Hoffman (1990), drawing on the mounting feminist critiques of circularity, was explicit that the absence of a concept of power in circular causality was a strong motive in moving away from Bateson and cybernetics into strong constructionist Family Therapy Part 2. (However, the paradox of wishing to hold onto the concept of the *real* causal power of patriarchy, while in all other respects departing further from *realism* into strong linguistic constructionism seems to have remained hidden in plain sight as I haven't seen it commented upon.) Dell's (1989) discussion of power tries to deal with the anomaly between the everyday experience of power and its theoretical absence in circularity by stating that experience (in this case, of being physically assaulted) is in a different domain from that of scientific explanation. Although circularity in this hypothetical case properly challenges the reduction of the woman to that of a passive victim, I do not find the domains account particularly helpful, preferring that explanation may shed light on experience, rather than appear to call experience into question.

In contrast to the apparent *disappearance of power* in a Batesonian universe, in Bhaskar's critical realism the system is *made up of causal powers* which may or may not be actualised.

Looking again at the same hypothetical case, the dominant (but currently non-violent) behaviour of the husband is empirically observed to be the sole context for the wife's submission and vice versa—her submission being the sole context for the husband's behaviour. Power appears to have absented itself. However critical realism says this explanation is simply wrong, created by the use of a shallow form of realism—empiricism. What we can apprehend empirically through our senses cannot give a complete account. It also commits the *fallacy of actualism*—assuming that one event invariably leads to another event, in this case in a circular manner. This is basically a circular form of positivism, relying solely on surface empirical observation.

Critical realism looks deeper than the observable circularity to attempt to retroductively discover the causal powers that have interacted to create the behavioural events of dominance and submissiveness. This gives a very different kind of explanation in which power is real but concealed from the observer. In this case, actual violence is no longer part of the regularity of the system, but the woman's *traumatic memory* of the historical violence is a currently actualised causal power. This is not only hidden from the observer's shallow reliance on the experience of his senses (empiricism), but it may even be hidden from the participants, depending how the trauma has been processed. The effect of the traumatic memory is to remind the woman that violence can become re-actualised if the unspoken requirement for submission is breached. For the man, the 'successful' use of violence is also memorised and reinforced.

The positivist shallow realism of empiricism and actualism (that causes are invariant) in the observed circular pattern is replaced, using Bhaskar's term, by 'depth realism'. There is more to coercive power (and everything else) than meets the empirical eye.

However, this is still, so far, a reductionist example. Many other causal powers in different layers of context ('strata' in Bhaskar's terminology) may play a part in the actualised behaviours of the couple. I will mention just a few possibilities. As I write, the England men's football (soccer) team is taking part in the European Championships. The *National Centre for Domestic Violence,* albeit in a comparatively small study, quotes an increase of nearly 40% in incidents of domestic violence whenever England lose a tournament game (Kirby et al., 2013). The woman in this example may be particularly cautious not to do anything which 'provokes' the England-supporting man after such a loss. The couple may be constrained from separation because of the causal powers of structural poverty and limited housing, arising from neoliberal economic policy. Patriarchy and misogyny may be a lower stratum causal power for both, emergent from which might be a socialised norm of toxic masculinity and compliant femininity, reinforced in family relationships, schoolyards, peer groups, and wider culture. And a reminder that all such theorising depends on (but is not solely determined by) the vantage points in

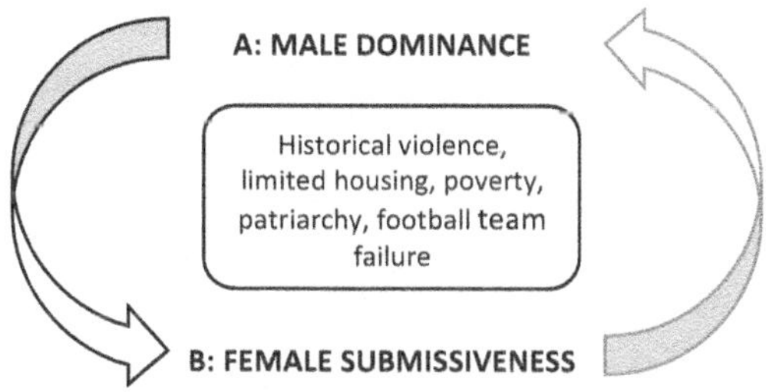

Fig. 4.2 Hidden causal powers generate apparently 'powerless' circularity

the mind of the observer. Figure 4.2 shows this more complex picture, in which the observed *apparently* 'powerless' circularity is no longer compelling as a complete explanation.

In the critical realist approach, the explanation of power sheds light on experience and does not stand in contradiction to experience as it appears to in Dell's (1985) account. In one family I worked with, the teenage girl had decided that she must never allow herself to become angry after experiencing her father smashing the window of a car she was travelling in with her mother and step-father. We came to understand this event as the one that most set the terms for her internal management of ordinary anger and influenced, thereafter, a preference for destructive self-regulation (Beebe & Lachmann, 2002) of difficult feelings—especially anger—through self-harm. The traumatic memory was a hidden active causal power, the significance of which was not apparent to anyone including herself. Cutting simply made her feel safer, so she repeated it until it became her only method of affect-management. We will return to this in Chaps. 6 and 11.

Where I am fully aligned with Bateson is with his concept of the stochastic process (Bateson, 1979). He introduces this as follows:

> A general assumption of this book [*Mind and Nature*] is that both genetic change and the process called learning (including the somatic changes induced by habit and environment) are stochastic processes. In each case there is, I believe, *a stream of events that is random in certain aspects* and in each case there is a non-random selective process which causes certain of

> the random components to "survive" longer than others. Without the random, there can be no new thing. [My emphasis.] (Bateson, 1979, p. 139)

Whether we call these random events lineal or not, they are clearly not simple punctuations of pre-existing circular patterns. Every utterance by the therapist is one such novel moment (causal tendency) regardless of whether the therapist is systemic, humanistic, analytic, cognitive, or none of those things. Whether these speech events become a *difference that makes a difference:* in other words, whether they survive as information to become lasting perturbations is what constitutes systems change. From a Batesonian-Bhaskarian viewpoint every therapist is a systemic therapist. Like dolphins we can't help being systemic because we and our world simply are an open system. The only question that remains is whether the result of our words and other inputs (causal tendencies) trend in the direction of *helpful* systemic change. That too is not an easy thing to define (who, for example, is doing the defining?) but clients and therapists often know it when they see it.

Adding systemic awareness to non-systemic therapy traditions means, first, allowing a host of other influences onto the therapist's conceptual map, as we discussed with Catherine of Siena and, second, that the therapist anticipates and tracks the systemic implications of her inputs. A *second-order systemic awareness* means including oneself in the system under observation and examining, as far as possible, one's premises. Fortunately, encouraging the therapist to look within is a regular part of humanistic and psychoanalytic practice alongside systemic therapy's reflexivity. It may simply need to be widened and deepened.

References

Bateson, G. (1979). *Mind and nature: A necessary unity*. Dutton.

Beebe, B., & Lachmann, F. (2002). *Infant research and adult treatment: Co-constructing interactions*. The Analytic Press.

Benjamin, J. (2017). *Beyond doer and done to: Recognition theory, intersubjectivity and the third*. Routledge.

Bertrando, P., & Arcelloni, T. (2006). Hypotheses are dialogues: Sharing hypotheses with clients. *Journal of Family Therapy, 28*, 370–387.

Bion, W. (1988). Notes on memory and desire. In E. Spillius (Ed.), *Melanie Klein today: Developments in theory and practice, Vol. 2. Mainly practice* (pp. 17–21). Taylor & Frances.

Cecchin, G. (1987). Hypothesising, circularity, and neutrality revisited: An invitation to curiosity. *Family Process, 26*, 405–413.

Collier, A. (1994). *Critical realism: An introduction to Roy Bhaskar's philosophy.* Verso Books.

Collier, A. (1999). Language, practice, and realism. In I. Parker (Ed.), *Social constructionism, discourse, and realism* (pp. 47–58). Sage.

Crittenden, P. (2008). *Raising parents: Attachment representation, and treatment.* Routledge.

Crittenden, P., Dallos, R., Landini, A., & Kozlowska, K. (2014). *Attachment and family therapy*. Open University Press.

Dallos, R. (2006). *Attachment narrative therapy: Integrating narrative, systemic and attachment therapies*. Open University Press.

Dallos, R., & Vetere, A. (2022). *Systemic therapy and attachment narratives: Applications in a range of clinical settings*. Routledge.

Dell, P. (1985). Understanding Bateson and Maturana: Toward a biological foundation for the social sciences. *Journal of Marital and Family Therapy, 11*, 1–20.

Dell, P. (1989). Violence and the systemic view: The problem of power. *Family Process, 28*, 1–14.

Efran, J., & Clarfield, L. (1992). Constructionist therapy: Sense and nonsense. In S. McNamee & K. Gergen (Eds.), *Therapy as social construction* (pp. 200–216). Sage.

Flaskas, C. (2002). *Family therapy beyond postmodernism: Practice challenges theory.* Routledge.

Golann, S. (1988). On second-order family therapy. *Family Process, 27*, 51–65.

Goldner, V. (1993). Power and hierarchy: Let's talk about it! *Family Process, 32*, 157–162.

Goldner, V., Penn, P., Sheinberg, M., & Walker, G. (1990). Love and violence: Gender paradoxes in volatile attachments. *Family Process, 29*, 343–364.

Haley, J. (1993). *Uncommon therapy: The psychiatric techniques of Milton H. Erickson, M.D.* Norton.

Heimann, P. (1950). On counter-transference. *International Journal of Psychoanalysis, 31*, 81–84.

Hoffman, L. (1990). Constructing realities: An art of lenses. *Family Process, 29*, 1–12.

Howe, D. (1989). *The consumers view of family therapy*. Gower.

Kirby, S., Francis, B., & O'Flaherty, R. (2013). Can the FIFA World Cup (soccer) Tournament be associated with an increase of domestic abuse? *Journal of Research in Crime and Delinquency, 51*, 259–276.

Korzybski, A. (1933). *Science and sanity*. Science Press.

Larner, G. (2000). Towards a common ground in psychoanalysis and family therapy: On knowing not to know. *Journal of Family Therapy, 22*, 61–82.

Larner, G. (2002). Towards a critical therapy. *The International Journal of Critical Psychology, 6*, 9–29.

Larner, G. (2011). Deconstructing theory: Towards an ethical therapy. *Theory and Psychology, 21*, 821–839.

Lebow, J. (2019). Current issues in the practice of integrative couple and family therapy. *Family Process, 58*, 610–628.

Mason, B. (1993). Towards positions of safe uncertainty. *Human Systems, 4*, 189–200.

Miller, L., & Wrate, R. (2014). *Integrated family therapy: A paramodern position*. Ebook.

Orange, D. (1995). *Emotional understanding: Studies in psychoanalytic epistemology*. Guilford.

Peirce, C. (1877). The fixation of belief. *Popular Science Monthly, 12*, 1–15.

Pilgrim, D. (2020). *Critical realism for psychologists*. Routledge.

Pocock, D. (2005). Systems of the heart: Evoking the feeling self in family therapy. In C. Flaskas, B. Mason, & A. Perlesz (Eds.), *The space between: Experience, context and process in the therapeutic relationship* (pp. 127–140). Karnac.

Pocock, D. (2013). A philosophy of practice for systemic psychotherapy: The case for critical realism. *Journal of Family Therapy, 37*, 167–183.

Reimers, S., & Treacher, A. (1994). *Introducing user-friendly family therapy*. Routledge.

Rober, P. (2005). The therapist's self in dialogical family therapy: Some ideas about not-knowing and the therapist's inner conversation. *Family Process, 44*, 477–495.

Rober, P. (2024). *Becoming an effective family therapist: Research, practice, and case studies*. Routledge.

Shotter, J. (1993). *Conversational realities: Constructing life through language*. Sage.

Smith, G. (2023). A 1.5-order therapy: Between knowing and not-knowing. *Family Process, 62*, 1281–1289.

Speed, B. (1984). How really real is real? *Family Process, 23*, 511–517.

Tomm, K. (1987). Interventive interviewing: Part 1. Strategizing as a fourth guideline for a therapist'. *Family Process, 26*, 13–31.

Watzlawick, P., Bavelas, J., & Jackson, D. (1967). *Pragmatics of human communication: A study of interactional patterns, pathologies, and paradoxes*. Norton.

Woodcock, J. (2009). Love and hate and the Oedipal myth: The perfect bridge between the systemic and the psychoanalytic. In C. Flaskas & D. Pocock (Eds.), *Systems and psychoanalysis: Contemporary integrations in family therapy* (pp. 129–146). Karnac.

Woodcock, J. (2021). *Families and individuals living with Trauma: A guide for therapists, relatives and friends*. Palgrave.

5

Theory Choice

> Things should be made as simple as possible, but not any simpler.
> Albert Einstein.

> They muddy the water to make it seem deep.
> Friedrich Nietzsche, *Thus Spoke Zarathustra*.

As I glance along my bookshelves I spot Stephen Hawking's *A Brief History of Time,* said to be the shortest book that most readers never finish. I appreciate Hawking's attempt to make this strange and complex world accessible, but quantum mechanics is beyond me. I can live with that. It isn't Hawking's fault or my fault, we did our best: him *trying* to explain, me *trying* to understand—the quantum world simply is very hard to grasp. On another shelf I can see another group of books and another failed project—attempting to understand the postmodern psychoanalytic theories of Jacques Lacan. In this second project the failure is not, I think, shared equally between me and the author. I am now conducting a small experiment which is to flick through the pages of Lacan's *Écrits*, putting my thumb at random on a passage and attempting to understand it. I've done this five times in a row now and each time failed to grasp the meaning. This is the fifth attempt:

D. Pocock, *Expanding the Limits of Individual and Family Therapies*, Palgrave Texts in Counselling and Psychotherapy, https://doi.org/10.1007/978-3-031-76309-0_5

> Let us return to our symbolic object, which is itself extremely substantial [*consistant*] in its matter, even if it has lost the weight of use, but whose imponderable meaning will produce displacements of some weight. Is that, then, law and language? Perhaps not yet. (Lacan, 2006, p. 64)

Of course, it is a little unfair to pick a small passage at random since meaning is provided by context, but *none of it* makes consistent sense to me. I don't give up easily. I have also read—or tried to read—various commentaries on Lacan, and even a cartoon book attempting to explain the basics, which was fun but still didn't help much. I get that he reinterprets Freud through structural and post-structural conceptions of language, and I *know* many of the things that he says, but my *understanding* doesn't grow coherently from those starting points.

What are we to make of dense theorising that, unlike Hawking's book, does not seem to want to explain? If we are in a relatively powerless position—as a trainee, for example—when we are expected to understand, the temptation is to think "this sounds brilliant so maybe I'm a bit dim". Even asking clarifying questions then becomes anxiety-provoking in case one reveals one's 'inadequate' grasp, so perhaps it's best to keep quiet and hope that understanding will come along later. (Pro-tip: it rarely does.) Another bad solution is to suspend one's capacity for critical thinking and take ideas on trust. If I had attended one of Lacan's regular seminars as a trainee—assuming I could get a seat since he was a rock star in French cultural circles, attracting big audiences—I would probably have thought that everyone else was understanding him, so it *must* be me. Maybe I would have learned to just mouth the language by rote rather than truly understand. But I know about suspending my critical faculties from my religious years, and I'm not going down that road again—in that way cults are formed.

Noam Chomsky, not a man overly eager to fit in, and knowing a thing or two about language, did sit in the audience and, many years later, talked about his experience in a podcast:

> Jacques Lacan I actually knew. I kind of liked him. We had meetings every once in a while but quite frankly I thought he was a total charlatan, just posturing before the television cameras the way many Paris intellectuals do.

> Why [his ideas are] influential I haven't the slightest idea. I don't see anything that should be influential. (Chomsky, quoted in Wolters, 2013)

The book on Lacan that I finally did understand was an enthusiastic biography by Katherine Millot (2018), his one-time patient, trainee, and lover—not an unusual combination of roles in Lacan's relationships. Lacan's personal narcissism shines through in the book and, indeed, I think his view of the human condition is best understood as an attempt to normalise and even celebrate narcissism (Flax, 1990). It is at odds (exemplified by the 'mirror stage') with *all* other models of human development. This, I believe, is both a reason for considerable scepticism (of which more later) and a partial explanation of Lacan's success, since membership of a radical group holding a quietly superior arcane knowledge at odds with established ideas has always sold well. This is evidenced by the rampant spread of conspiracy theories in our post-truth world and indeed the uncritical 'success' of postmodernism itself as the replacement metanarrative across many fields of study from the mid-60s.

As the Nietzsche quote at the start of this chapter suggests, obscurantism is easily confused with depth, but it is also marketable. Michel Foucault told his friend John Searle that he made his writing deliberately obscure to please his French audience. "In France, you've got to have ten percent incomprehensible, otherwise people won't think it's deep—they won't think you're a profound thinker". When Searle later asked Pierre Bourdieu if he thought this was true, Bourdieu insisted it was more like twenty per cent (Searle, 2013).

But obscurantism comes with a cost, not just to the baffled reader, but also to the obscurer. Jacques Derrida frequently complains that deconstruction has been widely misunderstood. For example:

> Every week I receive critical commentaries and studies on deconstruction which operate on the assumption that what they call 'post-structuralism' amounts to saying that there is nothing beyond language, that we are submerged in words—*and other stupidities of that sort.* [Instead] deconstruction tries to show that questions of reference [referring to reality] is more complex and problematic than traditional theories supposed. [My emphasis.] (Derrida, 1984, p. 123)

Systemic family therapists still enamoured by the 1990's strong linguistic turn please note! In my view, Derrida's clarification brings him closer to the epistemological and philosophical assumptions of critical realism, a conclusion also reached by Larner (2002), but reading Derrida in the original, one has to say that he can hardly blame his readership for misinterpreting. Take, for example, his famous statement "The text is all, and nothing exists outside it" (Derrida, 1967). Either he changed his mind in his 1984 clarification or didn't mean what he appears to mean in the first place. As discussed in Chap. 2, I think there is a double-bind in operation, since to provide clear unambiguous statements is to undermine the postmodern precept that words cannot reliably reference meaning or the world. To be clear is to automatically disqualify oneself as postmodern.

When it comes to training, it is not the sole responsibility of trainee psychotherapists to understand, it is also the responsibility of writers and teachers to meet them at least half-way, to try to make their ideas understandable. And, as we will come to, the same is true of therapists with their clients. *Expecting the other to accept ideas without understanding undermines autonomous meaning-making and can lead to colonisation, infantilised regression, and an idealised dependency.* Attempting to hold a safe space for not-knowing, questioning, open disagreement, argument, and play is the identical task for whether teacher, supervisor, or therapist. When it comes to theory choice, for a teacher or therapist to use an idea that they themselves have not digested simply allows mystification and inauthenticity to spread.

Finally in this section, a reflexive moment is required since Bhaskar's work can be difficult to read for those (including me) without a deep background in philosophy. While the postmodern assumption is that any attempt to encapsulate the world will fail, so postmodern texts are dense, ironic, celebrate ambiguity and must never reach a conclusion, critical realism, in contrast, at least struggles for clarity and simplicity (López & Potter, 2001).

Finding a Secure Base for Theory

Lacan is a particularly strong example but over-investing in major theorists and their associated movements is, I believe, a problem in the mainstreams of both psychoanalytic and systemic traditions. In Chap. 2 I attempted to deconstruct postmodern strong constructionism in systemic family therapy to reveal its hidden realist assumption. To repeat, *the idea that 'realities' are constructed only in dialogue and therefore are all equally valid is itself a powerful realist assumption. If this is not acknowledged, it becomes a first-order metanarrative placing powerful constraints on what counts as legitimate knowledge.* As described, this has to be compensated for with unacknowledged (covert) forms of realism which can then escape reflexive accountability. To acknowledge the paradox of realism inherent in strong constructionism's rejection of realism is to break out of the double-bind and, in doing so, one is on the way to becoming a critical realist (!) Rather more importantly, *many decades of clinical knowledge and research into the human condition are then re-opened as potential resources to those who seek our help in the very reasonable expectation that we, as therapists, will know some things that they don't.*

The degree of confidence that we can place in our theories is almost never discussed, but we now know very clearly—or should do—that therapist confidence can be misplaced. Theories can simply be wrong. Switching focus to the psychoanalytic world, Freud, for example, catastrophically abandoned his 'seduction theory' in favour of oedipal fantasy when he didn't—or couldn't—sustain belief in the extent of child sexual abuse reported by his patients, helping to set back the 'discovery' of the true prevalence of sexual abuse by around eighty years (Dell, 1989). When the now famous and harrowing film, *A Two-Year-Old Goes to Hospital* (made in collaboration by John Bowlby and James Robertson), was shown to the British Psychoanalytic Society, Wilfred Bion maintained that the little girl's distress at dangerous separation from her parents was solely a manifestation of her envy at her mother's pregnancy (Holmes, 1995).

Use of familiar sets of theories produces effects *understandable only through those lenses*, reinforced by case reports in books and journals. Over time there can be a tendency to forget that the lenses exist in the mind of the observer; confirmation bias is strengthened and, like Saxe's blind men, the dangers of slipping into first-order omniscience increase. 'Success' in the work may confirm the correctness of theory but leave unmapped other curative factors. For example, the reliability, regularity, and mindful attunement to the patient, inherent in the frame of long-term individual work, supply some basic requirements for the emergence of attachment security (Crittenden, 2008). This may occur regardless of the content of the sessions, or of the therapist's understanding of the true process of change.

The Value of Research

Treatment 'failures' tend not to be discussed in systemic work. In analytic work they might be framed as negative therapeutic reaction based on the defences of the patient (e.g. fear of change, or a non-conscious desire to spite the therapist) rather than any theory-driven or technical rigidity on the part of the therapist. The near ubiquitous and unquestioned use of interpretation in classical psychoanalytic technique is, for example, challenged by a major study of outcome, tracking patients over thirty years. The study showed no correlation between interpretation and good outcome and, instead, emotional support by the therapist emerged as the major 'curative' factor (Wallerstein, 1989). A third position combining—but emergent from—the two is offered by Orange (1995): creating emotional understanding together, between patient and therapist.

As shown in Chap. 1, institutions can protect established training curricula from destabilising encounters with the reality-testing provided by science, evidenced by the side-lining of attachment theory and other caregiver-infant dyadic research from both systemic and psychoanalytic mainstreams (Knox, 2013). I still occasionally encounter Kleinian colleagues who believe in the death instinct as an explanation for aggression, despite this being grounded in Lamarck's outdated theory of evolution, and Jungians who substitute realist notions of coincidence with paranormal 'synchronicity'.

While the dynamics of triadic, tetradic and larger sets of relationships cannot be fully explained by the dyadic, the lenses of attachment theories and research and numerous caregiver-infant observational studies provide, in my view, the most reliable standpoints for understanding the emergence of an autonomous relational self; a whole person capable of giving and receiving love in relationships without feeling diminished or at risk (Knox, 2011). Dyadic studies also provide maps of the way children adapt, at a cost to themselves, to try to make the best of their caregiver relationships and avoid the worst: these experiential templates being used unconsciously in later relationships (e.g., Beebe & Lachmann, 2002). These are ecosystemic adaptations and, while partial, fit in to the systemic whole.

I think it is unfair to expect major theorists to continue to bear the weight of expectations that they can still act as reliable guides. Brilliant, they may have been, but all were human, and therefore fallible, building on the socially constructed knowledge of their day while stumbling in the dark, as we all must, to make sense of that which is always ultimately imperfectly knowable. In *Faces in a Cloud: Intersubjectivity in Personality Theory*, George Atwood's and Robert Stolorow's (1993) fascinating psychobiographical analyses of Freud, Jung, Reich, and Rank shine a light on how the theoretical interests of each relate to their own unresolved psychological and relational issues. Yet that serves to helpfully contextualise and rehumanise their theoretical contributions, not discredit them.

More remarkable is not what the pioneers got wrong but the fact that many ideas have stood the test of time. As examples, I have already mentioned Freud's theory of melancholia in relation to Catherine of Siena. Jung's early writings prefigure contemporary Relational Psychoanalysis (Mitchell & Greenberg, 1983); and, while I reject Klein's acceptance of Freud's death instinct (and I reject Freudian drive theory as a whole), I find her theories of projective and introjective identification have good explanatory powers as discussed in the cases of Emma in Chap. 1 and Steve in Chap. 4. Indeed, I find it hard to understand the ubiquity of phenomena such as racism and sexism without the theoretical vantage point describing how one group of people can narcissistically shore-up their identities by non-consciously splitting-off and projecting feared inferiority or other disavowed parts of the self into another group: the other half of the story being the introjection of the corrosive projections by those being othered.

But the psychoanalytic tradition that I find most complementary to a realist systemic ontology is, as said, that of the broad collection of ideas known as Relational Psychoanalysis (e.g. Mitchell & Aron, 1999; Mitchell, 2000; Kuchuck, 2021), incorporating as it does attachment, parent-infant research, systems, mentalization, trauma-focus, moderate constructionism, object and subject relating, as well as sensitivity to culture and social justice (Layton, 2020). The relational therapist strives to include her conscious and unconscious influence in her understanding of the developing relationship with the patient. She is a second-order participant-observer, trying to keep herself in view, as much as the patient, and what is growing between them (Pocock, 2018). The one-way flow of non-conscious information from patient to therapist in Paula Heimann's (1950) conception of countertransference is augmented by assuming a fully interactional mingling of subjectivities at both conscious and unconscious levels, represented by Orange (1995) in her helpful term 'co-transference'.

Family Resemblance, Convergence, and Predictability

Scientific validation is important in theory choice, but we should not, I think, fall into scientism where only that which has been empirically researched counts as usable knowledge. The evolutionary functions of attachment in survival and producing the next generation can only give a partial account of the human condition. Bowlby has little to say about sexuality, dreams, or art, for example. But in pluralism, theories grounded in science can act as anchor points for other similar ideas. I feel more confident about object relations theory than, say, Lacan's metapsychology *because* object relations theory shares a family resemblance to scientifically researched attachment theory. Similarly, while much of the theorising in the relational psychoanalytic tradition moves beyond the findings from the extensive caregiver-infant observational studies, importantly it does not stand in contradiction to those findings.

While the map is not territory, when socially constructed maps from quite different theoretical standpoints seem to be pointing to something similar, the convergence suggests that reality is nearby. The theories then confer on each other some reliability in apprehending that part of the territory. Theories that are outliers to a convergence such as Lacan's mirror stage of development should, I think, be treated with suspicion unless and until they are supported by more than anecdotal evidence. As the American astronomer and science communicator Carl Sagan famously said, extraordinary claims require extraordinary evidence. In the case of Emma in Chap. 1, theories of parentification (Boszormenyi-Nagy & Krasner, 1986), moral defence (Fairbairn, 1952), and the Dynamic Maturational Model (Crittenden, 2008) strategies of compulsive compliance and compulsive caregiving all speak to internal adaptations by dependent children to reduce anxiety in the face of the danger of caregiver limitations. In brief, they all converge in their different ways to indicate that Emma adapted to make herself wrong to try to make her father right.

Theories make educated guesses about how part of the system works and, if they succeed in those predictions, they can earn their keep. My question to Emma after learning that she had seen her father taken away by ambulance "Did you think you had made Daddy tired?" contained an educated guess based on the information from the family members filtered only part-non-consciously through a range of vantage points given by theories and clinical experience. Her enlivened answer—not a flat compliance—"Yes, I thought I had worn Daddy out" provides some support (although not conclusive evidence) for the theories. In the case of Steve, in the last chapter, after a further three years, when the summer break came around, he reported that even the quiet sound of my breathing triggered his intense irritation. The break was no longer a "perfect arrangement" and the sharp abdominal pains had been replaced with a hard-earned capacity for anger and self-agency (Knox, 2011) as news slowly arrived that I was different to his internalised retaliatory mother, and he was not at risk with me. This lends support to, but doesn't absolutely confirm, the validity of the theory maps of adaptive somatisation and projective identification since in an open system there can be many hidden causal powers. It is unwise to hold any theory with a tight grip if it is not assisting in the work/play of understanding (Orange, 1995). Fortunately pluralism and transdisciplinarity usually provide other vantage points from which to look and think.

Critical Realist Science

Psychoanalytic therapies are fast disappearing from public agencies like the NHS, at least in the UK, in favour of brief therapies such as cognitive behavioural therapy which more readily satisfy the need for practice to be seen to be evidence-based and cost-effective. The situation is different for systemic family therapy which has, so far, retained a foothold especially in child and adolescent mental health settings, despite the dire UK economic circumstances. This is largely due to the willingness of a minority to conduct research into effectiveness. Ironically, large numbers of systemic family therapists who overtly reject realism owe their employment, at least in part, to quantitative research. This may not be sustainable in the longer term as the need for systemic therapists to provide evidence to justify what they do will only grow.

In the UK there is a requirement for systemic family therapy trainees to undertake a research module. Qualitative methods tend to be greatly favoured since they *appear* to be more in tune with social constructionism than quantitative methods which are generally understood to be an empirical and positivist search for objective, value-free knowledge and therefore unacceptable to so-called 'second-order' sensibilities.

So the apparent gap between quantitative and qualitative research methods maps onto the split between realism and strong constructionism. As we've discussed, critical realism bridges that gap by occupying a third position that it is simultaneously moderately realist and moderately constructionist. It assumes an objectively real and structured intransitive world which can only be known subjectively (and intersubjectively) and therefore fallibly in the transitive domain through the human construction of knowledge. Given that ideas can be tested against the constraints of the world, it also assumes that there are rational grounds for finding some ideas more object-adequate than others, science being one method.

The rejection of quantitative research on positivist grounds is, from a critical realist perspective, to misunderstand science and, as discussed in Chap. 2, to commit the fallacy of actualism. Scientific experiments are conducted by artificial closure of an open system so that the causal power of a single variable—for example, a drug or a psychotherapy method—can be tested. Critical realism sees no problem with that. *The problems start (the fallacy of actualism) with the positivist assumption that once the causal power of a variable has been established it is constantly operating in that manner.* To recap, critical realism says that constancy of the actualised power of a variable is *only* true in the artificially closed system of the experiment. In the everyday world of open systems, whether the power of that variable is active and produces an event depends entirely on the interaction with other variables. Laboratory testing of the waterproofing power of umbrellas by spending hundreds of hours pouring water on them in a controlled environment is all very well but once released from the closed system into the open air, the confounding variable of a single strong gust of wind changes everything, as many of us have found when our brolly inverts leaving us soaked to the skin.

Assuming that causal powers are always in play is the positivist error: the fallacy of actualism. *So quantitative science is not the problem when researching open systems, it is the positivist interpretation of science that creates the error.* If it was ever possible to control the variables to establish the efficacy of therapy with two parents and their out-of-control child, the day that the mother gets called into work on the day of the appointment and the father brings the child alone, all the research-based predictive bets of efficacy are off. Critical realism helps to *explain* open systems through retroduction but cannot *predict* how they will behave in the future, other than in the short-term when some regularities may endure.

Critical realism, alongside postmodernism, is therefore post-positivist. However, as well as avoiding the fallacy of actualism, critical realism avoids the *epistemic fallacy* of postmodernism which assumes that knowledge is solely produced by social means. *Critical realism favours neither qualitative nor quantitative research; it simply provides scaffolding. The choice of research methods depends solely on whatever is relevant to the subject being studied.* A mixture of methods is fairly typical in trying to map interacting systemic causal powers but depending entirely on the requirements of that which is being studied.

The argument for mixed methods is not a new one: William Pinsof and Jay Lebow (2005) write:

> Quantification does not … confer an inherent objectivity on the knowledge it generates. As a consequence, this [interactive constructivism] paradigm incorporates both quantitative and qualitative methods. They are not incompatible. On the contrary, within this paradigm, they exist in a circular, reiterative relationship. They generate somewhat different, yet compatible, types of knowledge that are complementary and mutually enriching. (p. 8)

This debate has recently been re-energised through a trio of papers from a Norwegian group, published in *Family Process* (Lorås et al., 2023; Whittaker et al., 2024) and the *Journal for Family Therapy* (Tilden et al., 2024), re-examining and challenging mainstream strong constructionist ontological assumptions from a critical realist standpoint. I anticipate more of these re-evaluations as, with the passage of time, systemic family therapy gains more distance from the powerful hegemony of the 1990s postmodern strong linguistic turn.

The depth realism inherent in critical realism suggests that what an observer can see empirically is, like an iceberg, merely the surface presentation of the system. As we discussed in relation to the example of power in the last chapter, a violent act in the history of a couple is no longer visible to an observer who, from the surface (empirical) presentation, may assume a power-free circularity between a dominant partner and a submissive one; the behaviour of each being the sole context for the other. Out of sight is the hidden active power of the traumatic memory of an act of violence, itself influenced by multiple hidden causal factors that may include misogyny, structural poverty, culture, racism, family scripting, early relational trauma, and so on.

A study that attempted to understand, for example, financial decision-making between couples would need a variety of quantitative and qualitative tools to adequately map deeper aspects of the system if crucial causal powers are not to be missed. Some tendencies will not routinely be activated. For, example, the availability of money as a causal factor may be more crucial the further away a couple are from payday. One partner may tend to dominate the decision-making only when money is scarce. A study undertaken soon after payday might lead to conclusions about financial decision-making that were increasingly inaccurate as the couple's available cash dwindled. Mixed-method research designs may provide a better chance of capturing the causal tendencies that may or may not be activated depending on their interaction with other hidden tendencies. As said, critical realism provides scaffolding but does not dictate methods: those are chosen to best suit the subject under investigation.

If it seems odd to my readers that critical realism joins depth realism to social constructionism in this way, I can assure you that it still sounds peculiar to me even after a decade and more of thinking this way; so powerful is the dominant discourse that insists that constructionism and realism are in opposition.

The Dynamic Maturational Model of Attachment and Adaptation (DMM)

What might a critical realist take on a scientifically researched theoretical model look like? I'll illustrate with the DMM which is one of the lenses that is always somewhere in my mind when working clinically. But first, I'll repeat a brief sketch of the DMM from earlier papers (Pocock, 2010a, 2010b). For those who wish to explore further, I highly recommend Pat Crittenden's (2008) *Raising Parents* which weaves a compassionate narrative, rich with clinical experience, into careful model-building.

- Attachment is seen in the DMM, not as a stable property of the individual (as in 'attachment disorder'), but an acquired strategy, or range of strategies, used mostly non-consciously and variably to attempt to keep safe within relationships and to produce the next generation. Survival of the self and the species is paramount.

- While genetic factors are recognised, the individual can only adequately be understood within his or her relational-cultural contexts: a central systemic premise. Research in varying cultural contexts is a strong feature of the model.
- There has been a tendency to assume that early categories of attachment may be valid throughout the life-span, but the DMM tracks how, as children mature, they are capable of a more elaborate range of emotional expression and operate within a wider relational-cultural field of siblings and peers. In older children affect can be consciously denied, exaggerated, or falsified in order to elicit certain responses from caregivers in order to feel safe. For example, the falsification of true affect in order to please an emotionally dismissing caregiver in pre-school years.
- Crittenden elaborates the basic Ainsworth et al. (1978) ABC model, where A is the avoidant attachment pattern, B the secure, and C the ambivalent, identifying new adaptive strategies within these broad categories. For example, Crittenden identifies nine sub-categories at pre-school age and thirteen by adulthood. This outlining of subcategories—e.g. A3 compulsive caregiving, C5 punitive—is a major strength of the model.
- The model meshes with the idea of co-evolutionary processes (Maturana and Varela 1980) in which individuals attempt to find the best fit with each other. Although mutual adaptation is at work, the DMM would anticipate this mutuality being frequency asymmetric, with children who have not had consistent and attuned responses adapting more to their caregivers than the other way round (Steirlin, 1959) given the greater danger arising from childhood vulnerability.
- Maladaption is viewed in the DMM as the continuing use of a once-adaptive strategy that has, other than in extreme circumstances, outgrown its usefulness. This is a good fit with the Mental Research Institute (Watzlawick et al., 1974) notion of problems being maintained by the misapplication of a solution or class of solutions often applied with even greater intensity as they fail—a state of affairs described in both the higher-numbered C (ambivalent) and A (avoidant) strategies.

- The idea of cognitive distortion as an aspect of relational adaptation runs parallel to both the concept of psychoanalytic transferential distortion and systemic psychotherapy's interest in beliefs as part of the second-order interests in meaning-systems.
- Splitting is theorised, for example the cutting off of fear in favour of omnipotence and controlling aggression in the C3 (aggressive coercive) strategy. It is only a short theoretical stretch to projective identification in which, for example, the fear that would otherwise be experienced by an adolescent boy using a C5 (punitive) strategy is, instead, experienced by the victim of his bullying.
- The model's theorising of multiple memory systems encompasses the need to act quickly, without reflection, to avoid danger, as well as the possibilities of reorganising strategies through processes of reflection and higher-order integration. This is in line with contemporary views on the role for mentalising in psychoanalysis (Fonagy et al., 2002), reflective process in systemic psychotherapy (Donovan, 2009), and forms of collaborative narrative therapy that work with autobiographical memory. (See Dallos, 2006, and Dallos and Vetere 2022, for an integrative model for family therapy.)
- As well as having considerable clinical scope, the DMM is built upon propositions that are clear enough to be tested through research.

The DMM has been developed through forty years of research and clinical application, and has over two hundred publications from around twenty countries so should definitely count as reliable positivist, objective, and value-free knowledge, yes?

Well no. First, critical realism recognises that all knowledge is socially constructed and is therefore fallible and subject to bias. The idea that attachment is being decided on the basis of data alone is naive. There is a bitter rift in the attachment field between the ABCD model of Main and Goldwyn (the D standing for disorganised attachment) and the DMM group who do not recognise disorganisation or, rather, have many subdivisions of it. Two editions of the giant *Handbook of Attachment* (Cassidy & Shaver, 1999, 2008) don't mention the DMM at all. This rift contextualises the DMM and the attachment field as a whole but doesn't invalidate it. In practice this means that, despite my enthusiasm for the clinical value of the DMM, especially its disambiguation of the 'disorganised' category, I am wary of the temptation to place all my eggs in the DMM basket, and I continue to keep at least a partially open mind on other attachment models.

Second, all theory is reductionist, and that is particularly the case in models where the key propositions have to be clear and simple enough for research purposes. There is no problem with reductionism as long as it is noticed and kept in mind. Mindful reductionism need not become mindless, naïve realist, reification.

Third, the DMM strategies need to be understood as tendencies that may or may not be actualised depending on other variables. Indeed, this is understood within the model. So, for example, the A3 compulsive caregiving strategy (parentification) and A4 compulsive compliant strategy hypothesised in the case of Emma who feared she had worn her father out would not be considered to be invariant but activated only under stress, perhaps when the father seemed to be especially 'tired' (depressed) or perhaps when tensions between the couple grew. Other, less extreme, attachment strategies may be used at other times.

Fourth, from a second-order perspective, no matter how well researched, the attachment strategies do not simply exist 'out there'. They are selectors and organisers of data in the mind of the therapist: a mixture of outside and inside. In a paper commissioned for a special issue on the DMM in the *Journal of Child Psychology and Psychiatry* (Pocock, 2010b), I raised concerns about the temptations of reifying strategies. Such temptations are all the greater when there is much empirical support:

> … I have a nagging concern which grows in proportion to my increasing appreciation of the potential strength of a model using validated assessment tools. That which a community agrees to name is a powerful influence on what will be perceived and what will be cast into shadow. Could the evidence-based zeitgeist, in which contemporary psychotherapy is struggling to survive, encourage the hubristic growth of DMM experts rather than the spread of cautious DMM expertise to mingle with other expertise? Given the vast complexity of the human condition, might awareness slip, that a model—no matter how good and well-evidenced—is inevitably reductive such that the DMM strategies become seen as reified

> categories? In the same way that a person with a DSMIV diagnosis of borderline personality can, for a busy clinician, become a person "who has a borderline personality disorder" or eventually "a borderline", will our clinics become populated with C3s and A4s. The latter point is not so fanciful—I have begun to notice this tendency in myself. (Pocock, 2010b, p. 307)

I was pleased to learn from Pat Crittenden (personal communication 2023) that this paper is included early in the DMM trainings to try to help guard against reifying dangers. Clinical value is lost when any theories, no matter how well researched, slip to first-order (out-there) observation and are held onto with a tight grip even when they are no longer working in the co-constructive process of therapy—a risk from which I am not immune. It needs constant vigilance. Strong constructionism in family therapy deals with this problem by (overtly) rejecting realist theorising, assuming that all such generalised 'expert' knowledge will subjugate the autonomous meaning-making of those we try to help. This can surely happen in a state of mind of first-order over-confidence in one's hypothesising, but the idea that this is inevitable is, I believe, a myth: *one that is at risk of denying those who seek our help the rich resources of understanding that come from decades of research and clinical practice in psychotherapy and related fields.*

Summing up, just how different is a critical realist science from what one might simply call 'good science'? Bhaskar (2016) writes:

> Critical realism is indeed a new philosophy but … it is not a new practice; genuine science, whether great or ordinary, revolutionary or normal, has always been critical realist. (p. 41)

What critical realism brings is a challenge to the reduction of knowledge to language and discourse on the one hand, and reduction to shallow forms of realism on the other. It is how critical realism *understands* science that makes if fit for open systems.

References

Ainsworth, M., Blehar, M., Waters, E., & Wall, S. (1978). *Patterns of attachment: A psychological study of the strange situation*. Erlbaum.

Atwood, G., & Stolorow, R. (1993). *Faces in a cloud: Intersubjectivity in personality theory*. Aronson.

Beebe, B., & Lachmann, F. (2002). *Infant research and adult treatment: Co-constructing interactions*. The Analytic Press.

Bhaskar, R. (2016). *Enlightened common sense: The philosophy of critical realism*. Routledge.

Boszormenyi-Nagy, I., & Krasner, B. (1986). *Between give and take: A clinical guide to contextual therapy: Conversations in theory and practice*. Basic Books.

Cassidy, J., & Shaver, P. (Eds.). (1999). *Handbook of attachment: Theory research and clinical applications*. Guildford.

Cassidy, J., & Shaver, P. (Eds.). (2008). *Handbook of attachment: Theory research and clinical applications* (2nd ed.). Guildford.

Crittenden, P. (2008). *Raising parents: Attachment representation, and treatment*. Routledge.

Dallos, R. (2006). *Attachment narrative therapy: Integrating narrative, systemic and attachment therapies*. Open University Press.

Dallos, R., & Vetere, A. (2022). *Systemic therapy and attachment narratives: Applications in a range of clinical settings*. Routledge.

Dell, P. (1989). Violence and the systemic view: The problem of power. *Family Process, 28*, 1–14.

Derrida, J. (1967). *Of grammatology*. Les Éditions de Minuit.

Derrida, J. (1984). Deconstruction and the other: An interview with Jacques Derrida. In R. Kearney (Ed.), *Dialogue with contemporary continental thinkers* (pp. 105–113). Manchester University Press.

Donovan, M. (2009). Reflecting processes and reflective functioning: Shared concerns and challenges in systemic and psychoanalytic therapeutic practice. In C. Flaskas & D. Pocock (Eds.), *Systems and psychoanalysis: Contemporary integrations in family therapy* (pp. 149–165). Karnac.

Fairbairn, R. (1952). *Psychoanalytic studies of the personality*. Tavistock and Routledge.

Flax, J. (1990). *Thinking fragments: Psychoanalysis, feminism, and postmodernism in the contemporary west*. University of California Press.

Fonagy, P., Gergeley, G., Jurist, E., & Target, M. (2002). *Affect regulation, mentalization, and the development of the self.* Other Press.

Heimann, P. (1950). On counter-transference. *International Journal of Psychoanalysis, 31*, 81–84.
Holmes, J. (1995). "Something there is that doesn't love a wall." John Bowlby, attachment theory, and psychoanalysis. In S. Goldberg et al. (Eds.), *Attachment theory: Social, developmental, and clinical perspectives* (pp. 19–43). The Analytic Press.
Knox, J. (2011). *Self-Agency in psychotherapy - attachment, autonomy, and intimacy*. Norton.
Knox, J. (2013). The analytic Institute as a psychic retreat: Why we need to include evidence in our clinical training. *British Journal of Psychotherapy, 29*, 424–448.
Kuchuck, S. (2021). *The relational revolution in psychoanalysis and psychotherapy*. Confer Books.
Lacan, J. (2006). *Écrits*. Norton.
Larner, G. (2002). Towards a critical therapy. *The International Journal of Critical Psychology, 6*, 9–29.
Layton, L. (2020). *Towards a social psychoanalysis: Culture, character, and normative unconscious processes*. Routledge.
López, J., & Potter, G. (2001). *After postmodernism: An introduction to critical realism*. Athlone.
Lorås, L., Whittaker, K., Stokkebekk, J., & Tilden, T. (2023). Researching what we practice—The paradigm of systemic family research: Part 1. *Family Process, 62*, 947–960.
Maturana, H., & Varela, F. (1980). *Autopoiesis and cognition: The realization of the living*. Reidel.
Millot, C. (2018). *Life with Lacan*. Polity Press.
Mitchell, S. (2000). *Relationality: From attachment to intersubjectivity*. Routledge.
Mitchell, S., & Aron, L. (Eds.). (1999). *Relational psychoanalysis: The emergence of a tradition*. Analytic Press.
Mitchell, S., & Greenberg, J. (1983). *Object relations in psychoanalytic theory*. Harvard University Press.
Orange, D. (1995). *Emotional understanding: Studies in psychoanalytic epistemology*. Guilford.
Pinsof, W., & Lebow, J. (2005). A scientific paradigm for family psychology. In W. Pinsof & J. Lebow (Eds.), *Family psychology: The art of the science* (pp. 3–19). Oxford University Press.
Pocock, D. (2010a). Debating truth, error, and distortion in systemic psychotherapy: A contribution from the DMM. *Context, 210*, 2–6.

Pocock, D. (2010b). The DMM – wow! But how to safely handle its potential strength? *Clinical Child Psychology and Psychiatry, 15*, 303–311.

Pocock, D. (2018). You, me, and us. In S. Lord (Ed.), *Moments of meeting in psychotherapy* (pp. 199–208). Routledge.

Searle, J. (2013). John Searle on Foucault and the obscurantism in French Philosophy. https://www.openculture.com/2013/07/jean_searle_on_foucault_and_the_obscurantism_in_french_philosophy.html

Steirlin, D. (1959). The adaptation to the 'stronger' person's reality. *Psychiatry, 22*, 143–152.

Tilden, T., Solem, M., Thuen, F., Loras, L., Stokkebekk, J., & Whittaker, K. (2024). Taking empirical evidence seriously v.2.0. *Journal of Family Therapy, 46*, 89–102.

Wallerstein, R. (1989). The psychotherapy research project of the Menninger Foundation: An overview. *Journal of Consulting and Clinical Psychology, 57*, 196–205.

Watzlawick, P., Weakland, J., & Fisch, R. (1974). *Change: Principles of Problem Formation and Problem Solution*. Norton.

Whittaker, K., Stokkebekk, J., Lorås, L., & Tilden, T. (2024). Researching what we practice – the paradigm of systemic family research: Part 2. *Family Process, 62*, 961–975.

Wolters, E. (2013). https://www.critical-theory.com/noam-chomsky-calls-jacques-lacan-a-charlatan/

6

Emotion in the System

The heart has its reasons which reason knows nothing of… We know the truth not only by the reason, but by the heart. Blaise Pascal (*Pensées* 1623–1662)

[Emotional] understanding is, among other things, a form of loving and it can be experienced that way by the patient. Donna Orange (1995, p. 171)

People come to—or in the case of younger children are taken to—psychotherapy, not primarily because of a faulty epistemology or belief system, but because they, or someone in relationship to them, feels bad. This is not a temporary bad feeling—everyone has those—but usually a mixture of persistent or recurring states of anxiety, sadness, anger, depression, shame, meaninglessness, self-hatred, hopelessness, or terror, and so on. High on the list of things of interest to the psychotherapist should therefore be emotional experience. But experience is, itself, not straightforward and can be unpacked. The self-psychologist and intersubjectivity theorist, Donna Orange (1995), defines *experience as both given and made.*

[E]xperience results from the endless and constant interaction between the given and the made. It emerges within and between the subjectivities

D. Pocock, *Expanding the Limits of Individual and Family Therapies*, Palgrave Texts in Counselling and Psychotherapy, https://doi.org/10.1007/978-3-031-76309-0_6

> involved in any intersubjective field. Individually and together we make sense of … what is partly brute, unorganised, surprising, or confusing. (Orange, 1995, p. 88)

The *given* is brute reality—the intransitive dimension in Bhaskar's terminology: a sexual assault in childhood, ghosting by a friend, redundancy at work, the absence of an emotionally attuned caregiver, the racial slur. The *made* (transitive dimension) is what is constructed out of the given: individually and socially. Will the sexual assault in childhood be made into a lifelong implicit feeling of pervasive shame for which the body has to be regularly punished or, instead, made into an outrageous event that happened in the past and was entirely the responsibility of the perpetrator? We are still in the critical realist domains of external reality and how we construct that reality internally, relationally, and culturally, but now it's not just theoretical and philosophical, it is personal and interpersonal, cognitive *and* emotional.

In the case of Emma in Chap. 1, who believed she had worn her father out, what is missing so far from my account is the emotional communication between the various family members and between each of them and me. They had agreed to video-recording, so I was able to review the tape on several occasions but, even so, emotional communication is hard to notice. It is harder still to express in words as it takes place mostly out of awareness through countless small moments of bodily posture, facial expression, tone of voice, speech rhythm and modulation, and, crucially, how well these behaviours are attuned to—and communicated with—others. Receiving and responding to these cues are all part of our knowing-within (Shotter, 1993) based on years of emerging as a person through relationships. For many of us, that includes experiences of personal psychotherapy in order to come to know about our own suffering so that we can bear to be in contact with the suffering of others (Orange, 1995).

I will now try to introduce some sense of the emotional quality of the encounter with Emma and her family. Overall, I experienced the meeting as warm and enjoyable with a willingness to explore. The obvious concern for Emma by both parents did not feel tinged with irritation and there was an absence of critical comments (Brown, 1985). I felt safe with them and they, I think, with me. There was no pressure on me to do other than I did. There was no detectable agenda from anyone to control the narrative and no implicit denigration or idealisation of my role. I could feel tension between the parents as they hinted at, through careful choice of words, the difficulties in their relationship. They were clearly anxious not to burden the children with their problems as a couple and were relieved when I said we could have the next meeting without the children. I could bodily sense what I felt to be the father's depressed feelings and shame, conveyed by his posture, flat tone, difficulty with eye-contact, and a tendency for his sentences to tail-off. Emma's stillness and flattened affect also affected me, as it did her parents. Only Emma's younger brother, Ian, seemed unburdened although his very liveliness may well have represented some unconscious adaptive compensation. I found it easy to begin to emotionally attune to each family member, and to convey to them non-verbally that their feelings mattered, were acceptable to me, and that their concern and distress had affected me, but not upset me. I noted the robust and sensitive qualities of the mother who, while burdened herself, was warm and empathic and able to take the lead in giving a clear and emotionally coherent account of the difficulties.

My question to Emma about whether she thought she had made her father tired was put gently and came about half-way through the session. This built on engagement, primarily with the children, but also involving the parents, over easier topics such as pets, hobbies, and schools, in which I found it easy to take a warm interest. Problem talk began after about fifteen minutes of this social getting-to-know-you talk: what the family therapist, Minuchin (1974), calls 'joining the family'. I had noted Emma listening intently when her mother told me, in a quiet voice, that Emma had seen her father taken away by ambulance and I sensed that she was then in touch with the memory. Outside of my awareness the first question to Emma (whether she remembered seeing her father being taken away) was intoned in a kindly manner and phrased in a way that she could answer with a simple yes or no, indicating in my tone that either was acceptable. Her immediate emotionally robust sounding reply in the affirmative encouraged the next riskier question, in the same tone, as to whether she thought she had caused his tiredness. Given my emotional experience of the family up to that point I was pleased but not surprised, both that Emma could use the question to elaborate her fearful experience of being the cause of her father's "tiredness", and that her parents could respond in such an emotionally supportive and cognitively correcting way. Emma was then able to feel emotionally understood and in receipt of parental care rather than anxiously providing it.

A major part of Emma's *given* was her father's depressed behaviour culminating in his traumatic removal from the home by ambulance staff. What she *made* of it to create the causal power of *memorised emotional experience* was, I think (using a variety of theory lenses discussed in Chap. 1), a cognitive distortion of self-blame and inhibition of affect that could be understood, not as an invariant and inevitable feature of her personality, but an adaptive ecosystemic response through drastic self-regulation to reduce her sense of danger and helplessness. This required and empowered her to make things better, but at personal cost to her development.

Questions of epistemology, ontology, and theoretical understanding discussed so far in this book are simply vehicles to try to take the therapist to the vicinity of the cognitively influenced emotional experience, which itself can only be understood within the systemic context of multiple and variable causalities using a plurality of lenses. Emotional understanding and feeling understood are always contextually influenced (Pocock, 1997, 2010). The self-torturing physical and emotional suffering of Catherine of Siena, hypothesised to be, among other causes, an internal adaptive solution to intense unresolved guilt at the death of her twin, begins to make sense only within the many contexts of her life including a search for autonomy and meaningful self-expression within the highly restrictive patriarchal religious culture of her time.

Theory maps within a critical realist frame can, like directions to someone's house, help us locate the front door, but they do not guarantee that we will find anyone home. The next step is that each person has to be met.

To Be Met as a Person

For Sally Box, my first family therapy supervisor, psychotherapy is a place for thinking (Box & Copley, 1977), but what are the conditions that make exploratory thinking possible? In her book, *To Be Met as a Person*, Una McCluskey (2005) writes movingly of an unsuccessful meeting between her mother, then aged fifty-five, and a consultant cardiologist to discuss the possibility of an operation on her mother's failing heart valves. In a twenty-minute meeting the brisk conclusion of the cardiologist was that her mother was not sufficiently ill to warrant the risk of an operation. Her mother, in line with her Scottish cultural upbringing, was polite and deferential throughout the consultation and the cues to her despair and the extent of her suffering were not picked up. Only when she left the meeting did she breakdown in tears. She died within six months.

In a rigorous series of videotaped studies of careseeker-caregiver meetings, and drawing on evidence from related fields, McCluskey concludes that *neither an empathic-sounding response, nor emotional attunement on their own by a caregiver, are sufficient for both caregiver and careseeker to experience the meeting as successful. It requires a combination of the two.* In her observational studies, meaningful exploration could only begin when the careseeker had the experience, as Dan Siegel (2012) puts it, of 'feeling felt'. Accurate emotional attunement by the caregiver that was not communicated empathically by facial/bodily expression or verbal tone failed to meet the careseeking need. Eventually, the careseeker would give up, indicated by a sense of dissatisfaction and distance, observable as a relational deadening or, as Daniel Stern (1985) terms it, diminished 'vitality affects'. Without an authentic emotional meeting, no safe base (Bowlby, 1988) was established, and exploratory thinking never properly got started. Psychoanalytic psychotherapists still tempted by classical notions of neutrality, and invariant systemic circular questioners, please note!

When the caregiver successfully conveys their attunement to the careseeker—facial expression or vocal tone may be enough—the careseeking goal is met and the subjective experience of both is one of relief. The relationship settles, lively vitality affects are observable, and genuine exploration can begin.

Emma was able and ready to let herself be emotionally understood once there were sufficient conditions of safety and support for her to elaborate her emotional experience. For patients with more adverse early histories, authentic emotion can be harder to locate.

John, a middle-aged white British man from an impoverished part of a large northern city, who I saw for long-term individual therapy, described routine denigration including cruel mocking behaviour by both his parents, but particularly his mother, who made it clear that she didn't like him and thought him a "moral coward". As a small boy she would flick him in the face with her fingers and, if he flinched or cried, she would berate him for his weakness. She would allow his brother to beat him up which became John's fault for not standing up for himself. As I write this, I can still feel fury on John's behalf despite the therapy ending some time ago, but when he first gave an account of this and many other emotionally abusive incidents, he did so in a light bemused tone which seemed to also deny me the possibility of any depth of feeling. This may be understood theoretically as the A (avoidant) attachment strategy and/or dissociation. John's kindly manner, high intelligence, and great career success hid enormous self-doubt in his personal relationships, periods of depression and suicidal ideation, secretive self-harm, and regular undiagnosed abdominal pain.

John was interested in global politics and would frequently bring world events into the conversation. When he did so his manner changed. His depressed feelings lifted, and he became enlivened, in touch with deep rage at the injustice of uncaring, self-serving, and oppressive regimes. He also had a deep distrust of the medical profession since he believed that any medical 'weaknesses' would be permanently held in his records and in some way used against him. We came to understand that politics and his view of doctors were—because they were sufficiently remote from him—the safest places that he could locate his adverse emotional experience with those whom he should have been able to trust in childhood. In these more distant domains he was free to have his authentic angry feelings and to register his sense of injustice. The phenomenon that psychoanalysis describes as transference is more widespread than the usual focus on the patient's relationship with the therapist.

The growing realisation of the link between his anger with distant authorities and his relationship with his early caregivers caused John immense bodily discomfort. He told me that daring to think this way felt like evidence of his cowardly and disloyal nature, so powerfully did this false attribution by his parents still define him: an alien part of the self, as described by Peter Fonagy et al. (2002). As a child, John had no alternative but to make the 'given' of his parents' treatment of him into a persistent self-denigrating assumption about his true nature. As George Orwell shows in *Nineteen Eighty-Four*, lies become truth under all tyranny. It took several years of work in the 'developmental second-chance' (Orange, 1995) of psychotherapy for John to exonerate himself and remake the attribution into a lie that he was required to accept on behalf of his parents.

This and similar experiences in psychotherapy make it impossible for me to accept highly relativist epistemological assumptions in strong constructionism. Without an externally real ontology there are no lies or truth, no authenticity or distortion, just different perceptions. Equally, I can't accept that John's hard-won capacity for anger at his unjust treatment (in place of his ubiquitous self-hatred) arises primarily from any inherited internal attribute such as a death instinct or an archetype (Knox, 2011). We are biological entities, born with a range of possible emotional expressions, but made experientially in relationships and culture.

Emotional Maps

Crittenden's Dynamic Maturational Model of Attachment and Adaptation, outlined in the last chapter, shows how affect can be transformed and cognition distorted by the child as adaptations to manage the dangers of adverse parenting. I will shortly introduce three other dyadic maps that I have found to be particularly helpful: Beatrice Beebe and Frank Lachmann's systemic model of self and interactive regulation; Peter Fonagy and colleagues' concept of mentalising; and Jessica Benjamin's intersubjectivity theory and the role of destructiveness in developing an empathic self. All are included as vantage points in the discussions of aggressive out-of-control behaviour in Chap. 11 and suicidality and self-harm in Chap. 12. (For a fuller discussion of the use of these maps in systemic family therapy, see Pocock, 2009.)

But, first, a note on cultural differences in emotional expression. Glenda Fredman (2004), writing from a strong social constructionist perspective, challenges (properly, in my view) the implicit assumption in more traditional analytic work that there is a common language of emotion which accurately transfers across culture. Instead, Fredman sees emotion as a social and cultural construct ungrounded in any commonalities. She contrasts two psychotherapeutic practices with regard to emotion: 'autonomous' in which emotion is seen as entirely the property of the individual, and 'relational' in which emotion emerges intersubjectively. Fredman favours the latter account. However, I think that the organising influence of the postmodern metanarrative takes Fredman too far in over-correcting assumptions of universality. Paul Eckman (1992)—after Darwin—identified six basic emotions common to all cultures: happiness, sadness, disgust, fear, surprise, and anger. Later he added pride, shame, embarrassment, and excitement. A 2017 self-report study identified 27 categories of emotion common across cultures—but more graded than distinct (Cowen & Keltner, 2017).

From a critical realist perspective, all human beings, as members of a single closely related species, are born with the same embodied *potential* set of emotions. This is the biological *given* of emotional experience, rather like a child's new box of paints. But the range of expression of a mature individual depends on what is *made* of those colours through mixing and selection within a range of causal intersubjective contexts, from caregiving relationships to enculturating norm circles (Elder-Vass, 2012—see Chap. 8). As we have discussed in all the cases so far, developing children adapt their emotional expression to maintain, as far as possible, safe acceptability to their caregivers, including cultural acceptability. Later, children seek to fit in to other acculturating groups (e.g. friendship circles, school, hobbies, work) which continuously encode acceptable and unacceptable emotional expression. This middle position, avoiding both universality and strong relativism, is found in the work of cultural anthropologist and systemic psychotherapist, Britt Krause (2002, 2012). That which humans have in common helps to account for the possibilities of sensitive communication across cultures if we take some care. We will explore this further in Chap. 8.

System of Self and Interactive Emotional Regulation

Beatrice Beebe and Frank Lachmann (2002) bring their thirty years of research experience, together with their work as adult psychotherapists, to propose a dyadic system, applicable from infancy to adulthood, in which each member of a dyad in relationship self-regulates their level of emotional arousal while simultaneously engaging in mutual interactive regulation. Through painstaking examination of videotaped face-to-face minute interactions between mothers and infants, the authors show that interactions of face, voice, and bodily orientation are co-constructed: caregiver and careseeker each being a context for the other.

In optimal relational dyads there is a balance between self and interactive regulation. A distressed infant, in interactive regulation with a secure caregiver, benefits from that caregiver's capacity to regulate his own emotional level. Through this experience the infant develops the ability to self-regulate. Infants are also born with some capacity to self-regulate, for example, by looking away from a caregiver to down-regulate the intensity of their arousal. Therapists self-regulate all the time when involved in interactive regulation with emotionally aroused clients—glancing away, self-stroking of arms or face, and gripping of fingers.

All caregivers have difficulties in self-regulation from time to time, but when there is a chronic difficulty in caregiver self-regulation the child may suffer in interactive regulation if the child's emotional response (rage, upset, need for attention or distance) leads to collapse in parental function or retaliation. Sometimes collapse and retaliation are combined when, for example, an overwhelmed parent says in angry exasperation to a child repeatedly demanding to stay up late "Oh, just do what you want!"

In the absence of caregiver self-regulation and safe interactive regulation, the child is thrown back on premature and destructive forms of self-regulation. For example, in a family I saw of an unsupported single mother and her one-year-old (non-autistic) child referred for assessment by social services after incidents of non-accidental injury, the child could only interact and play with the mother with his back permanently turned to her. At no time in one hour of observation, despite them both moving around did he face her. The unavailability—or inability to make use of—interactive regulation with a caregiver may make destructive self-regulation the sole means of managing arousal. This may take the form, later in life, of self-hatred, self-harm, self-starving, or alcohol or drug abuse. I have found this theory lens to be of particular value in understanding self-harm as we will discuss in Chap. 12.

Mentalising

Peter Fonagy and colleagues (2002) see the capacity to mentalise as a crucial achievement in mental health. Mentalising or, to phrase it differently, 'reflective function', is the ability to reflect upon one's own mental states as well as that of others in relationship. This maps some of the same territory as that of the post-Kleinian analyst, Wilfred Bion (1962), who describes the importance of a caregiver's capacity for 'containment': the ability to receive powerful feelings such as hatred from the careseeker and give back a less toxic version modified through what he calls 'reverie'. From both perspectives, an infant in relationship does not simply ingest the raw *given* of the relationship, instead she takes in how she is *made* by the other. So, for example, the way the careseeker may come to feel about her angry upset protest, if her needs are not being met, depends on how she finds herself being represented in the mind of the caregiver, as conveyed in the caregivers emotional and behavioural responses including facial expression.

Most of this is communicated non-verbally. I wrote previously (Pocock, 2009) of my experience of dentistry over the years, including a childhood dentist who bought himself time by lying about how much his procedures would hurt and how long they would take, at cost to my ability to trust him or other dentists thereafter. My best experiences were with a dentist of a few years ago who muttered a small exaggerated 'ooh' sound whenever I winced under her ministrations. This conveyed that she compassionately understood how I was feeling but, in a process that Fonagy et al. (2002) describe as 'marking', the sound was not a sign of her distress. It was a small performance conveying that she was aware of my pain, but not in pain herself. In this way the caregiver shows that the careseeker's state of mind has been empathically received, and that the caregiver has been affected by the distress but not overwhelmed by it.

The way the caregiver receives the feelings from the child and responds depends upon a non-conscious evaluation of the appropriateness of such feelings which depends, in turn, on upbringing and culture. As Krause (2002) points out, the idea of mentalising is, therefore, a crucial link in coming to understand how cultural variation in emotional acceptability is passed from one generation to the next.

Jessica Benjamin's Intersubjectivity

Prior to a cost-saving decision by my local NHS Child and Adolescent Mental Health Trust to discount aggressive, out-of-control behaviour as a mental health issue, around half of the referrals we received were for 'conduct problems', with around three-quarters of the identified patients being boys. I must have worked with, or supervised, several hundred such cases. What puzzled me for a long time was that, in combination with the behaviour, but rather cast into shadow by the focus that the aggressive behaviour commanded, seemed to be a low level of empathy in the child or adolescent. Parents, teachers, and peers (especially those bullied by the child) were barely seen as people, but as objects to either control or be controlled by. This seemed more understandable in situations where there seemed, for a variety of reasons, to be a history of unempathic caregiving but, in many cases, at least one parent seemed warmly allied with the child.

The influential feminist and relational psychoanalyst, Jessica Benjamin (1999) elaborates Donald Winnicott's (1969) theory of the developmental importance of destruction. Here, the story goes, the infant has, as part of ordinary development, an omnipotent sense of control of the mother (or other caregiver). By trying to force her to comply with his wishes, but failing, he progressively destroys the object representation he has of her, replacing this with the discovery of her as a subject—a person in her own right, not an extension of his wishes. Development passes through recurring phases of destruction of his internal representation of the mother and recognition of her as a real external subject. What is crucial here is her *mindful survival* as a parent in the face of the developmentally necessary attacks of rage. (Note the convergence, here, with the capacity for mentalising, and emotional self-regulation.)

Psychoanalysis, from Freud onwards, has traditionally seen maturity of the infant as arising from the father reclaiming the mother and, in the case of a boy, the child identifying with him. For Benjamin this Oedipal story sets the developmental bar too low leaving out the process of the infant's discovery of the mother as a real person with an equivalent centre of self with whom there can be genuine delight in mutual recognition (Pocock, 2009).

> When the destructiveness damages neither the parent nor the self, external reality comes into view as a sharp, distinct contrast to the inner fantasy world. The outcome of this process is not simply reparation or restoration of the good object, but love, the sense of discovering the other. (Benjamin, 1999, p. 192)

As we will discuss in Chap. 11, parents usually assume that setting limits is only about teaching the child appropriate behaviour and this can lead to much ambivalence about their parental role, especially if control was experienced as unloving or confusing in their family of origin. Benjamin's theoretical vantage point suggests that firm-kind parental control also contributes to an *empathic appreciation of others* as real people with minds of their own. In short, kindly limit-setting is also a pathway to love.

As said, these three theoretical vantage points are largely dyadic, tend to focus on mothers as the parent, are reductionist, and therefore need the support of other means of mapping the system to allow a more holistic appreciation. Without a fuller picture, the therapist risks reification and conscious or unconscious mother-blaming.

Emotional Resonance

In *The Mindful Therapist* Dan Siegel (2010) describes how, if the therapist is fully present, open, and attuned, this allows her internal emotional state to resonate with others. We will discuss in the next chapter how a theory-led approach can interfere with the therapist being present and open but here I want to focus on the non-conscious aspects of emotional resonance which, at times, may be uncomfortable—even destabilising.

I have written previously (Pocock, 2005) about a single session of consultation with thirteen-year-old Amy and her mother from a white British family. Single session consultations were used at that time as a response to growing waiting lists at the child and family consultation centre. Up to that point, assessment of urgency had been done as a paper exercise, and those not seen as requiring immediate help were simply left to wait for many months, with all the risks that necessarily entail. I will use Amy's case to try to illustrate how the therapist gets caught up in emotional currents that flow between those in the therapy room, partly unconsciously. I will put my emotional experiences in italics to assist focus.

Prior to the session I had only been able to take a cursory look at the referral letter from the GP as the file had, for some reason, been difficult to find. So *I was feeling flustered when I met Amy and her mother in the waiting room.* When I introduced myself, I was met with broad anxious smiles from them both. *It felt like an unusually long walk* to my room, and they chatted brightly to each other behind me *which seemed to add to my tension.* I *couldn't seem to steady myself* through my usual rituals of starting a first session and *I felt both incompetent and inauthentic.* Things went from bad to worse when it dawned on me, *accompanied by a small surge of panic*, that I had forgotten the name of the daughter and, try as I might, I couldn't bring it to mind. This is not unprecedented, but what was unusual for me was *a reluctance to own up. I didn't want to look as inept as I was feeling, and it also felt unforgivably uncaring to forget Amy's name.* I hung on fruitlessly, hoping that the mother would use her daughter's name but in the end I had to confess. "I'm so sorry, this is stupid of me, but I have forgotten your name". This too was unusual. I wouldn't normally put myself down as this might require someone to feel sorry for me and inhibit their freedom to feel about me as they wished.

There was, however, an *immediate easing of tension at this point*—not, I think, just in me but between us. Being able to speak to my own failure and attempts at covering up may have helped lift the anxiety from mother and daughter that they would be judged. (This was an afterthought—not available in-session.)

Amy said she had been feeling very low for no obvious reason. She had been getting into a lot of angry confrontations with teachers at school and had been excluded on five occasions in the last year. She also confessed, with considerable shame, that she had been cutting her arms. In exploring the history of the difficulties, her mother explained that Amy had no problems at junior school, but things went downhill quickly at secondary school. I explored what else might have been happening around this time and the mother said that "Amy's grandmother", with whom Amy had a close relationship, had died that year. Soon afterwards Amy's older sister returned to the family bringing her young son and, several months after that, Amy's mother began a new relationship. Shortly afterwards, he too joined the family.

I noted all these losses for Amy through death and displacement *but sensed some special emphasis on the grandmother* and I asked Amy how she felt the loss of her grandmother had affected her. She began to cry quite freely but, when her mother looked at her, the mother too filled up with tears and immediately Amy stopped crying and the mutual anxious smiling behaviour from the walk down the corridor was reinstated. I had assumed from the way the mother told me that "Amy's grandmother" had died (she didn't say "my mother") that she was referring to Amy's *paternal* grandmother but realised, belatedly, it was the maternal grandmother who had died. I pointed out my misunderstanding and said to the mother "So that was a great loss for you also". She agreed and looked sad, and *I became aware of Amy anxiously monitoring her mother's facial expression.*

Rather than ask Amy whether she worried about her mother (assuming that the only answer she could give that would not worry her mother would be "No") I said that *I was getting a feeling that Amy worried a lot about her mother* and wondered what they made of that. The mother agreed in a manner that conveyed that she might not need so much consideration from her daughter. Amy was then able to speak a little about her concern for her mother who had often seem depressed over the preceding two years. However, she quickly moved on to say that she also felt responsible for her father. *This felt a more comfortable topic* for mother and daughter. He had lived alone since the parents separated several years previously and Amy felt she had to visit him regularly or he too would get depressed. He "moaned" if she didn't go. She would sometimes prefer to be with her friends but couldn't tell him that.

After a while I sensed that it was possible to challenge both mother and daughter a little over what I took to be Amy's parentified role. I said what a pain it must be to have to be so concerned about both her parents and wondered if she needed to take the business of being an ordinary selfish teenager far more seriously. Amy laughed and said, with what I assumed to be a roguish pride, that "unselfish" was not one of the things she was known for among her teachers. *I felt she was much freer* in talking about her school-self than she was about her home-self. I then asked her what she thought she was known for among her teachers. At that point *I felt her withdraw* and realised, despite the bravado, that her "bad reputation" was painful for her. When I acknowledged this the connection between us felt restored and she was able to speak of her bad name in more general terms. She had been a "quiet girl" all through junior school but had now made quite a name for herself for anger and defiance with teachers. Amy said she was sorry about that but conveyed that it was hard to get out of the pattern now as both she and the teachers expected it.

I felt sad at this point and thought that Amy might be lonely. I said that it can be horrible to be at a new school where no one knows you and sometimes the need to be recognised can feel more important that the need to be well-behaved. She agreed and looked very sad and thoughtful, and *I felt she was, for the first time in the session, allowing both me and her mother to be compassionately in contact with her lonely self.* In this emotional shift it now seemed possible to risk gently suggesting that Amy may have felt forgotten at home given that her grandmother had died, her mother was grieving, her mother had a new partner, her sister had re-joined the family bringing a new baby *and* that Amy felt responsible for looking after both her parents. Amy seemed hesitant but her mother quickly and robustly affirmed that Amy might have felt left out. This emotional permission from her mother made it possible for Amy to say how bad and alone she felt at times, especially when she felt her mother take her new step-father's side against her.

I asked Amy what she thought she had done with the angry feelings that usually go with feeling unimportant. Had she been able to feel angry with her mother, for example, or otherwise make her feelings known in the family? Amy said that she was aware that her mother was not very happy with her new partner and that, together with her mother's grief at the death of her own mother, made Amy feel that she must try hard not to add to her mother's upset. I asked the mother whether she truly needed that much looking after by her daughter or whether she could, in fact, cope with some good teenage anger. She replied warmly and very robustly that she didn't need looking after at all and what she really wanted was for her daughter to be happy and to enjoy herself even if she was more difficult at home. *It did feel quite believable* that the mother could rise to the challenge of surviving ordinary anger and upset.

I said that angry, hurt feelings that can't be expressed in relationships have to be hidden and managed privately, and wondered aloud if Amy cutting herself was a way of trying to keep the hurt out of her mind and out of their relationship. I explained that the reason why children are protective of their parents is often because they are trying to protect them from their own mixed feelings, including fury, and wondered if, instead, Amy had been able to use teachers as safer targets for her fury at feeling unimportant. They both accepted that this might be the case and Amy helpfully added that some of the teachers who still seemed to like her even after she hated them, were the ones she got on with best now. There seemed to be a message to her mother in that. I agreed that we as human beings do seem to trust most those who can accept both our loving and hating feelings.

At the end of the session they agreed to go on a waiting list for further work and we parted on good terms with the agreement that I send them a letter summarising our conversation.

Reflecting afterwards and again now, I certainly didn't feel initially 'present' using Siegel's (2012) term but, my initial sense of ineptness, fear of confessing my vulnerability, trying to press-on inauthentically, and the attempt to protect Amy from the painful truth that I couldn't remember her name were, I think, a non-conscious resonance to these same important themes for Amy and her mother, especially the concealed pain of feeling forgotten. The mislaid file was clearly a causal mechanism that helped prime my contribution, but the intersubjective emotional resonance between and within us was, I think, helpful in Amy and her mother unconsciously inviting me in to the salient issues.

As I re-read this account, it strikes me how inadequate words are in trying to capture emotionally resonant communication. My questions and observations now sound a little pushy because I cannot adequately describe when the emotional context was invitational and other times when it suggested it was better to wait (see the next chapter). Sometimes my contributions caused a rupture—for example, when I hadn't realised the painful feelings that lay beneath her roguish pride at making a name for herself—although these moments were repairable since the rupture was also emotionally communicated.

I have made little attempt to include the light formulation of ideas, using multiple lenses, that was building somewhere in my mind but some of this can be surmised from things I said to Amy and her mother. We will explore in the next chapter how the second-order use of clinical theory within the emotional flow can further the collaborative search for contextual understanding and the feeling of being emotionally understood.

References

Beebe, B., & Lachmann, F. (2002). *Infant research and adult treatment: Co-constructing interactions*. The Analytic Press.

Benjamin, J. (1999). Recognition and destruction: An outline of intersubjectivity. In S. Mitchell & L. Aron (Eds.), *Relational psychoanalysis: The emergence of a tradition* (pp. 181–210). Analytic Press.

Bion, W. (1962). *Learning from experience*. Maresfield Library.

Bowlby, J. (1988). *A secure base: Parent child attachment and healthy human development*. Basic Books.

Box, S., & Copley, B. (Eds.). (1977). *Crisis at adolescence: Object relations therapy with the family*. Jason Aaronson.

Brown, G. (1985). The discovery of expressed emotion: Induction or deduction? In J. Leff & C. Vaughn (Eds.), *Expressed emotion in families* (pp. 7–25). Guilford Press.

Cowen, A., & Keltner, D. (2017). Self-report captures 27 distinct categories of emotion bridged by continuous gradients. *Proceedings of the National Academy of Science, 114*, 7900–7909.

Eckman, P. (1992). Are there basic emotions? *Psychological Review, 99*, 550–553.

Elder-Vass, D. (2012). *The reality of social construction*. Cambridge University Press.

Fonagy, P., Gergeley, G., Jurist, E., & Target, M. (2002). *Affect regulation, mentalization, and the development of the self*. Other Press.

Fredman, G. (2004). *Transforming emotion: Conversations in counselling and psychotherapy*. Whurr Publishers.

Knox, J. (2011). *Self-Agency in psychotherapy - Attachment, autonomy, and intimacy*. Norton.

Krause, I.-B. (2002). *Culture and system in family therapy*. Routledge.

Krause, I.-B. (2012). *Culture and reflexivity in systemic psychotherapy: Mutual perspectives*. Karnac.

McCluskey, U. (2005). *To be met as a person: The dynamics of attachment in professional encounters*. Routledge.

Minuchin, S. (1974). *Families and family therapy*. Harvard University Press.

Orange, D. (1995). *Emotional understanding: Studies in psychoanalytic epistemology*. Guilford.

Pocock, D. (1997). Feeling understood in family therapy. *Journal of Family Therapy, 19*, 283–302.

Pocock, D. (2005). Systems of the heart: Evoking the feeling self in family therapy. In C. Flaskas, B. Mason, & A. Perlesz (Eds.), *The space between: Experience, context and process in the therapeutic relationship* (pp. 127–140). Karnac.

Pocock, D. (2009). Working with emotional systems: Four new maps. In C. Flaskas & D. Pocock (Eds.), *Systems and psychoanalysis: Contemporary integrations in family therapy* (pp. 93–109). Karnac.

Pocock, D. (2010). Emotions as ecosystemic adaptations. *Journal of Family Therapy, 32*, 362–378.

Shotter, J. (1993). *Conversational realities: Constructing life through language*. Sage.

Siegel, D. (2010). *The mindful therapist: A clinician's guide to mindsight and neural integration*. Norton.

Siegel, D. (2012). *The developing mind: How relationships and the brain interact to shape who we are*. Guilford.

Stern, D. (1985). *The interpersonal world of the infant: A view from psychoanalysis and developmental psychology*. Routledge.

Winnicott, D. (1969). The use of an object. *International Journal of Psycho-Analysis, 50*, 711–716.

7

Collaboration and Change

> In the long history of humankind (and animal-kind, too) those who learned to collaborate and improvise most effectively have prevailed. Charles Darwin (1809–1882)

> The co-created Third has the transitional quality of being both invented and discovered. To the question of "Who created this ... you or I?", the paradoxical answer is "Both and neither." Jessica Benjamin (2017, p. 31)

In this chapter I hope to demonstrate how the theoretically informed therapist can participate in a genuine collaboration with those who seek our help in a joint pursuit of beneficial change. I will draw on my experiences, not only as an individual and family therapist, but also as a fifteen-year consumer (in two periods) of one to four times weekly psychotherapy. I plan to steer a central course between (and avoid) two myths:

Myth 1. *Let me tell you what's really going on.* A myth that the therapist will know what is wrong and will reveal this to the client(s), resulting in change. Classical psychoanalysis, for example, assumes that patients change largely or solely through the therapist's interpretation of the unconscious and the growth of patient insight.

D. Pocock, *Expanding the Limits of Individual and Family Therapies*, Palgrave Texts in Counselling and Psychotherapy, https://doi.org/10.1007/978-3-031-76309-0_7

Myth 2. *It's my way or the highway.* A strong social constructionist myth that a theoretically informed therapist will inevitably be non-collaborative, privileging her own theory-derived 'reality', and requiring clients to adapt to her expert 'essentialist' views.

I should stress that I don't believe that either of these myths correspond to real-world practice, other than temporarily, simply because they are unsustainable. All psychoanalytic therapists are engaged in a relationship with their patients, so the relational facilitation of growth may be available regardless of the therapist's conscious understanding of the process of change. Similarly, strong constructionists may claim that their moment-to-moment choices of what to say are not based on knowledge of individual and relational processes but, as discussed in Chap. 2, realist choices (for example, which subjugated narratives to be thickened) are inevitable, albeit cloaked as covert realism.

Critical realism assumes that beliefs don't need to be true to have influence: all have potential causal power. Each of the myths, for example, may become active in enabling selective inattention to the therapist's actual behaviour, excluding important information from reflective appraisal. Additionally, Myth 1 might inhibit therapists from learning about or even discounting relational and wider systemic processes, while Myth 2 might discourage therapists from studying any theories and research of child and family development.

As an aside, I appreciate I am in danger of perpetuating these myths through the act of naming and discussing them. Myth 1 is probably more active in systemic family therapy as a straw-man warning than it is representative of most contemporary psychoanalysis. But I can recall a conversation in the last five years with, of all people, *a Jungian,* who declared that he was not providing a relationship! Myth 2 was certainly active in some recent discussions with those generous enough to debate these ideas with me on a UK *Association for Family Therapy* online forum.

Collaboration as a Cognitive *and* Emotional Experience

For a period in the early 2000s I was still training as an adult psychoanalytic psychotherapist while working full-time as Head of Family Therapy in my local Child and Adolescent Mental Health Service. This, together with family commitments, was a particularly stressful period so, on the recommendation of a friend, I took up Tai Chi which combines gentle bodily movement with mindfulness. My favourite exercise was Push Hands. In pairs each faces the other at an arm's length with the right foot forward and the feet placed to give a balanced stance. The leading hand of each person is lifted to around chest height with the palm inwards and the backs of the hands of the two participants lightly in contact. The rear hand of each is placed gently on the other's leading elbow. The intention is to maintain the light contact at hands and elbows while exploring all the whole possible range of movement and retaining balance. A player who is pushed or pulled off-balance has to move their feet to regain their stance. Being able to unbalance the other gives a competitive side to the exercise which is quite fun. But after a while, when the pair have got used to each other, the wish to maintain contact with the other often leads to a new and more deeply satisfying experience of connection. *It is then no longer clear who is pushing and who is giving way.*

In the quote at the start of the chapter, the relational psychoanalyst Jessica Benjamin (2017) refers to this, in psychotherapy, as a surrender to "the Third": not your way or my way, but our way. Logically someone must be initiating the movement and someone following at every moment, otherwise the movements of the pair would become static, but who is doing the pushing and who the giving way becomes less noticeable and less important than the co-constructed experience of mutual exploration of the space between (Flaskas et al., 2005) through joint action (Shotter, 1993).

Maintenance of contact means that, for a time, one (in psychotherapy, the therapist or client) is happy to lead in a particular direction and the other is happy to follow. When the follower is reluctant to go that way, but the leader, rather than picking up the cue and taking a turn as a follower, insists on pushing, then a power struggle ensues, and each can feel pressure and potential loss of equilibrium. Benjamin (2017) describes these regular experiences in psychotherapy as "Push-me / Pull-you" dynamics: you versus me, in which the experience of "us" is temporarily lost (Pocock, 2018). How these inevitable, often subtle, power struggles are noticed and resolved seems to determine outcome: the mutual willingness to maintain contact being otherwise known as the therapeutic alliance. It is the ability to repair lost connection as much as the connectedness itself which seems to build safety and progress. Note, that if there is never any push then everything remains static, but pushing too hard, rather than taking a turn in following, leads to resistance in the other and eventually someone will lose balance and break away.

I can recall times, both as a patient and a therapist, in which periods of the work felt not only moving but joyous. The Boston Study Process Change Group (Bruschweiler-Stern et al., 2010) refers to these as "moments of meeting": each through connection gains a deeper implicit understanding of the authentic subjectivity of the other (Buber, 2008) which allows the work to move along. Sometimes these moments are ones of heightened shared affect: for example, the therapist being fully present and affected by a client's deep sense of desolation, or the mutual spontaneous burst of laughter at a joke.

Other moments of meeting are less obvious and perhaps only appreciated in hindsight. As a patient I recall turning up at completely the wrong time for a session and was able to experience my therapist, while evidently thrown, having some genuine care for how I felt at the error. Little of this was conveyed in words. A female patient who experienced terrifying abuse at the hands of her father told me, a year after a specific incident in a therapy session, that this was the moment she sensed she could begin to trust me. A woodlouse had crawled out from under some furniture and was slowly heading across the carpet towards her. I had carefully picked it up and took it to a window and dropped it out onto some grass, mumbling, "There you go!" She knew that everyone in her family would have enjoyed crushing it. I was different to how she expected me to be even though she was not previously aware of that expectation. No interpretation or other words were needed; the opportunity for a new relational experience was sufficient. Much therapeutic change takes place out of sight in this wordless experiential manner. In critical realist terms these are real, *actualised* events that are not empirically observable (Bhaskar, 1977). Many clinical examples are given in Susan Lord's (2018) helpful collection of essays *Moments of Meeting in Psychoanalysis.*

Surrendering to the third is very different to *submitting to the other* to avoid conflict (Ghent, 1990). Authentic collaboration to create new shared emotional experience and new meaning has an enlivened feeling. If the client (or therapist) goes along with the other for fear of damaging the relationship, the resulting pseudo-mutual relating (Wynne et al., 1958) can feel lifeless and static. The following part of a session with thirteen-year-old Jody illustrates moments of arrival at some authentic connection and the co-creation of new understanding (the Third), followed by what felt to me like a flat, falsely compliant, surrendering response when I pushed a little too much.

It is not unusual for adolescents, to find it hard to talk about their self-harm and about problems at home. For Jody it seemed exceptionally difficult. She had not wanted to be referred but her parents had insisted. She very reluctantly agreed on condition that she was always seen separately from them. This excerpt is from the second individual therapy session.

After starting by saying everything was "fine", Jody eventually told me that she had hurt herself on one particular day that week. There was great tension as she began to speak of this and, when I reflected this back to her, she told me that she'd had a lump in her throat all that day. The words cannot convey the emotional tone of the exchanges, especially the emotional effort that it took for Jody to speak, but some cues are given in brackets.

DP: Had anything happened that day?

J: Yes ... Mum had been upset. [Haltingly] I assumed it was my fault... My dad had come home late and had a go at her. Then he walked out, and she was upset.

DP: How was it your fault?

J: I don't know—I just assumed it was. My sister told me that Mum has been upset for the last two weeks because of Dad.

DP: But even though she had been upset for two weeks because of your dad, it stayed your fault all through Friday?
J: Yes.
DP: It sounds like you feel guilty.
J: Yes—that's the lump in the throat.
DP: Ah … that makes sense.

This felt like the first hopeful moment, that Jody could take the initiative in linking her bodily sensation to her emotional state *and* share that mentalised understanding with me creating a shared Third.

DP: Sometimes people feel less guilty after they have been punished or punished themselves—is that how it is with hurting yourself?
J: Yes, definitely.

Jody invests in my suggestion helping to build part of my formulation. Her enlivened response using an enthusiastic choice of words made it something we now shared: no longer mine but ours—another emergence of the Third—helping to move the work along. In these last exchanges there is a feeling of connection building between us. Moments later I push a little harder:

DP: [Feeling angry with her parents] Did you feel annoyed with Mum or Dad?
J No. Not really. [She looks uncomfortable.]
DP: Even though Dad behaved pretty badly?
J: No.
DP: [Evenly] I'm not surprised. I think most people who cut themselves have to protect their parents at all costs from their bad feelings. They hurt themselves instead. How does that sound to you?
J: Yes, that could be right.

Although this looks from the words alone like agreement, the affective tone and bodily posture in which they were said conveyed a flat compliance, very different from the emotional tone supporting her earlier "Yes, definitely". It felt to me that Jody had, using Ghent's (1990) term, 'submitted', since at this point in our relationship she had not experienced being able to safely disagree with me. I felt I had pushed her too far and needed to ease back and repair. However I am not suggesting that my statement offering a partial relational cause for her self-harm was incorrect. As we will discuss, it was 'an offer that can be refused'. Once made it remained food for thought that could be saved for later (or thrown away or made into something more palatable). It was, however, important to register in myself the hidden submission signalled by the flat affect and to try to restore the connection. Any further pushing would be to risk the alliance. Nothing can grow in a pseudo-mutual relationship. We return to Jody and her family in Chap. 12.

Aspects of Collaboration

In planning this chapter I had imagined a short list of guidelines to represent my thoughts on collaboration, somewhat along the lines of the three proposed by the Milan Group of systemic family therapists: hypothesising, circularity, and neutrality, augmented by a fourth—curiosity—in the Post-Milan development of Cecchin and Boscolo (Cecchin, 1987). In the event, something that comes fairly automatically in practice is, like riding a bike, much more complicated to describe. The following is a list of fourteen considerations, moving roughly from principles to practice. These overlap but cannot be completely reduced to each other. Space requires me to deal with each aspect quite briefly.

1. *Presence, attunement, and resonance*

This trio of concepts, drawn from the work of Dan Siegel (2010), is a foundation for human relating. When we are fully present we bring our open, receptive, caring, and authentic self to the other, ready for any possibilities to unfold. Attunement allows us to focus on the other(s) to take them inside ourselves, accepting *what is*, rather than what our preconceptions say *should be*. In a state of resonance we feel 'in tune', 'heard', 'connected' to the other(s) and they to us: we 'feel felt' (Siegel, 2007). But this is not the whole story. Jean Knox (2011), summarising extensive mother-infant research, cites the frequent lack of co-ordination between infant and parent in even healthy relationships. What is crucial "lies in re-achieving a matching from a mismatching state, a mutually regulated reparatory process" (p. 9). The same is true for psychotherapeutic careseeker-caregiver dyads. Repair builds trust.

2. *Generous listening*

Glenn Larner (2009) and Stephen Frosh (2009) translate the ethic of responsibility towards the other, described by the French and Jewish philosopher Emmanuel Levinas, into generous listening. The intention is to understand those we work with in their own terms, helping them to elaborate their experiences, while respecting their irreducible otherness. It is a complement to curiosity-motivated exploration (below). On a practical basis, generosity also includes providing drawing and other play materials to younger children as a means to enable communication. For example, I found a set of plain wooden figures of adult, child, and grandparent figures, included among other play materials, to be particularly helpful in sculpting perceived closeness and distance in relationships.

3. *Multi-directional partiality*

Ivan Boszormenyi-Nagy and Barbara Krasner (1986) describe this as a therapist attitude of empathy to *all* persons in the room. It embeds a principle of relational justice through conveying to each a sense of their personal worth. Each person's perspective is welcomed and taken seriously even though they may be in conflict. This does not negate the possibility of challenge—or inviting challenge—to a perspective. Empathy, welcome, compassion, and challenge should not be at odds with each other. In individual therapy this requires the therapist to empathically imagine those the client is, or has been, in close relationships with. Therapist *anger with others* (which may represent inhibited affect in the client through identification by the therapist) can be helpful if reflected upon. It should, however, be distinguished from unhelpful *blame of others*. Even abusive parents may be understood if their experiences are sufficiently known. Blame in the therapist's mind is thus a symptom of limited contextual information.

4. *Attending to the therapeutic alliance*

A meta-analysis of studies (summarised in Adito & Rabellino, 2011) shows a moderately strong association between perceived alliance and therapeutic outcome. The association is stronger still if only the client measures are used. There remains some debate as to what constitutes the ingredients of a successful alliance. How much do explicitly shared goals matter, for example? I won't expand on this debate here but will add that I think it is an error to assume that the alliance is only a *facilitator of change*. As discussed above, I would argue that the alliance inherently includes recreation of self in relationship and is *itself a major part of change,* especially in long-term work. This mirrors what is now understood about pathways for development in which the autonomous-secure self emerges through emotionally attuned and reliable relationships and is sustained in relationships throughout life (Knox, 2011; Mitchell, 2000; Crittenden, 2008; Beebe & Lachmann, 2002). Autonomy and relationality (mediated through cultural variation) are thus understood to be two sides of the same coin rather than in opposition, as positioned by some strong constructionist accounts.

Although it may seem obvious, a successful alliance also means being responsive to what clients request even though this may fall outside the preferences of the therapist. Judging from user surveys in family therapy (e.g. Reimers & Treacher, 1994), unwillingness to respond to requests for advice, or for the therapist own views (rather than simply facilitating the views of others) features fairly highly in accounts of user dissatisfaction. In my experience, clients have no problem accepting that some joint exploration and understanding of the issues is necessary before any advice can be given. At that point advice can usually be collaboratively constructed, for example, finding ways in which parents can work together more effectively once divisions over how to set limits on behaviour of children have been collectively understood.

5. *Reflecting on the past in the present*

Resonance is both intersubjective *and* partly non-conscious. In the 'inner conversation' (Rober, 1999) of therapists when sitting with clients, two valuable questions to ask oneself are "Who am I to you?" and "Who are you to me?" All humans (including therapists) use old internal relational-cultural templates to make sense of the other in relationship, much of this out of awareness. A male with the designated authority that comes with the title 'Psychotherapist' is not a fresh start for teenage boy who has been abandoned by his father, mocked by his step-father, and suspended by his male headmaster. The memory of these experiences may readily be transferred non-consciously to the therapist. Disentangling what is old and what is new in the therapeutic relationship(s) is one of the processes of change, partly in awareness and partly outside, as with the above example of me removing the woodlouse. Conversely, the therapist, no matter how extensive their self-knowledge (through personal therapy or other forms of self-reflection), will inevitably get caught up in misperceptions of clients based on old internal relational-cultural templates. Donna Orange (1995) uses the term 'co-transference' as a vantage point to describe this mingling of subjectivities of patient *and* therapist at conscious and unconscious levels.

6. *Second-order participant-observation*

In a state of second-order reflexivity, the therapist tries to become aware that what she is experiencing of the other(s), and how she then responds, depends on the information she is receiving from her senses—including somatic information—*and* how that information is selected and filtered through what she already has in mind, including theoretical ideas and clinical and life experiences. So the field of observation ideally embraces both what is ontologically 'out there' and epistemologically 'in here' in the mind—the given and the made of the therapist's experience of the part of the system under observation.

There are two caveats. First, this second-order state of mind is never complete, is quite demanding, and can be lost from moment-to-moment. Observation then returns, via the ever-present regressive pull, to first-order naïve realism. This may happen particularly when emotion is high since it can then be harder to reflect especially if this connects with an old hidden emotional preoccupation or trauma in the therapist. In a previous book chapter (Pocock, 2018) I described my failure to meet a patient who suddenly burst into tears when describing the death of her sister. I had felt unmoved and slightly irritated and, in my mind, had fallen back on the theoretical idea of 'narcissistic crying' (Alexander, 2003)—as if my response was being controlled and demanded. Rather than surrender to the Third, or even allow myself a state of not-knowing, my heightened emotional response had led me to cling defensively to theory: in the words of Benjamin (2009), "much as a drowning man clings to a straw". I am normally fine to receive distress of all kinds. It was only years later that I realised that it was the specific *suddenness* of her tears breaking through that had triggered implicit (non-conscious) memories of my mother bursting into tears when I had done something wrong which, as an adult, I can see was usually quite trivial. I now understand this was because of the death of my mother's mother, father, and brother all within the previous four years and the limited support available to help her mourn. However, the tears were experienced by me as a child, and in that moment with the patient, as an accusation—"Look how you've hurt me!"—from which I needed to distance myself. I should add that this limitation on my self-knowledge came despite lengthy periods of personal therapy. Understanding oneself is a lifelong process and never completed. We inevitably expose clients to our wounds—our unthought knowns (Bollas, 1987)—alongside our generous attempts to understand.

Second, and linked to the above example, there is a limit to what one can understand of the otherness of the other *and* the otherness of oneself (Frosh, 2009). For example, as Britt Krause (2002) explains, it is very difficult to give a full account of one's culture. These taken-for-granted norms—what Bourdieu (1990) refers to as the 'doxa'—arise from a lifelong social integration into culture and are largely non-conscious. We explore the implications of this in the next chapter.

7. *Curiosity-motivated exploration*

The emphasis on the role of curiosity in Post-Milan systemic therapy (Cecchin, 1987) was, I think, a transformative moment in family therapy development. Key moments for the initiation of curiosity are when something apparently significant makes little immediate sense inviting the question in the mind of the therapist "What are the contexts (causal powers) in which this may become understandable?" Why, for example, does this person remain with his abusive spouse? Why does this child smile so broadly even in risky situations? Why does this kinship relationship outside of the immediate family seem to matter so much? And so on.

8. *Co-constructing emotionally coherent narrative*

Systemic family therapists are likely to identify the term 'narrative' with the work of Michael White and David Epston (1990), and others. This is a valuable social justice approach helping clients to 're-story' their lives to counter dominant discourses that have defined them in adverse, 'problem-saturated', ways. Perhaps less well known in systemic, humanistic, and psychoanalytic mainstreams is the concept of 'coherent narrative'; for me, one of the most influential research discoveries, transforming my individual and family therapy practice.

I am speaking of the work of Mary Main and colleagues (1993) and their use of the Adult Attachment Interview. Their staggering finding was that they could *predict with 85% accuracy a child's attachment status at one year of age based on the coherence of their parent's biographical narrative.* Just as remarkable, adverse relational and other traumatic experiences *were not* the deciders of the parents' ability to facilitate security in their child, it was the *ability to provide in their account of their childhoods "a steady flow of ideas, intent, thoughts and feelings that are clear, truthful, consistent, plausible and complete"* (Main, 1993).

Importantly, parents could arrive at this 'earned secure' status by several means, all allowing reflection and higher-level integration of life experiences (including adverse experiences) leading to neural integration (Siegel, 2007). The pathways might involve one or more of: thoughtful conversations with a supportive partner or friend, reading novels or biographies, identifying with characters in film or on TV, working with a therapist interested in relational history, and quiet personal reflection. Collaborative systemic understanding that includes exploration of attachment narratives is a strong facilitator of coherence. A fine example of this being the Attachment Narrative Therapy of Rudi Dallos and Arlene Vetere (Dallos, 2006; Dallos & Vetere, 2022).

9. *Searching together for exceptions to same-old patterns*

Judging by the storyline of numerous successful time-shifting films—*Back to the Future, The Time Traveller's Wife*—audiences are fascinated by the dangers of radically changing the future by making tiny differences in the past. We might do well to consider which small changes in the present might radically alter the future! Critical realism describes how actualised causal powers can be quickly deactivated by others, changing the system. This might be as simple as a new idea—Bateson's (1979) difference that makes a difference—or even applied carpentry as in the raised cot-side example at the end of Chap. 2. The intervention of removing any single part from a flashlight (bulb, battery, switch, or case) denies the emergence of light despite every other part of the system remaining intact. Substitute 'symptom' for 'light' to illuminate the analogy!

Systemic family therapy—Strategic, Brief Solution-Focused, and Narrative therapies—has a commendable track record of searching for and strengthening overlooked solutions. In Chap. 4 I mentioned the case of a man I worked with who reported long-term depression and strong suicidal ideation. In one session he became in touch with anger at a friend who had let him down badly. I noticed how robust he sounded and enquired how depressed he was now feeling. He had previously told me that he had been continuously depressed for about ten years but in that moment he could not locate any depression. He became very interested in the notion that depression might be an alternative to healthily accepted anger (disallowed in childhood) and started to use a journal whenever 'depressed' to try to locate repudiated emotion.

Individuals and families caught in a generalised problem-saturated state of demoralisation (White & Epston, 1990) may be gently challenged by the therapist exploring and underlining hitherto neglected experiences when things went better than expected. These exceptions can easily fall into the shadow of the dominant narrative—"My daughter *never* listens"—eroding any motivation to change. A question to the daughter, "what helped you to listen on *that* occasion?", may help to uncover previously unmapped causal tendencies. Maybe it was better at a weekend when everyone was less stressed from work and therefore calmer, or perhaps when the parents themselves had first listened carefully to *her*. I find it best not to explore exceptions too early. Complaints often need to be properly heard by the therapist first as long as they don't hurt the complainee—an opportunity to model generous listening.

10. *Reworking the made and acknowledging the given of experience*

Strangely, given how different the traditions are, psychoanalytic and strong constructionist therapies both tend to concentrate on the *made* aspect of experience at the expense of what is given (brute reality). For example, it is not unprecedented for trainees in psychoanalytic trainings to find that negative feedback about aspects of the training is sometimes responded to with an implicit—or sometimes explicit—suggestion that the solution lies in the trainees doing more work on themselves, assuming that internal constructions made from old object relations are the entire source of the problem! Without ontological realism, traumatic life events, structural poverty, racism, and a host of other injustices can be just another story.

Therapists have no more power than anyone else to change societal racism, for example, but failure to acknowledge the *given* reality of racism on clients' lives, both in wider society and, as it may play out, for example, between a white therapist and a black patient, is at least a missed opportunity. At worst, it is a corrosive denial of toxic reality, limiting the healing potential of the relationship. Bearing witness (Miller, 1990) and naming as unjust the brute reality of racism in the life of a client or family members as a first step allows a second step of exploring what is being *made* of that potentially toxic *given*, consciously and unconsciously. How much, for example, is racism allowed to define the self as inferior? I can recall a black child, adopted into a white British family, who was found trying to scrub her skin to make herself whiter. What internal or relational resources are there for making the given into a profound experience of injustice that speaks of the defensive projective needs of the racists? Helen Morgan (2014) gives a helpful account of these issues in a psychoanalytic setting.

11. *Dynamic formulation and the use of theory*

I need to distinguish dynamic formulation from Milan and Post-Milan group hypothesising. The latter generally assumes a single deductive hypothesis based on the functionalist premise that symptoms are needed for the system to be stable. In the case of Emma, in the introductory chapter, a functional hypothesis would be that her symptoms distract from the couple's marital difficulties and help to keep the family together. In Post-Milan work the hypothesis is more of a starting point for questions which develops depending on the ongoing responses to curiosity-motivated questioning. Nevertheless, despite this more flexible approach, I think functionalism is, on its own, too restrictive a premise for formulation.

Dynamic formulation is a light, ever-evolving structure of ideas in the therapist's mind (Vetere & Dallos, 2003). It is an always-incomplete loose model of the systemic ontological reality, being constantly informed and changed by the meeting of theoretical maps with the cognitive and emotional information emerging from the developing relationship(s). It is both an abductive process, joining information from disparate multiple overlapping maps (Harries-Jones, 1995), and a retroductive one (Bhaskar, 2016), attempting to retrospectively track the causal influences that combine to generate the problem(s). It is part of the therapist's inner conversation (Rober 1999), partly conscious, partly non-conscious.

Nothing is certain, but aspects of the formulation become strengthened if they seem to add to joint understanding *as defined by the client feeling understood.* Other parts may be discarded or weakened if they do not seem to help in the work-play of understanding. One strengthening moment is when Jody said "Yes, definitely" to my question whether self-harm made her feel less guilty. Similarly Emma's response "I thought I had worn Daddy out" strongly supported the parentification aspect of the formulation.

Despite shared aspects I think it is important for the therapist to own that the formulation is *her* construction to help guard against the pull of naïve realism. (Clients will have their own internal construction—*co-construction does not mean everyone will understand things in the same way.*) Sketching a formulation in writing at the end of each session is valuable self-supervision since it may help to bring to mind therapist assumptions that otherwise remain out of awareness. I recommend starting with the words "I currently think that …" in order to help guard against an objective description. The world is real, but description is always a human—and therefore fallible—product of construction, influenced by theoretical and experiential standpoints, which needs to be owned by the therapist.

Theory needs to be held with a loose grip (Orange, 1995). The availability of multiple theories in the therapist's collection means that a theoretical idea, or layers of ideas, can be selected, in a bottom-up manner, by association to the clinical moment. By contrast, using a single theoretical model tends to *select information to fit that model* in a top-down, deductive manner. (Minuchin, 1974, often said "I have seen this family a thousand times".) This sounds complex, but in practice ideas (theories, similar experiences), that may fit the content being discussed, simply pop into the mind through association. This happens in the same way that, in any interesting conversation, listening carefully to the other naturally brings rich associations to mind in one's inner dialogue. These may or may not be shared when it is our turn to speak.

12. *Deciding when to speak and what to say*

These are immensely complex decisions, too complex to try to tease apart here, drawing on—and further developing over time—the resource of clinical experience, emergent from which is the therapist's idiom. I agree with Peter Rober (2024) that both *fast* (intuitive) thinking and *slow* (reflective) thinking (Kahneman, 2011) are needed at different moments in psychotherapy. Fast intuitive responses allow the therapist to be present and spontaneous in emotionally meeting clients. Slow thinking enables reflection and can be an important corrective to any fast therapist responses which have proved to be ill-judged as picked up from the verbal or—more frequently—non-verbal feedback from the client(s).

I have found two guidelines to be helpful in slow thinking. First, as an idea for a statement or a question begins to form in the therapist's inner talk, the therapist can empathically place themselves in the shoes of the client(s) to imagine how this may be received. Patrick Casement (1985) refers to this as 'trial identification'. Second, a question to oneself about whether the new information or question is likely to fall within the 'zone of proximal development' (Vygotsky, 1978) of the client at their present level of age and/or understanding. Information that may be new and meaningful to the client with the help and clarification of others falls within the zone. Information that is too similar to what they already know or too different falls outside. This can also be tested, before speaking, through trial identification. Shaping one's response through imagining what it is like to be the other, in order that the response may be understandable, sounds convoluted but is one of the ordinarily unnoticed skills of human relating. However, like all skills, it can be improved (Flaskas, 2013).

13. *Making a refusable offer*

Therapists of all traditions in training can probably recall times when they have been presented with new ideas which don't fit but feel uncomfortable to reject. This occasionally happened to me as a patient, early on in therapy, when receiving interpretations based on what the therapist thought was occurring in my unconscious. I hadn't yet discovered that it was safe to disagree with her without damaging the relationship. It was an uncomfortable feeling of having to choose between risking rejecting her or negating my own experience. I had the same feeling rather more regularly in supervisions as a systemic and later a psychoanalytic trainee when it was assumed that the supervisor, through virtue of their experience and training, would inevitably know more than me about what was going on between me and my client(s). Of course this is sometimes the case, but it is not invariably true—more frequently no one knows. My worst experience was of being a mouth on the end of an ear-bug when my work with a couple was live-supervised in a family therapy training clinic. I recall one low moment when I was about to repeat a very lengthy message from my supervisor to the couple. The bug was loud and one of them interrupted me to say with weary sarcasm, "Yeah. we heard..." Fortunately systemic therapy seems to have mostly let go of its fetish for technology (one-way screens, and ear-bugs) and hidden teams which, as Reimers and Treacher (1994) document, are frequently disliked by clients.

The paediatrician and psychoanalyst Donald Winnicott used to carry a shiny metallic spatula in his pocket. If placed gently within reach an infant might ignore it, use it as a spoon to feed the mother, bang it on the table, and many other creative uses. But any attempt to force it on the child would result in a sudden threat and loss of creativity turning the spatula into an alien object. This is opposite to the classic Mafia strategy in the first *Godfather* movie as mumbled by Brando "I'll make him an offer he can't refuse". Offering ideas in a spirit of uncertainty—"I don't know whether this fits, but I found myself wondering ...."—supports the right to safely refuse and therefore enables play and the creation of the Third. Individual autonomy, as an essential part of relationality, is therefore respected (Knox 2011).

14. *Taking a stand*

Finally in this list, I think there are times when the therapist *does* need to take a strong position even if it risks a rupture to the alliance. There is a limit to collaboration when therapists need to address behaviour that is clearly abusive or simply continuously counterproductive and/or controlling within a session. All therapists, for example, have child protection responsibilities. In psychoanalytic therapy Neville Symington (1983) speaks of 'acts of freedom' as an agent of therapeutic change where the therapist speaks from the heart to free herself from a cloying conviction that there are things that must never be said.

Robust, frank exchanges are to be preferred to prolonged and stale pseudo-mutuality in which the therapist has submitted for fear that conflict will not be manageable. Ged Smith (2023) provides plenty of examples of robust talk in family therapy:

> You know, in all the years I have been doing this I find that stories of bad behaviour don't get us anywhere. Without any detail, what is the real point that you want to be understood?
>
> What are you hoping for in telling me this, other than to get me on your side which most people do?

You have to listen to these in a Scouse (Liverpool) accent said with an undercurrent of dry humour to sense how Smith calibrates these down-to-earth interventions. It helps that his idiom has evolved over thirty years of practice, working in the city he grew up in, enabling these words to work for him.

In a chapter, *Constructionist Therapy: Sense and Nonsense*, Jay Efran and Leslie Clarfield (1992) provide a relatable quote on robustness:

> To act as if all views are equal and that we—as therapists—have no favourites among them undercuts the very sort of frank exchange we want and expect to have with our clients. It patronizes them, compromises our own integrity, and treats open dialogue as if it was an endangered species needing 'hothouse' protection. (p. 208)

After-thoughts

Psychotherapy cannot successfully be reduced to a painting-by-numbers formula. In the space available these fourteen considerations will have to suffice to try to convey the balance between being authentically responsive to the other in the therapeutic relationship(s) alongside a freedom for the therapist to think, feel, and make choices. This is a process partly served by theory, but not driven by it: attending to the relationship(s) needs to come first. I hope the guidelines will, at least, provide some sense of my intentions as we move more deeply into clinical practice in the later chapters.

References

Adito, R., & Rabellino, D. (2011). Therapeutic alliance and outcome of psychotherapy: Historical excursus, measurements, and prospects for research. *Frontiers of Psychology, 18*, 270.

Alexander, T. (2003). Narcissism and the experience of crying. *British Journal of Psychotherapy, 20*, 27–38.

Bateson, G. (1979). *Mind and nature: A necessary unity*. Dutton.

Beebe, B., & Lachmann, F. (2002). *Infant research and adult treatment: Co-constructing interactions*. The Analytic Press.

Benjamin, J. (2009). A relational psychoanalysis perspective on acknowledging failure in order to restore the facilitating and containing features of the intersubjective relationship (the shared third). *International Journal of Psychoanalysis, 90*, 441–450.

Benjamin, J. (2017). *Beyond doer and done to: Recognition theory, intersubjectivity and the third*. Routledge.

Bhaskar, R. (1977). *A realist philosophy of science*. Harvester.

Bhaskar, R. (2016). *Enlightened common sense: The philosophy of critical realism*. Routledge.

Bollas, C. (1987). *The shadow of the object: Psychoanalysis of the unthought known*. Columbia University Press.

Bordieu, P. (1990). *The logic of practice*. Polity Press.

Boszormenyi-Nagy, I., & Krasner, B. (1986). *Between give and take: A clinical guide to contextual therapy: Conversations in theory and practice*. Basic Books.

Bruschweiler-Stern, N., Lyons-Ruth, K., Morgan, A., Nahum, J., Sander, L., Stern, D., Harrison, A., and Tronick, E. (Collaborators), & The Boston Change Process Study Group. (2010). *Change in psychotherapy: A unifying paradigm*. Norton.

Buber, M. (2008). *I and thou*. Simon and Schuster.

Casement, P. (1985). *On learning from the patient*. Routledge.

Cecchin, G. (1987). Hypothesising, circularity, and neutrality revisited: An invitation to curiosity. *Family Process, 26*, 405–413.

Crittenden, P. (2008). *Raising parents: Attachment representation, and treatment*. Routledge.

Dallos, R. (2006). *Attachment narrative therapy: Integrating narrative, systemic and attachment therapies*. Open University Press.

Dallos, R., & Vetere, A. (2022). *Systemic therapy and attachment narratives: Applications in a range of clinical settings*. Routledge.

Efran, J., & Clarfield, L. (1992). Constructionist therapy: Sense and nonsense. In S. McNamee & K. Gergen (Eds.), *Therapy as social construction* (pp. 200–216). Sage.

Flaskas, C. (2013). The therapist's Imagination of self in relation to clients: Beginning Ideas on the flexibility of empathic Imagination. *Australian and New Zealand Journal of Family Therapy, 30*, 147–159.

Flaskas, C., Mason, B., & Perlesz, A. (Eds.). (2005). *The space between: Experience, context, and process in the therapeutic relationship*. Karnac.

Frosh, S. (2009). What does the other want? In C. Flaskas & D. Pocock (Eds.), *Systems and psychoanalysis: Contemporary integrations in family therapy* (pp. 185–201). Karnac.

Ghent, E. (1990). Masochism as a perversion of surrender. *Contemporary Psychoanalysis, 26*, 108–136.

Harries-Jones, P. (1995). *A recursive vision: Ecological understanding and Gregory Bateson*. Toronto Press.

Kahneman, D. (2011). *Thinking fast and slow*. Farrar, Straus, and Giroux.

Knox, J. (2011). *Self-agency in psychotherapy - Attachment, autonomy, and intimacy*. Norton.

Krause, I.-B. (2002). *Culture and system in family therapy*. Routledge.

Larner, G. (2009). Intersecting Levinas and Bion: The ethical container in psychoanalysis and family therapy. In C. Flaskas & D. Pocock (Eds.), *Systems and psychoanalysis: Contemporary integrations in family therapy* (pp. 203–220). Karnac.

Lord, S. (Ed.). (2018). *Moments of meeting in psychotherapy*. Routledge.

Main, M. (1993). *Attachment across the life cycle*. Routledge.

Miller, A. (1990). *For your own good: Hidden cruelty in childhood and the roots of violence*. Noonday Press.

Minuchin, S. (1974). *Families and family therapy*. Harvard University Press.

Mitchell, S. (2000). *Relationality: From attachment to intersubjectivity*. Routledge.

Morgan, H. (2014). Between fear and blindness: The white therapist and the black patient. In F. Lowe (Ed.), *Thinking space: Promoting Thinking about race, culture, and diversity in psychotherapy and beyond* (pp. 56–74). Karnac.

Orange, D. (1995). *Emotional understanding: Studies in psychoanalytic epistemology*. Guilford.

Pocock, D. (2018). You, me, and us. In S. Lord (Ed.), *Moments of meeting in psychotherapy* (pp. 199–208). Routledge.

Reimers, S., & Treacher, A. (1994). *Introducing user-friendly family therapy*. Routledge.

Rober, P. (1999). The therapist's inner conversation in family therapy practice: Some ideas about the self of the therapist, therapeutic impasse, and the process of reflection. *Family Process, 38*, 209–208.
Rober, P. (2024). *Becoming an effective family therapist: Research, practice, and case studies*. Routledge.
Shotter, J. (1993). *Conversational realities: Constructing life Through Language*. Sage.
Siegel, D. (2007). *The mindful brain in human development: Reflection and attunement in the cultivation of well-being*. Norton.
Siegel, D. (2010). *The mindful therapist: A clinician's guide to mindsight and neural integration*. Norton.
Smith, G. (2023). A 1.5-order therapy: Between knowing and not-knowing. *Family Process, 62*, 1281–1289.
Symington, N. (1983). The analyst's act of freedom as agent of therapeutic change. *International Review of Psychoanalysis, 10*, 283–291.
Vetere, A., & Dallos, R. (2003). *Working systemically with families: Formulation, intervention, and evaluation*. Karnac.
Vygotsky, L. (1978). *Mind in society: The development of higher psychological processes*. Harvard University Press.
White, M., & Epston, D. (1990). *Narrative means to therapeutic ends*. Norton.
Wynne, L., Ryckoff, I., Day, L., & Hirsch, S. (1958). Pseudomutuality in the family relationships of schizophrenics. *Psychiatry, 21*, 205–220.

8

Sameness and Otherness

> [O]therness might be something we are compelled to stand in awe of, not to make comprehensible, and this might constitute its challenge and also its humanizing core. Stephen Frosh (2009, p. 187)

> [T]herapists may get 'meta' to a family's discourse (this is the expertise for which we are trained and paid), but we can't get 'meta' to culture since culture (through its discourses) constructs us all. Virginia Goldner (1993, p. 2)

In planning this book I have probably spent more time thinking about the content of this chapter than any other. The word 'culture' was originally going to appear in the chapter title, but one problem is that 'culture' is a slippery term with multiple meanings and I am not entirely surely I know what I mean by it myself; rather, it can mean different things to me at different times. This is, perhaps, no surprise. Anthropologists Alfred Kroeber and Clyde Kluckhohn, writing in 1952, cited 164 definitions of culture from a critical review of the literature and the number has, if anything, increased in the last seven decades.

I have a fair handle on the usual meaning of 'cross-cultural' work (towards the end of this chapter, for example, I describe individual therapy with a Brazilian woman). The other side of that binary description is

D. Pocock, *Expanding the Limits of Individual and Family Therapies*, Palgrave Texts in Counselling and Psychotherapy, https://doi.org/10.1007/978-3-031-76309-0_8

'intra-cultural' which represents the great majority of my clinical experience. Have I only been working with people who are the same culturally as me? Sometimes it does feel like that, but quite often it does not. Conversely, cross-cultural work often has an unexpected ease of connection. That leads us immediately to three questions:

1. How meaningful is it to distinguish intra-cultural from cross-cultural therapy?
2. What accounts for the otherness of the other in intra-cultural work and how are we to theorise that?
3. What makes possible the occasional unexpected ease of connection in cross-cultural work?

For the moment, I will put these to one side as I don't think I should go further without allowing myself to be known as a cultural and 'racial' subject, as far as I am able to understand that. 'Racial' is placed in scare quotes since race is a socially constructed category based on minor genetic variations within the single closely related human species. But like all social constructions—true or false—it has real causal power.

I was born in July 1953, a month after the coronation of Queen Elizabeth II. I choose that reference point to honour my mother's passionate interest in the British Royal Family, alongside my own ambivalence. For the first eighteen years of my life I lived in the Pewsey Vale between the Marlborough Downs and Salisbury Plain, deep in rural Wiltshire, UK, and I now live less than ten miles from my birthplace. Both my parents came from families that are white British as far back as anyone can remember. We were rural working class, living in a cottage tied to my father's job as a farm labourer. This arrangement meant that losing a job meant the immediate loss of a home: a causal factor underlining the notable class/power difference between us and the boss's family and the absolute necessity of performing deference in the presence of the young boss and his father, The Old Man. One unspoken rule (non-conscious norm) was that you didn't speak to The Old Man unless he first addressed you. His family lived in a big house visible from ours. We had an open fire in the living room, an outside toilet, a bath in the 'scullery' that was brought out on Sundays, a back garden for vegetables, and a motorbike and sidecar. Their house came with multiple bedrooms, central heating, wooded grounds, tennis court, ponies for the children, shooting parties, and a Bentley, changed every two years.

My parents never went abroad in their entire lives. My mother had a single holiday in Edinburgh, with a friend, when on leave from her wartime duties as a WAAF (Women's Auxiliary Air-Force). This was a daring event for her since it meant defying her mother's expectation that she should go home to visit. The wartime was the most eventful—and for my mother, at least, the most thrilling—period of their lives. The likely alternative was that she continued as a live-in domestic servant; work she had taken up straight after leaving school. My father tried to join the armed forces at the outbreak of the war but his reserved occupation as a farm labourer meant he was rejected. He joined the Home Guard and did not enjoy seeing it lampooned in the popular BBC TV series *Dad's Army* which we, nevertheless, watched every week.

When I was in the last years of junior school my mother was able to work full-time stacking crates in the local brewery and, after a difficult start, loved her job because of the regular social contact. She had been quite isolated before then as a stay-at-home mother in a tiny village, caring for me and my sister who was four years older.

My parents were very careful with money, saving all of the time. Later—at a time when interest rates were high—my mother (who had sole charge of the finances) invested sensibly, and they were able to buy their own home when my father retired. This had been one of their two dreams—the other being able to see both of their children "settled". Christmas was the one time of the year they allowed themselves to spend freely, and there was always a large pile of presents on Christmas Day.

I have written previously about my relationship with my father (Pocock, 2013). I won't repeat the details here except to say that the circumstances of his early life were difficult. His mother—my beloved Grandma—came from a wealthy upper-middle-class family of solicitors in London but, when working as a Land Girl between the wars, she became pregnant to the villainously named Percy Pocock, a First World War veteran and amputee. In line with the cultural expectations of the day, she married him, but her family essentially cut her off for marrying 'so far beneath' herself. Faithful to his villain's script, Percy drank through her small inheritance and then abandoned her, my father, and my father's sister. Grandma worked as housekeeper from then on but had to move frequently (for reasons that were never explained to me) resulting in my father attending a total of thirteen schools.

Both my parents were keen on supporting mine and my sister's education. She passed all three stages of the exam for Grammar School but was then deferred for a year on the grounds of being too young. She then passed the first two stages again but was failed at interview. Only later did I learn how male privilege was embedded in the selection process. As mentioned in Chap. 3, entry to Grammar School was intentionally rigged to smooth the way for a fixed quota of averagely less-able boys. My parents were delighted that I passed (easier to detect in my mother) and, later, fully supported me financially at degree level to study biology, unlike the wealthier parents of some of my fellow students who declined to pay their share.

I grew up surrounded by a low-key Church of England Christianity which was encouraged in a routine way by my mother (with nothing like her passion for royalty) probably under the influence of her mother, with neither objection nor endorsement from my father who neither attended church nor expressed any religious view. I was encouraged to say prayers before bedtime, went to a Church of England Primary School, attended Sunday school and, later, was taken (reluctantly) each Sunday after lunch by my mother to the tiny Methodist Chapel in the village to join in with the droning cacophony of hymn singing and endure the endless tedium of the sermons. I mentioned in Chap. 1 my 'capture' and eventual escape from Baptist Chapel; that whole period roughly coinciding with my secondary school education, most of that at Grammar School.

Incredible as it seems now not a single person of colour attended either my primary school or Grammar School and it was well into my late teens before I talked to anyone black or Asian. But race—or I should say 'racism'—was everywhere. Racist (alongside sexist and homophobic) jokes and other tropes were simply a part of everyday conversation. My father was not at all unusual in his racist views, expressed quite casually as self-evident truths, rather than with venom: "black people's houses smell"; "don't send money to Africa as 'they' breed like flies"; and, bizarrely, without context, "never trust a Frenchman". To my mother's credit she always tried to challenge him. At the Baptist Chapel we were reassured that the holocaust must have been part of God's plan (because everything was), most likely as punishment because the Jews killed Christ. And so on and so on. Even Catholics were seen as a bit odd and had to be mysteriously taken away for their own daily assembly at Grammar School.

Until a decade ago I might have said with some confidence that I had, with the benefit of my social work and family therapy trainings, unlearned the racist, homophobic, sexist, and other discriminatory lessons of childhood and young adulthood. I then joined a Thinking Space Group with fellow psychoanalytic psychotherapists from my membership institute using the collected essays in Frank Lowe's (2014) edited book *Thinking Space: Promoting Thinking about Race, Culture, and Diversity and Beyond* as a starting point for discussion. The outcome—not one I had expected—was to peel away (slowly at first, then rapidly) the thin layer of political correctness that had kept these discourses out of consciousness. I had simply learned to hide them from myself. For the first time the readings and discussion confronted me with what lurked within, and, for many months, this was deeply disturbing. It did, however, allow a deeper updating of those views and some working through of the associated shame.

Until five years ago I would have described myself as an atheist with regard to all religious matters, but now think, that 'atheist cultural Christian' is more accurate. I had always been struck, and indeed puzzled, by how the actions and sayings of Christ seemed modern and in tune with a liberal centre-left sensibility. (This is where my political affiliation ended-up after a flirtation with Marxism, during my social work training in the late 70 s, followed by membership of a far-left Labour Party Ward after moving to the South Wales Valleys for my first post-qualifying job as a probation officer.) The penny dropped when reading historian Tom Holland's (2019) *Dominion: How the Christian Revolution Remade the World.* He argues that the humanistic values which seem intrinsic to western liberal culture are primarily the product of Christianity and would not exist in the same way without the two thousand years of Christian dominance of the culture. What I took to be Christ's modern-sounding humanism, Holland argues, was secularism's hidden derivation from Christianity.

I use the term 'atheist cultural Christian' very reluctantly since I was more content to feel I had been able to turn away from *all* religion. I am fully aware of the history of persecution, murder, and oppression which resulted from Christianity which continues to the present day in some form. The rise of the Christian right in the US deeply troubles me, for example. But we do not choose our cultural influences, they shape us whether we like it—and know it—or not.

Experiences of Otherness

You might think, from the above, that I was about as integrated into British culture as it is possible to be, but I would argue that full integration at a national level is not only a dangerous ideal for countries to aspire to, with its constant risk of othering recent immigrants (we are all immigrants of different periods), it is also an impossibility for *any* person to achieve, whether born in this country or not. 'Intra-cultural' as indicative of a homogenised group is, I suggest, a fallacy which collapses under closer examination. (For further discussion on 'the myth of cultural integration' see Archer, 1996.) To make my case I will start by listing a few experiences of otherness up to the age of eighteen.

1. From as far back as I remember I was puzzled by what it meant to be me. In fact I can remember these thoughts quite vividly from when I was a small child. Why am I me and not someone else? Why are other people them and not me? Why am I the only me? Do other animals think and, if so, what? There seemed to be no answers to any of these questions, not that I would ever have voiced them to anyone.
2. For the majority of my childhood things happened around me, within social groups, that I did not understand. Older tough gangs of boys roamed around the villages on bikes, like the bandits in the film, *The Magnificent Seven.* They had ways of behaving and talking that made no sense to me: hyper-sexualised talk, smashing things up when adults weren't around, destroying bird's nest, and making false calls to the fire brigade. My sister's group of friends had their own games and secrets which were not for boys, or certainly not for younger brothers. Older

people in the village spoke in a broad Wiltshire accent peppered with West-Country dialect that seemed almost defiantly incomprehensible to me, as if they didn't want to be understood.

3. Infants' school was initially a complete mystery. In those days there was no pre-school, and it was many years before anyone realised that children needed a gradual introduction. I remember, on my first day, eating my sandwiches just after getting off the school bus in the morning, until my sister told me to save them for lunchtime.
4. The eventual relative comfort and informality of junior school was replaced by an entirely new set of expectations that had to be learned at Grammar School which had public school pretensions. Teachers were now more distant authority figures who addressed pupils by surname, wielded heavy sarcasm and the power of referral to the headmaster, who regularly reported at assembly the list of those he had caned along with their misdemeanours. Rugby and cricket (hockey and netball for the girls) were now taken more seriously than football. Membership of the Grammar School tribe was at odds with the majority of secondary school boys who yelled "Gutter Snobs!" and worse at us. It created a strong social division in friendship groups outside of school, which were then never the same.
5. My early social class encounters with the Boss and his family were supplemented by displays of comparative wealth at school, with the compulsory uniform making little difference. Clothes, shoes, satchels, briefcases, and sports' gear looked the same only from a distance. Every pupil knew where they stood in the wealth hierarchy. While we working-class kids had 'dinner' at midday, 'tea' as a main meal, and 'supper' was a small snack before bed, *they* had 'lunch' for dinner and, confusingly, 'dinner' or 'supper' for tea. 'Breakfast' was the only classless meal name.

In summary, even before I left home, my 'intra-cultural' experience included several social groups that I was either to remain outside of (upper-middle-class farmers, girls/women, thuggish older boys, elderly country-folk, non-elite secondary education, wealthy peers) or ones with unfamiliar norms that I needed to accommodate to (infants' school, Grammar School, Baptist chapel). Along the way there were perpetual 'lessons' in racism, sexism, homophobia, social class, gender conformity, and educational privilege provided through every-day discourse but varying across the groups. The next half-century has added (and in some cases subtracted) other groups and their norms, too numerous to list but including both my systemic and psychoanalytic trainings each of them with subdivisions (models and traditions) with their own norms.

Models of Culture

How are we to make sense of these multiple influences which are obscured in the intra-cultural / cross-cultural binary? Issues of culture and race were entirely absent from my psychoanalytic training which, as said, tended to assume that unconscious processes were universal. (That situation has improved greatly in psychoanalytic training in recent years.) In contrast, the period of my systemic training occurred at a time of increasing interest in gender, race, and culture. However, this came with some confusion. By-and-large, respecting culture was seen as a good thing; culture was to be understood, even celebrated, rather than challenged. On the other hand, patriarchy, as expressed in the imbalance of power between a heterosexual couple, was definitely a bad thing that ought to be challenged. Given that roles of men and women are always shaped by culture, what is one to do, respect or challenge?

Further confusion arose from strong constructionist assumptions of culture that over-emphasised difference. This didn't fit at all with my experiences during summers spent working in Germany during student vacations and months travelling overland to, and through, India after graduating. During these times, I was surrounded by people whose language I didn't understand but where limited—but often surprisingly warm—connection was possible through gesture and facial expression supplemented by a few words.

The Social Graces approach developed by John Burnham and Alison Roper-Hall (see Burnham, 2012 for a history and the development of the approach) lists aspects of identity, that might otherwise be invisible and/or unvoiced, in a mnemonic—GGGRRAACCEEESSS—(gender identity, geography, generation, race, religion, age, ability, appearance, class, culture, education, ethnicity, employment, spirituality, sexuality, sexual orientation). Yet this flat list doesn't take account of the superordinate position of culture. As examples: social class seems best understood as the set of cultural distinctions associated with wealth, property, education, and other forms of social capital (Bordieu, 1986); gender roles, as mentioned, are surely an inherent aspect of every culture; and what is religion if not a cultural organisation around belief in gods? And so on.

More helpfully, as mentioned in earlier chapters, I have found the centrality of culture, its non-conscious aspects, its transmission from caregiver to child through mentalising, its strong association with emotion, and the notion that culture is *both* socially constructed *and* constrained by universal aspects tied to embodiment, are all well represented in the work of anthropologist and systemic psychotherapist, Britt Krause (2002, 2012).

Systemic psychotherapy also deserves considerable credit for providing a platform for the ongoing project that has become known as 'decolonising', making new demands on therapists' reflexivity in terms of their unconscious assumptions and mapping the long reach of partly concealed colonialising practices, including the use of normative Eurocentric theoretical lenses (e.g. Reynolds, 2012; Cottrell-Boyce, 2022; Jordan, 2022; Roy-Chowdhury, 2022; Afuape & Oldham, 2022; Afuape et al., 2022). Similarly, the 'social psychoanalysis' of, among others, Lynne Layton (2020) recognises the causal power of 'normative unconscious processes' on identity formation:

> [These] are the lived effects on identity formation of unequal power arrangements and dominant ideologies that split and differentially value straight from gay, rich from poor, masculine from feminine, white from black and brown. Social hierarchies of sex(ism), class(ism), race(ism), heterosex(ism) mandate what one will have to split off to attain a "proper" identity. (p. xxxii)

The work of Krause and others has significantly shaped my thinking, but I also turn to two other authors to deconstruct the 'intra-cultural'.

Multidimensionality, Norm Circles, and Intersectionality

Celia Falicov (1995) provides the following *multidimensional* definition of culture:

> Those sets of shared world views, meanings and adaptive behaviours derived from simultaneous membership and participation in a multiplicity of contexts, such as rural, urban, or suburban setting; language, age, gender, family configuration, race, ethnicity, religion, nationality, cohort, sexual orientation, socioeconomic status, employment, education, occupation, political ideology; stage of acculturation. (p. 373)

Here, culture is properly given a superordinate position with regard to other distinctions. She distinguishes *Multidimensional* from three other positions: *Universalist*—that all families are very alike; *Particularist*—each family is unique; and *Ethnic-Focussed*—that difference is entirely due to the single factor of ethnicity. *Multidimensional* has no conflict with the notion of 'cross-cultural' work, but it gives a nuanced and, in my view, a more object-adequate account than 'intra-cultural' and fits my life and professional experiences considerably better.

Critical realism is well placed to account for intersectionality since *absence* as well as *presence* are both recognised as real causal tendencies (Bhaskar, 2016). An individual may experience advantage—an *absence* of obstacles—in some aspects of identity (e.g. a white skin) but disadvantage—the *presence* of obstacles—in other aspects (e.g. being gay, a woman, and of low socioeconomic status) (Martinez Dy et al., 2014).

The critical realist sociologist Dave Elder-Vass' (2012) concept of norm circles provides an even finer-textured understanding of culture. A norm circle is any group with a tendency to support and enforce a particular norm: a social practice, belief, attitude, prejudice, way of speaking, ethic, knowledge, 'race', rules for what counts as knowledge, and so on. Membership of a norm circle may be conscious or non-conscious. I am conscious of the normative influence of numerous circles: eating with my mouth closed, white professional-middle class, supporting Liverpool Football Club, queuing for buses rather than a free-for-all, centre-left politics, not standing right next to another person in public urinals if there is a choice, critical realism, avoiding eye-contact on the London Underground, relational psychoanalysis, the rules of chess, and so on. These multiple norm circles—some small, some large or very large—do not absolutely determine behaviour but are social structures which *encourage a tendency to accept and enforce their norm.* In that sense they are real (they arise from material embodied individuals) but are also socially constructed between individuals. Like all real tendencies, whether or not they are actualised depends on how they intersect with other tendencies. For example, there are some social contexts in which I might use swear words, and others in which I would not.

For Elder-Vass (2012), norm circles are the dynamic source of cultural change.

> Cultural change occurs when some norm circles grow in size and/or influence at the expense of others and when innovation produces new or altered norms which develop their own norm circles and enter this fray. It is not a question of whether some norms disappear and others appear in the archive that matters here; it is a question of which norms can secure the allegiance of the population. (p. 47)

Awareness of *previously unconscious* membership of norm circles requires the arrival of a Batesonian (1979) 'news of a difference'. I wrote previously (Pocock, 2012) of my reaction to reading Bateson's (1958) account of the important role that headhunting had, until recent times, played in the culture of the male Iatmul in Indonesia. I had found this disturbing but, on reflection, it was not the headhunting itself which particularly bothered me, it was my perception of what I can only describe as the lack of 'fair play' in the manner of the killing. Bateson records that it made no difference at all to the Iatmul men if the victims were killed in a 'fair fight' or whether they were stabbed in the back. I cannot completely map the origins of my reaction to this, but I sense that it is linked to some old white imperial association of Englishness with 'fair play', reinforced by a childhood watching, and acting out with peers, war and 'western' movies in which 'cowardly' acts by 'baddies', such as back-stabbing, legitimised their ultimate demise, providing some guilt-free excitement and re-establishing the moral order. This non-conscious membership of norm circles maps onto Bordieu's (1990) concept of 'habitus'—a cultural unconscious.

In turn, it is quite possible that an Iatmul man of that period would be no less shocked with my norms of intimacy between a father and grown-up sons.

> While I was on Sepik, a European father and son settled together on the Ceram River many miles away, where they started a small, isolated tobacco plantation. The Iatmul heard of this and were surprised and shocked. They came to me to ask if the two were really father and son and were disgusted when I told them it was so. They said, "Has the father no shame?" (Bateson, 1958, p. 41)

Consider a meeting between two persons. Figure 8.1 (modified from Elder-Vass, 2012) provides a simplified map of just a few of the many possible norm circles that intersect both within and between them as individuals. Person 1 is a member of norm circles A, B, and C but not of norm circles D and E. Person 2 is a member of some of the same norm circles as Person 1 but not all of them and is also a member of D that does not include Person 1.

Turning this into a highly reduced case example, I am Person 1, and Person 2 is the client. We have a common ethnicity (Circle A) and are of the same educational level (Circle C). But I am an atheist cultural Christian (Circle B), and Person 2—the client—is a committed

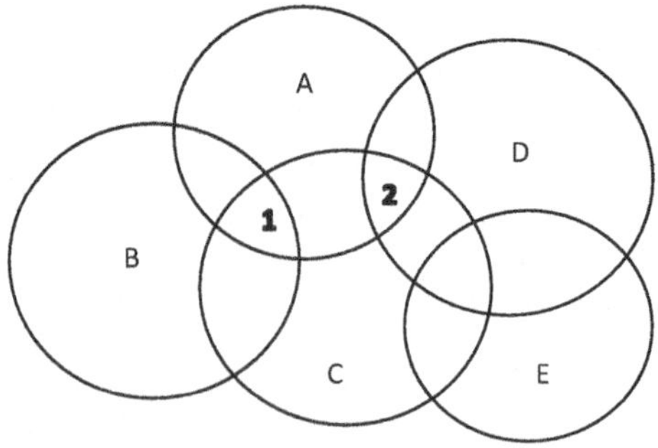

Fig. 8.1 Intersecting norm circles

right-wing Christian fundamentalist (Circle D). From these intersections one might predict that there would be some shared norms casing communication and understanding in certain areas but with potential conflict over active versus deactivated religious belief.

Assumptions of Sameness

Addressing now the title of this chapter, I want to argue (after Benjamin, 1999 and Frosh, 2009) that *coming gradually (albeit incompletely) to recognise the other in their subjective otherness is the only path to an authentic, non-colonising, relationship*. As soon as we are confident that we know the other, the relationship is in trouble. I think most of us realise that the statement "I know *exactly* how you feel" is among the crassest things we could possibly say.

Descartes is not my favourite philosopher since his mind-world dualism has caused no end of trouble (Collier, 1999). But his pursuit of certainty, connected with his obsessive drive to try to prove the existence of God, did at least clear up one matter: the only thing we can know with absolute certainty is what we have already made in our heads. In evolutionary terms, one of the greatest threats to people is other people so, as a species, we reach judgements about strangers very rapidly and partly non-consciously (Gladwell, 2005). If we know something about someone with certainty it is because we have made them fit our pre-existing constructions including theoretical ones. In psychoanalytic terms this, as a non-conscious process, is called projective identification; we see something from our own mind in the other but assume that this really belongs to them. *We are then actually relating to part of ourselves, not to the other.* For example, as discussed, racism and sexism are ways of locating feared inferiority (and other repudiated aspects) safely in the other. In relationships of differential power, where the other may feel they have no choice but to accommodate the views of the projector—for examples in childhood or periods of dependency in individual psychotherapy—this becomes colonisation. For Fonagy et al. (2002) the other in a dependent relationship can become a host for the projected part of the self. This projection then turns into an alien object in the mind of the other.

In summary, we start off relating via quick judgements to people as internal objects of our own (e.g. stereotypes, prior experiences, theoretically derived representations). Then, if there is sufficient time and space for not-knowing, we may discover them as subjects in their own right, allowing many of our preformed object-assumptions to break down along the way. However, such assumptions can be stubbornly durable especially, as Goldner (1993) says, in the quote that begins this chapter, we cannot stand outside of ("get meta to") our culture; we bring our norm circles to every encounter.

To illustrate, I will now add some details to the norm circle example that I began to illustrate above. The eldest teenage son from a white professional family from the North American Mid-West was referred to our child and adolescent mental health service out of concerns that he was depressed. The father telephoned me in advance of the session to ask if he and his wife could meet me without the children in order to talk to me about how I proposed to conduct the therapy. He didn't want to elaborate on the phone, so I agreed, feeling somewhat apprehensive about what lay ahead. When we met, the father did most of the talking and soon explained that *his* family were Baptists, and it was *his* responsibility to ensure that they were not subjected to any bad influences that would be contrary to their religion. Was I, he asked, a Christian? My reply—that I was brought up in the Baptist tradition, was no longer a person of religious faith, but tried to be respectful of the beliefs of those I worked with—did not satisfy him. He was willing to be referred instead to another family therapist who was a practicing Catholic but, in the event he did not pursue that either.

Although we had norm circles in common (two of the many possible, as shown, were professional white middle class, and higher education) it was not possible, I think, to get past the assumptions each of us made about the other based on our relationship to religion. We each remained *objects of sameness* to the other: I was for him, perhaps, a personified representative of the Devil, ready to seduce his family from the true path. He was for me a representative of my experiences of the hated dogmatic religious patriarchy of my youth. With time we might have got past this to begin to find each other as subjects, but he was not willing to take the risk. How much of his decision was influenced by my projection onto him is unknown but I was relieved not to have to work with him, although concerned for the son.

Our aim in psychotherapy is different to that of cultural anthropologists: not to gain knowledge of the other for its own sake but to understand sufficiently to enhance the possibility of positive change. In practice that may mean avoiding the misunderstandings and defences (including in the therapist) that stand in the way of that possibility. To illustrate, I am going to quote verbatim and at length from an earlier published case example (Pocock, 2012).

> In individual therapy with Nina, a bright engaging Brazilian trainee solicitor [recently married and living permanently in the UK] who was depressed and convinced that she was failing in her career, we had struggled to understand how she had become convinced that she was deficient in mental capacity. It seemed to me that her investment in the belief that she had less "brain power" than her peers, robbed her of motivation to work for her exams in which she frequently under-performed. In turn she interpreted her underachievement with the same low-brain-power schema: her beliefs and behaviours forming a closed self-reinforcing loop. Explorations of the potential origins of this led to a traumatic memory of her failing some school exams as a nine-year-old. She had been told that, because of this failure, she would not be able to accompany the family on holiday but would have to stay with relatives to do summer school. Although this punitive sanction had later been lifted, her predominant memory was that of shame and the associated idea that she was not clever enough.
>
> This self-blaming adaptation to her parents' sanction seemed understandable to me in the light of an apparently insecure avoidant [A-strategy] attachment to them both. She had been raised by her maternal grandmother for the first few years of her life and had struggled to find her place in the family when returned to her parents at the age of five, around the time of the birth of the second child. It seemed to me that a more secure child would have felt entitled to be angry with her parents about this sanction, and that her self-blame and the specific assumption that there was something wrong with her brain was an adaptive unconscious avoidant strategy of turning the negative affect against herself in order to fit in (Crittenden 2008; Pocock 2010a, 2010b). This way of thinking of these experiences felt right to Nina but made no real difference to the strength of

> her self-blaming schema. Little progress seemed to be made on this key issue and the work began to feel stuck.
>
> Only slowly over many sessions did news arrive of a more pervasive sense of shame in relation to the circumstances of her birth. She was illegitimate: a fact we knew but had not sufficiently understood emotionally since it initially seemed to mean little to Nina and *does not have strong emotional significance in my relational-cultural history.* What took time to slowly and painfully emerge was a never-spoken shame of this illegitimacy that needed to be understood in the context of the family's Catholicism, poverty and an internalised self-denigration which was gendered and linked to her 'dark' skin and 'inferior' indigenous status. The shame of educational failure, which I assumed we had the measure of, seemed to be fed by this more corrosive subterranean shame from earlier unprocessed relational-cultural experiences.
>
> The stuckness was caused by the apparent irrelevance of her illegitimacy being 'in the bag'. It had slipped there, unbeknown to either of us, through the seductive illusions of knowing and sameness. Nina had been temporarily colonized in the therapy by an account in which both of us had failed to recognise the importance of emotional issues that gathered around the circumstances of her birth. (The extent to which echoes of European colonization of Brazil contextualised that process between us—a Brazilian patient and a European therapist—remains an open question.) I thought I had understood her, and she had thought she had been understood, but we were both wrong: the narrative fitted too poorly with her unformulated experience (Flaskas, 2009) and the therapy stalled. The gradual recognition of this error was much needed, allowing a renewal of curiosity, a rebalancing of knowing with not-knowing, and eventually some recognition and progress. (pp. 11–13. [My emphasis])

I can now add a post-script to this account. Note in the penultimate paragraph the highlighted phrase: illegitimacy "*does not have strong emotional significance in my relational-cultural history*". My mother died a year after this chapter was published and at her funeral an elderly relative, whom I had never met, or even heard about before, asked me about my mother's sister. To my knowledge my mother didn't have a sister. I was then astonished to learn that her mother's first-born child (half-sister to my mother) was born illegitimate and raised in another family. I am sure my mother must have known but concealed this her whole life. The unspoken shame of illegitimacy—unrecognised by me in the work with Nina—applied to us both. Again, difference was not the problem in understanding the meaning of her shame, the barrier was my unacknowledged sameness over an issue that both of us needed to keep out of awareness.

My Position in Summary

Snap judgements are part of the human condition and, presumably, have conferred an evolutionary advantage. This involves relating to the other as if they are the same as our preformed constructions ('racial' or national stereotypes, diagnoses, theoretical categories, and prior experiences). We are then only relating to parts of ourselves projected into the other. This is the greatest risk of first-order naïve realism exemplified by Saxes' blind men. *Unexamined sameness—expecting the other to be just how we expect them to be consciously and non-consciously—is thus a greater problem than difference.* These object relations have to break down for each in a relationship to discover the other as a subject in their own right. I see psychotherapy (especially individual therapy where the therapeutic relationship is more central) as an attempt by each to discover the other in their subjective otherness, sufficient to enhance positive therapeutic change. This must be collaborative and can never be complete. In the same way we also remain something of a mystery to ourselves.

Culture, in the form of norm circles, is superordinate to other aspects of identity: class, 'race', gender, sexuality, disability, etc. Norm circles provide many points of similarity and difference in a therapeutic encounter and this intersectional and dynamic model is preferred to the intra-cultural/cross-cultural binary. Norm circles are made up of real (materially embodied) individuals, but the norms are socially constructed and often unconscious. They have real causal power in the form of tendencies that may or may not be actualised depending on interaction with other tendencies. It is not possible for anyone to give a full account of their norms, but these can be discovered in moments when difference is encountered. Reflecting on these moments is part of therapist second-order reflexivity.

References

Afuape, T., & Oldham, S. (2022). Beyond 'solidarity' with Black lives matter: Drawing on liberation psychology and transformative justice to address institutional and community violence in young Black lives. *Journal of Family Therapy, 44*, 20–43.

Afuape, K., Bisimwa, N., Campbell, K., Jemmott, R., Jude, J., Nijabat, N., et al. (2022). Black and proud: Impact of intergenerational racism upon global majority family systems. *Journal of Family Therapy, 44*, 5–19.

Archer, M. (1996). *Culture and agency*. Cambridge University Press.

Bateson, G. (1958). *Naven: A survey of the problems suggested by a composite picture of the culture of a New Guinea tribe drawn from three points of view*. Stanford University Press.

Bateson, G. (1979). *Mind and nature: A necessary unity*. Dutton.

Benjamin, J. (1999). Recognition and destruction: An outline of intersubjectivity. In S. Mitchell & L. Aron (Eds.), *Relational Psychoanalysis: The emergence of a tradition* (pp. 181–210). Analytic Press.

Bhaskar, R. (2016). *Enlightened common sense: The philosophy of critical realism*. Routledge.

Bordieu, P. (1986). The forms of capital. In J. Richardson (Ed.), *Handbook of theory and research for the sociology of education* (pp. 241–258). Greenwood.

Bordieu, P. (1990). *The logic of practice*. Polity Press.

Burnham, J. (2012). Developments in social GRRRAAACCEEESSS: Visible-invisible and voiced-unvoiced. In I.-B. Krause (Ed.), *Culture and reflexivity in systemic psychotherapy: Mutual perspectives* (pp. 139–160). Karnac.

Collier, A. (1999). Language, practice, and realism. In I. Parker (Ed.), *Social constructionism, discourse, and realism* (pp. 47–58). Sage.

Cottrell-Boyce, J. (2022). Addressing white privilege in family therapy: A discourse analysis. *Journal of Family Therapy, 44*, 142–156.

Elder-Vass, D. (2012). *The reality of social construction*. Cambridge University Press.

Falicov, C. (1995). Learning to think culturally: A comparative framework. *Family Process, 34*, 373–388.

Fonagy, P., Gergeley, G., Jurist, E., & Target, M. (2002). *Affect regulation, mentalization, and the development of the self*. Other Press.

Frosh, S. (2009). What does the other want? In C. Flaskas & D. Pocock (Eds.), *Systems and psychoanalysis: Contemporary integrations in family therapy* (pp. 185–201). Karnac.

Gladwell, M. (2005). *Blink: The power of thinking without thinking*. Little, Brown and Co.

Goldner, V. (1993). Power and hierarchy: Let's talk about it! *Family Process, 32*, 157–162.

Holland, T. (2019). *Dominion: How the Christian revolution remade the world*. Hachette Book Group.

Jordan, L. (2022). Unsettling colonial mentalities in family therapy: Entering negotiated spaces. *Journal of Family Therapy, 44*, 171–185.

Krause, I.-B. (2002). *Culture and system in family therapy*. Routledge.

Krause, I.-B. (2012). *Culture and reflexivity in systemic psychotherapy: Mutual perspectives*. Karnac.

Kroeber, A., & Kluckhohn, C. (1952). *Culture. A critical review of concepts and definitions*. Harvard University Press.

Layton, L. (2020). *Towards a social psychoanalysis: Culture, character, and normative unconscious processes*. Taylor and Francis.

Lowe, F. (Ed.). (2014). *Thinking space: Promoting thinking about race, culture, and diversity in psychotherapy and beyond*. Karnac.

Martinez Dy, A., Martin, L., & Marlow, S. (2014). Developing a critical realist positional approach to intersectionality. *Journal of Critical Realism, 13*, 447–466.

Pocock, D. (2012). Objectification, recognition, and the intersubjective continuum. In I.-B. Krause (Ed.), *Culture and reflexivity in systemic psychotherapy: Mutual perspectives* (pp. 71–90). Karnac.

Pocock, D. (2013). How to make a man: Moritz, Maurice, and me. *Context, 129*, 38–41.

Reynolds, V. (2012). An ethical stance for justice-doing in community work and therapy. *Journal of Systemic Therapies, 31*, 18–33.

Roy-Chowdhury, S. (2022). Talking about race, culture, and racism in family therapy. *Journal of Family Therapy, 44*, 44–55.

9

Who to See, and Other Choices

> We alternate choosing places to go, but we also have to be willing to go where the road takes us. This means the grand, the small, the bizarre, the poetic, the beautiful, the ugly, the surprising. Just like life. Jennifer Niven, *All the Bright Places.*

My psychoanalytic, humanistic, and family therapy readers might find it odd that, up until this point, I have not sought to draw strong distinctions between individual and family therapies. The reason for this, as I hope is becoming clear, is that I use the same theories and metatheories (epistemology and ontology) for both. My assumption of an ontologically holistic systemic world, which includes the therapist, applies equally, regardless of who is present in the therapy room and who is left out. Historically, the dominant narrative, especially on the side of family therapy, was to emphasise difference. Indeed, I think one of the foundational myths of family therapy is that only family therapy is systemic. (Boscolo & Bertrando, 1996, provide a notable exception.) As previously discussed, if we are (as Bateson was implicitly) systemic ontologists, then it follows that, regardless of how we think, and regardless of what we do (or don't do), *everything*, including our minds and bodies, is part of the

D. Pocock, *Expanding the Limits of Individual and Family Therapies*, Palgrave Texts in Counselling and Psychotherapy, https://doi.org/10.1007/978-3-031-76309-0_9

system. This is Bateson's (1972) 'immanent mind', and Bhaskar's 'metaReality' (2012) or 'co-presence' (2016):

> … at the deepest level of being, all is in all: that the starry heavens are within us, and we are within them. (Bhaskar, 2016, p. 202)

While the world itself is almost certainly ontologically systemic our capacity to apprehend its multiple influences is another matter altogether. That depends on the therapist's epistemology—the ability to think systemically and to retroductively map significant causal tendencies. But work with the *whole* system would be to attempt 'universe therapy'. No room would ever be large enough! Choices have to be made.

In this chapter, I want to elaborate how the choices of who to see in psychotherapy create a range of contexts which powerfully open up some pathways to change while closing down others. I plan to indicate how, in family therapy, there is often untapped potential for flexibility in choosing who to see, and how in other areas—especially long-term individual therapy—holding a consistent boundary is necessary to enhance the possibility of the therapeutic relationship becoming a 'developmental second chance' (Orange, 1995). Within these large choices of who to see other choices become available. Such choices constitute an aspect of technique or, using Shotter's (1993) term, 'know-how'.

Agreement about who to include in therapy involves choices by both therapist and client(s). I'll start by considering the position of the client. One of the reasons that I left the Gwent (South Wales) Probation Service in my early thirties, after four years, was the difficulty in working with those who had *no choice* (other than opting for something worse) whether to meet with me regularly under the terms of a probation order, supervision order, or prison after-care licence. I soon found that compulsory relationships are, to say the least, not the most facilitating basis for change. However, after arrival at the Swindon Child and Family Guidance Centre as a social worker, I discovered that 'voluntary attendance' was not at all like I had assumed. Many parents and children were far from the idealised eager-to-work clients that I had fondly imagined in my probation service years. I learned that a productive first line of enquiry was not to explore *what* problems they were seeking help with, but *how* the 'agreement' to referral had been made. This helped to reveal what I came to think of as 'gun-to-the-head referrals': parents who agreed to be referred by schools or social services under the implicit (or occasionally explicit) threat that something worse would happen if they didn't accept the offer. In turn, children in those families were sometimes similarly coerced by parents or professionals. It was also comparatively rare to find a parental couple in which each was as motivated as the other.

I had no training in family therapy for the first two years at the child and family guidance centre, so it took me a while to work out that engagement with family members went more smoothly when their relative reluctance to attend and any coercion that informed their 'choice' was understood and accepted. Reluctance is mostly communicated non-verbally, and in the case of angry adolescents, often loudly so. For example, to a teenage boy with his back firmly turned to me, who had made it clear that he would not speak, I might say something like, "I've never met anyone who actually *wants* to come here—in fact *wanting* to come here would probably be a bit strange". I might add that I didn't mind if he chose not to speak, stating that, very often, people prefer just to listen to others. The crucial factor is not just normalising and positively connoting reluctance in words but coming to see it this way oneself (Kraemer, 1988), such that one's emotional communication does not contradict the words. Inauthenticity is easily picked up by most people and inauthentic positive connotation of behaviour is a small step away from sarcasm. Supporting some level of autonomy (the right not to want to be present and the right not to talk) within the wider context of coerced attendance usually resulted in adolescents joining in when they were ready. I can't recall any that held out in silence for an entire session.

Client choices will thus be relatively constrained or unconstrained, but choices are also relatively informed or uninformed. No one, including the therapist, can predict with accuracy what will happen in any psychotherapy, since it is an open system, but without the provision of basic information of roughly what might be expected, both in advance and at the start of a first session, client expectations and anxieties can run high. In public agency family therapy the knowledge gap may be filled with idealised hopes (e.g. the therapist will know exactly how to fix the problem) or terrifying ones, such as the discovery in the user-surveys, reported by Reimers and Treacher (1994), that a high proportion of parents secretly feared that their children might be removed. In the light of such findings our service commissioned an independent researcher to undertake a large survey covering every stage of the user experience, from first discussion with a referrer, through initial contacts, experiences of the building, reception, the therapist, the therapy, and the outcome. Provision of good information, prior to the first appointment, emerged as a key issue and, alongside leaflets, some of us offered the opportunity of contact with a parent by telephone to talk through what might be expected and address any immediate concerns.

Individual Psychotherapy

Remarkable as it now seems, there was a period in the late-1980s and early-1990s when our NHS Child and Family Guidance Centre was not running with impossibly long waiting lists and the continuous pressure to keep the work brief, which has been a feature of the last decade or so given the great increase in referrals but limited public funds. It was then possible to offer longer-term individual therapy to a few parents. I offered this when there seemed to be particularly strong negative attributions, made by the most involved parent about the referred child, which didn't seem to change during family therapy. These attributions seemed often present in binary pairs distributed between pairs of siblings. So, for example, a 'bad aggressive' child appeared paired with a 'good compliant' child, a 'selfish' child with a 'giving' one and so on. I wrote about this work and a later study which found, in a small sample, some evidence that the biggest differences that a parent perceived between pairs of siblings were linked to unresolved traumatic relational issues for that parent. I named this causal tendency 'triadic projective identification' (Pocock, 1992). I was also more likely to offer this kind of work when the parent was at least partly aware that their negative attribution was linked to *their* perception of the child and they were beginning to own the issue and express some guilt and curiosity about their role. For example, "I was a surly child like her", "my brother was like that" or, in relation to a violent ex-partner, "my son has that same look when he's swearing at me".

In my 1992 paper I described individual therapy with Jennifer. She and her white Irish siblings and half-siblings had been placed in a Catholic orphanage when she was a few weeks old. She was the only child not to be returned to any part of the family over subsequent years. As she grew up she was described as "bad" and "mad" by the nuns. In her adult life her intelligence and academic ability enabled her to stave off feelings of badness by performing tasks to a very high level. However, any slip in performance (for example, in exams) triggered depressed feelings. She described herself as severely depressed after the birth of Samantha and received little support from her husband. Despite this, up until the birth of her second child, she saw her relationship with Samantha as "perfect". Samantha's demanding behaviour after the birth of her brother reactivated Jennifer's feelings of failure and she and Samantha became distant from that point. Samantha began stealing (the same as one of Jennifer's 'crimes' in the orphanage), and Samantha then became the recipient of attributions of badness and greediness. Samantha's brother became the acceptable child and was seen as "naughty but charming", said in an indulgent tone. Individual therapy allowed a relationship between us in which Jennifer's experiences in childhood could be revisited and re-evaluated. As we slowly became more compassionately understanding of her emotional deprivation and understandable envy of other children, her relationship with Samantha improved. I think, the causal projective process was no longer needed by Jennifer, and the stealing stopped. Individual therapy inevitably has systemic consequences—everything does.

All psychotherapy offers a facilitating relationship with the therapist, but the choice of longer-term individual therapy allows the therapeutic relationship to develop a deep attachment not possible in family therapy. Donna Orange (1995) refers to this as the provision of "a developmental second chance". At its simplest, the process allows the patient to move gradually through from old ways of relating to self and others, to new ways, revisiting earlier points in development along the way. I have come to understand that there are always two kinds of relating *going on simultaneously* in individual psychotherapy—the old object-relationship(s) in which the therapist is perceived mostly non-consciously as if they were the same as prior experiences with caregivers, and a new relationship in which the therapist is gradually discovered as a new subject. (As discussed in the last chapter, the therapist *also* has to discover the patient's unique subjectivity, gradually but incompletely. Discovery of the other is a mutual, gradual, and error-prone process.)

Within this large choice to meet individually, there is, I think, a smaller but crucial choice, different with each patient, and varying at different times with the same patient: how much to make oneself available. I appreciate this may seem odd to my family therapy readers, so I'll elaborate. By the therapist holding back a little in immediate responsiveness, this opens a gap for not-knowing. Minds—like nature—abhor a vacuum and this not-knowing space becomes filled with the patient's expectations based on the mostly non-conscious memory of old relationships (transference). For example, with a patient who told me that the previous week I had said something that really irritated her, I would probably not move to quickly reassure her that her irritation is entirely acceptable (in other words I would not respond immediately as me) but instead I might neutrally ask her to imagine what I'm thinking and feeling about her in the light of what she has just said. Her answer, based on old relational experience, might be "I think you probably hate me now". This might be explored a little further in order that we might find the originating context (causal tendency) for that assumption: a silently withdrawing, punishing father for example. However, before too long, having given sufficient time to the search for the original relational context, I would want to respond authentically as me: something like "actually, I felt that your ability to feel irritated with me and to tell me about that shows that there is new trust in our relationship. I enjoyed your new moment of freedom". *The contrast between what the patient assumes I think and feel about her, and what I authentically think, allows the possibility of news of a difference and a small moment of change. The new subject-relationship is strengthened a little, and the old object relationship is incrementally weakened.* Along the way the patient learns more about how her mind works and adds to the co-constructed coherent narrative.

Under Freud's influence, the default position for the therapist was that of a neutral blank screen to stimulate projections. However, the invariant use of blankness and too much not-knowing can be deeply inhibiting for many patients. It can deny, or at least slow down, the discovery of the therapist as a new subject. My experience as a patient in training therapy was that a warm relationship with my analyst, far from avoiding 'negative' feelings, actually made their expression safer. Psychoanalysis, from Klein onwards, has made much of the therapist's ability to work with the patient's hate and envy (the negative transference). Much less is spoken about the capacity to safely allow and manage loving feelings which will also grow in a productive long-term therapy. Hate and envy are not pleasant to accept but at least they come with a safe distance. Love—especially its erotic dimension—is both harder to speak about and to manage by therapists, judging from the history of boundary violations in psychoanalysis and many other therapies, especially between male therapists and their female patients. (See Reimers & Treacher, 1994, pp. 36–37, for a review of the evidence of boundary violations in family therapy and Steinberg & Alpert, 2017, for a recent discussion from a psychoanalytic perspective. See also Crittenden & Landini, 2024, who describe how sexual and attachment behaviours are almost identical, and that therapists need to understand that sexual signalling can substitute for attachment when more usual routes to relational safety are closed.)

Mary

I have still not fully conveyed the co-constructive process of the developmental second chance of individual therapy. Partly this is undertaken through language, in which the therapist and patient co-construct a coherent narrative (Main, 1993): a new story in which the patient's life experiences are woven together to allow the patient to become more emotionally understandable and acceptable to himself. But a more foundational co-construction occurs at a preverbal level if the therapist is able to emotionally meet the patient. Christopher Bollas (1979) refers to this as the therapist needing to become available as a 'transformational object'. Here the therapist is a willing partner in a co-evolutionary process, with patient and therapist each adapting to the other—a dynamic that Beebe and Lachmann (2002) refer to as self-and-interactive regulation. This is in contrast to the patient having to fit into, and make the best of, what might be experienced as a rigid caregiving environment in order to make the relationship work. As said, a minimally responsive neutral therapist will certainly help evoke the patient's old relational experiences. But understanding these experiences verbally (the insight and interpretation model of change) may not be sufficient for transformation at the preverbal level, since change requires difference: something new needs to meet—and eventually, at least partially, replace—something old. Difference allows the old to stand out, to be recontextualised, and compassionately understood. Finding a meeting point between what the patient needs preverbally, and what the therapist is willing to provide, is another aspect of Benjamin's (2017) Third—not my old way, or your old way, but our new way. This was a particular feature of the work with Mary.

Mary was a single white British woman in her early thirties when I first met her. From age sixteen, for all but a year or two, she had been an inpatient in psychiatric hospitals. She had recently begun living independently, supported by a psychiatric nurse. For the previous two years she had received group and individual psychotherapy in a specialist hospital. She had a diagnosis of borderline personality disorder following multiple serious incidents of self-harm. Among the worst was the use of an electric carving knife on her arms, severing several tendons, causing permanent restrictions in the use of her hands. She had jumped from bridges causing skeletal damage and damage to her urinary system for which she needed a permanent catheter and bag to collect urine. There were dangerous overdoses with paracetamol, and more passive self-harm such as not managing her catheter well resulting in frequent infections. I was somewhat anxious about taking her on but, by then, I had worked with many teenagers who had self-harmed, and in the first meeting I liked her and there was something admirably determined about her. She had taken the initiative in contacting me and did a lot of the chasing up of NHS funding, for example.

Mary's self-harming behaviour and admission to the adolescent unit began after she had travelled to Scotland—a rare defiance of the wishes of her parents—to meet a boyfriend. She and her boyfriend had fallen out one evening and she became separated from him. She was picked up outside a nightclub by a serviceman who took her to his house and raped her. Except she didn't call it rape: her reasoning being that he was never convicted so it must be her fault. She couldn't feel the slightest hint of anger towards the serviceman. This black and white rigid thinking and cutting-off of feelings was a regular part of her self-management. More specifically, as we gradually worked out, it became in her mind the fault of her body, and particularly her arms, for failing to fight back, hence her specific rage-filled attacks on them. Finding words for anything emotionally difficult was initially extremely hard for Mary. However, after many months she did give me details of the events leading up to the incident in Scotland. It was clearly rape since she was entirely coerced and had not given consent. I told her that, even though it might annoy her, I would always think of it—and refer to it—as rape since calling it anything else was a lie for which she had to permanently blame and attack her body.

Her parents were initially idealised in her descriptions. What slowly emerged was that Mary had internalised a highly reactive and critical mother who seemed to have been overwhelmed and couldn't cope with Mary as a baby and, while supportive in practical ways, was routinely critical ever since. Mary's mother had been adopted as a child and there seems to have been much neglect in her own early life. Mary eventually told me that if she was on a bus and saw a mother threaten to hit a child she would have to get off. She didn't know why. When I said, carefully, that this made me wonder if she was hit as a child, she immediately cut off and said nothing for the remainder of the session, not in a consciously angry way, more like a psychic retreat (Steiner, 1993) where she was safe and unaffected. She called this "wiping people out". She could walk away from quite longstanding relationships with doctors or other professionals if they upset her, and they then meant nothing to her, thereafter. Several times she wiped me out but always told me about this after the event. I had to endure several mostly silent sessions followed by a week of anxiety about whether she would safely return.

Mary struggled to speak at the start of sessions. It was my usual practice to wait for patients to start, but this quickly seemed too persecutory for her, so we worked out a new response (surrendering to the Third) where I would leave a short silence but then speak before it became oppressive. (E.g. "I'm only speaking so you can hear in my voice that I'm OK with you being quiet".) Even then it would, in the first year, often take up to half a session until she could find some fluency to speak—there were many false starts. My main message to her, mostly conveyed non-verbally, was that however she was in the session was acceptable to me: she might *feel* wrong, but she couldn't actually *be* wrong. The ends of the sessions were also very difficult for her, and she would begin to go quiet about ten minutes before the ending. We worked out that she couldn't bear to be cut-off when the time ran out, so she simply stopped talking. So, a further accommodation was for me to give her a ten-minute warning of the ending. It was a year or two before she could tolerate me linking endings to memories of her mother withdrawing from her (and perhaps worse) if she protested or was demanding. Breaks from therapy were initially an issue. The first Christmas break was the worst, during which she took a serious overdose and was briefly hospitalised. She was mortified, feeling that I would not want to continue the therapy, assuming, I think, that I would be the same as the internal retaliatory and abandoning mother object in her mind.

The majority of the work consisted, I believe, not only what I did, but in what I didn't do. I didn't retaliate or abandon her as expected when she blanked me. Much of the work consisted in her having a new preverbal relational experience rather than an interpretative one. However, her capacity to think about her feelings—to mentalise (Fonagy et al., 2002)—grew alongside and supported the new pattern of self-and-interactive emotional regulation developing between us. There was initially great splitting between me—the good mother in her mind—and the community nurse whom she initially found annoying and disappointing. Surprisingly, Mary was very open to me talking about this split in terms of how she was trying to keep me good by making the nurse carry all the bad. I could often joke with her near the end of a session (in which, for example, I had encouraged her to go further to explore difficult feelings on an issue, often to do with her family) by saying "I expect 'Susan' is going to get it this week" and she would laugh in acknowledgment. Later she would sometimes say at the start of a session—"Yep—Susan got it in the neck this week!" Although I took her seriously, I found that she tolerated challenges more readily when they had a gentle teasing quality. Spontaneous warm humour played an important part in the work, not as a technique but a natural enjoyment of her, which grew over time. Gradually, as she felt safer and more able to mentalise, she risked expressing more anger and upset with her mother and with me, and the relationship with Susan was eventually allowed to become warm and highly supportive.

In the second half of her six-year therapy there were significant changes. She became employed for the first time in her life, successfully taking on a responsible role in a charity. She passed her driving test and could then drive herself to sessions, which felt a very big move into greater autonomy. She became pregnant by an old boyfriend in a brief relationship, and this became a true second-chance at a mother-baby relationship. Despite her considerable fear that she would harm the child, she became a good mother. This gave her another reason for taking better care of herself and, from then on, she attended regular medical appointments for her catheter and other health issues. She was always sensible with money and a further achievement was to buy her own home on a shared financing deal with a housing association. She contacts me each Christmas to send a card or a short video of her daughter. To the best of my knowledge, both continue to do well without any professional involvement.

In passing, for any commissioners of services who might happen to read this, the total cost of Mary's six years of weekly psychotherapy was roughly the same as a three-week stay in psychiatric hospital. Despite this, it took many months to arrange funding and, for the first year or two, there were periodic, intrusive, and destabilising requests for reports from both me and Mary *to justify the cost* which raised anxieties that the funding would cease if there was insufficient progress. Fortunately these requests ceased following the intervention of a supportive psychiatrist, and we were left to get on with it.

I have intentionally left out the pluralistic use of theory and dynamic formulation in this account in order to highlight the relational adaptations needed to meet Mary. We will return to plural use of theory in a fuller discussion of self-harm in Chap. 12.

Choices in Family Therapy

In family therapy, the relationship with each person present still matters but this is less central as the crucible of change. What is gained, instead, are the possibilities of enhancing understanding and relational change *between* those present. Many choices open up requiring, in a child and adolescent service, negotiation between therapist and parents over who initially attends. My preference for a first appointment is to invite the parent(s) and as many members of their family who are able to attend. This allows the parents to define what 'family' means to them, which will vary within and between cultures. For most white British families this is the household, but often, especially with a single-parent household, one or more grandparents also attend. One needs to be mindful of real impediments to attendance and not always assume that non-attendance is avoidant or defensive. It is, for example, generally easier for parents in professional occupations to get time-off for appointments than those in manual occupations. The loss of a day's pay may also be much more significant for the latter. The old family therapy label 'peripheral father' can judge a father who simply has fewer choices by virtue of social class. Gathering up several children as a lone parent and taking one or more buses may leave everyone exhausted and irritable before a first meeting. All such, so-called, 'external factors' are, of course, an *integral* part of the system and have causal powers.

First meetings with a larger household or family group allow the therapist to join the family (Minuchin, 1974), to emotionally meet each individual (McCluskey, 2005), and to observe patterns of interaction—the "family dance" (Minuchin & Fishman, 1981). Who is close and who is distant? Where are the alliances? Who gangs up against whom? Who is in charge? How is parental authority exercised? Who speaks over whom? Who remains silent? What are the competing narratives? What is the emotional quality of the various relational combinations? This empirical, non-verbal information is non-conscious and therefore more freely available (and sometimes more reliable in helping to map patterns) than verbal information.

There is a trade-off to be made in choosing how to continue. A larger group brings the immediacy of alternative views through direct communication and can harness untapped relational resources more directly. However, like others (e.g. Reimers & Treacher, 1994; Crittenden, 2008; Crittenden et al., 2014) I prefer to mix up who to meet rather than always continue in a large group which, as said, also makes great demands on families' time and money. I find that smaller combinations tend to create safer, boundaried spaces in which family members can speak more freely. I cannot imagine there are any teenage girls who are comfortable in speaking openly about their anxieties about sexuality in front of a younger brother, for example, or indeed many younger brothers who would want to listen! I always include sessions with parents alone, especially if the couple relationship appears troubled. A child who appears parentified (e.g. Jody, in Chap. 7), who needs to protect her parents from her anger or other 'true' affect, may only be free to speak when seen alone or in a sibling group.

There can be unintended consequences from some combinations. I generally avoid combinations of two parents and the identified patient child in order to protect the child from too much punishing negativity. In situations where there is ongoing conflict between separated parents, in which a child is triangulated (see the next chapter), I usually meet each parent separately. This avoids the risk of inadvertently reinforcing a child's symptomatic behaviour if that appears to have causal power in keeping them engaged in a passionate (albeit hate-filled) relationship. Separate meetings with separated parents allow the therapist to experience triangulating, divided-loyalty pressures as each parent pulls the therapist into their narrative. Conflict between family members and professionals, such as teachers and social workers, may be addressed by bringing professionals and parents together. I found these meetings particularly useful in working with children showing aggressive, out-of-control behaviour (Chap. 11).

Working in these various smaller combinations provides richer verbal—and more emotionally authentic—information but demands more from the therapist in holding several boundaries of confidentiality simultaneously. However, it is usually possible to negotiate things that can be shared and, quite often, this proves easier than anticipated once the issues have been spoken of, and thereby rehearsed, with the therapist. I have often found, for example, that a young person's assumption that her parents have no idea what is troubling her to be surprisingly incorrect, as in the following case.

I wrote previously about seventeen-year-old Jo and her white British single-parent household in an article about adolescent self-harm (Pocock, 2011). I met with Jo and her mother for a first session after Jo had taken an overdose and had cut her legs on several occasions. Jo's mother was concerned about her daughter but, in the first part of the session, when I saw them both together, she was baffled about the reasons for Jo's behaviour. Jo was not able to give any kind of explanation, other than she had felt bad on occasions before harming herself but didn't know why. Both agreed that I should spend some of the session having a confidential meeting with Jo alone.

In the second part of the session, having negotiated that I would not share anything with her mother unless I had Jo's permission, Jo immediately told me how angry she was with her mother. Six months previously her mother had a serious row with her own mother who lived next door. That same night, her mother moved with Jo and her younger sister to a town sixty miles away, initially staying with friends. Thereafter, her mother had become very stressed, attempting to rebuild her life without the practical support of the maternal grandmother. Jo also lost contact with her friends and had a difficult time adjusting to her new school. I asked Jo to rank, in order of intensity of feelings, the things that she was angry with her mother about. She was quite able and willing to do this. I had sensed that her mother would be robust enough to hear about some of these and I attempted to negotiate with Jo if she would be willing to risk opening up some discussion on one of the issues. She was very reluctant but agreed that I could ask her mother if she could *guess* if there was anything that Jo might be angry with her about.

For the third and final part of the session I saw them both together again. The mother immediately and accurately guessed the thing that Jo was most angry about which was the loss of her friends. There was nothing retaliatory in the mother's response when Jo confirmed that this was an accurate 'guess' and Jo was then willing for her mother to guess further. Her mother then named each of the things on Jo's list, with most of them in the correct order of intensity—losing regular contact with her maternal grandmother was ranked second. It seemed to be a relief to Jo's mother to do this and it certainly was for Jo. Her mother had long regretted her impulsive action but seems to have felt too guilty to allow herself to reflect on how her emotionally driven behaviour had really affected her children. The hypothesised causal mechanism of destructive self-regulation of anger and distress through self-harm, to protect her relationship with her mother, was then replaced by a more benign process of self-and-interactive regulation of emotion between them, once the silence between them was breached.

In the next chapter we discuss the tensions in three-person relationships. I should add here that for those with emotionally impoverished primary dyadic relationships, painful feelings of exclusion for individuals in triads seem much greater. Therefore, a useful and I think under-used systemic choice can be, as above, to work dyadically with the symptom-bearing child and the most involved parent or caregiver to strengthen that relationship. Less is sometimes more.

Summary

If we as psychotherapists are (as I believe we should be) systemic ontologists as well as systemic epistemologists, then none of the case examples mentioned above, or in this book as a whole, is more or less ontologically systemic than any other. Whole systems are impossibly complex and massive, so choices need to be made, each choice opening some possibilities for understanding and change, and closing others. What facilitates our role in positive change is how much we are able to map, understand, and influence those parts (causal powers) of the systemic territory which become available for focus through our negotiated choices. However, few choices are well-informed, and unconstrained. The therapist gets a say but, in open systems, we can never predict what will happen, so we also have to be flexible enough to make the best of where the road takes us.

References

Bateson, G. (1972). *Steps to an ecology of mind*. Balantine.

Beebe, B., & Lachmann, F. (2002). *Infant research and adult treatment: Co-constructing interactions*. The Analytic Press.

Benjamin, J. (2017). *Beyond doer and done to: Recognition theory, Intersubjectivity and the third*. Routledge.

Bhaskar, R. (2012). *The philosophy of metareality: Creativity, love, and freedom*. Routledge.

Bhaskar, R. (2016). *Enlightened common sense: The philosophy of critical realism*. Routledge.

Bollas, C. (1979). The transformational object. *International Journal of Psychoanalysis, 60*, 97–107.

Boscolo, L., & Bertrando, P. (1996). *Systemic therapy with individuals*. Routledge.

Crittenden, P. (2008). *Raising parents: Attachment representation, and treatment*. Routledge.

Crittenden, P., Dallos, R., Landini, A., & Kozlowska, K. (2014). *Attachment and family therapy*. Open University Press.

Crittenden, P., & Landini, A. (2024). Sexual signals and behaviour in children: Building hypotheses about the function of sexuality in childhood. *Human Systems, 4*, 21–49.

Fonagy, P., Gergeley, G., Jurist, E., & Target, M. (2002). *Affect regulation, mentalization, and the development of the self*. Other Press.

Kraemer, S. (1988). Letter to the editor. *Journal of Family Therapy, 10*, 412–414.

Main, M. (1993). *Attachment across the life cycle*. Routledge.

McCluskey, U. (2005). *To be met as a person: The dynamics of attachment in professional encounters*. Routledge.

Minuchin, S. (1974). *Families and family therapy*. Harvard University Press.

Minuchin, S., & Fishman, H. (1981). *Family therapy techniques*. Harvard University Press.

Orange, D. (1995). *Emotional understanding: Studies in psychoanalytic epistemology*. Guilford.

Pocock, D. (1992). Parental perceptions of sibling differences: Towards a theory of sibling differentiation. *Journal of Family Therapy, 14*, 123–144.

Pocock, D. (2011). When anger endangers relationships: Self-harm as a systemic solution. *Context, 115*, 63–66.

Reimers, S., & Treacher, A. (1994). *Introducing user-friendly family therapy*. Routledge.

Shotter, J. (1993). *Conversational realities: Constructing life through language*. Sage.

Steinberg, A., & Alpert, J. (2017). Sexual boundary violations: An agenda demanding more consideration. *Psychoanalytic Psychology, 34*, 221–225.

Steiner, J. (1993). *Psychic retreats: Pathological organizations in psychotic, neurotic and borderline patients*. Routledge.

10

Triangles

> Jefferson's hatred of Hamilton was complicated by jealousy of Washington's affection for the younger man [Hamilton]. The continuing intellectual debate over the Jeffersonian and Hamiltonian rival systems of government takes on a new and richer dimension if seen against the backdrop of the personal drama of this remarkable triangle. Fawn Browdie (*Thomas Jefferson: An Intimate History,* 1974)

Theories of three-person relationships offer a rare bridge between systemic family therapy, attachment theory, and psychoanalysis (Byng-Hall, 1995; Dallos & Vetere, 2012; Flaskas, 2012; Crittenden, 2008; Woodcock, 2009). Lynn Hoffman (1981) in *Foundations in Family Therapy* devotes no less than three chapters to the subject. However, in the wake of the linguistic turn in family therapy—itself, strongly led by Hoffman (1990)—there seems to be a danger for postmodern family therapists of such theorising becoming dusty artefacts in a museum of dubious therapist ethics.

The postmodern assumption is, as discussed, that such theories of structure are essentialist and expert-led, inevitably subjugating the local meaning-making of family members. Theories of triads tend, therefore, to be associated with so-called 'first-order family therapy'. To recap on

D. Pocock, *Expanding the Limits of Individual and Family Therapies*, Palgrave Texts in Counselling and Psychotherapy, https://doi.org/10.1007/978-3-031-76309-0_10

my earlier argument (especially Chap. 2), theories themselves can make no contribution to whether they are used in a first-order (naïve realist) manner or a second-order (critical realist) manner. A critical realist approach understands various kinds of triangular theorising as social constructions, made in knowledge communities as a result of numerous encounters (including research) with the ultimately unknowable world of clinical practice.

In Chap. 7 I tried to demonstrate how theory can be used in a fully collaborative manner if held lightly and reflexively to serve the process, rather than dominate it. In other words, if the therapist can hold onto uncertainty and a second-order appreciation of her role in the observation. In this chapter I want to underline the value of understanding triangulation for all psychotherapies and, along the way, introduce individual therapists from psychoanalytic and humanistic traditions to a much wider range of triangular formulations developed in family therapy from its origins up to the present day.

The Oedipal Myth

Freud (1975) wrote that a man who has been the indisputable favourite of his mother keeps for life the feeling of a conqueror. At first glance this looks like the characterisation of a two-person relationship but the word 'favourite' points to at least two triangular configurations standing behind the mother-son dyad. The most prominent of these for Freud was the Oedipal triangle with the main person conquered, we may reasonably assume, being Freud's father, especially as the father became progressively diminished by illness (Atwood & Stolorow, 1993). The Oedipus Complex took the place of seduction theory in Freud's mind and became central to his understanding of male sexuality and, more broadly, how instinctual drives and defence mechanisms shape personality.

Despite the prominence of Oedipal theory and its further development in Freudian and Kleinian psychoanalytic traditions, there is little evidence for its supposed universal role in shaping sexuality. (In contrast, the evidence supporting the widespread sexual abuse of children in Freud's time and ours is now vast.) I prefer the broader formulation of the psychoanalyst, Maureen Marks (2002, p. 95), who notes the stresses for *all* participants in the triangle: "The task for mother, father and infant involves tolerating the link between two people that they love and desire, which excludes them". As noted at the end of the last chapter, if any person in a triad has felt unloved in their (dyadic) primary attachment, feelings of exclusion in a triangular relationship are all the more painful.

A revision of the Oedipal Complex is found in the work of the post-Kleinian psychoanalyst Ronald Britton. An internal triangular space in the mind "provides us with a capacity for seeing ourselves in interaction with others and for entertaining another point of view whilst retaining our own" (Britton, 1989, p. 87). In individual therapy this third would include the therapist's relationship with theory. However, there is a tension between Britton's third and Benjamin's third: how much to hold onto theory and how much to surrender to something newly created between therapist and patient (Pocock, 2018). In Chap. 7, as an example of the dangers of Britton's third, I described defensively clinging to the theoretical idea of narcissistic crying, because of an enactment of my own, rather than being able to emotionally meet my tearful patient to create some new experience (Benjamin's Third). A moderate solution is that proposed by Donna Orange (1995): namely, "holding theory lightly"; or, one might add, 'lightly and self-consciously', to locate this in a second-order frame.

Perhaps the most significant legacy of the Oedipus Complex is a broader conception developed more fully in the systemic family therapy world: *that three-person relationships have within them a range of dynamics: some developmentally progressive, some stabilizing, some regressive, and some destabilizing, but all, I would argue, relevant in understanding individuals within their relational contexts.* Indeed, Jeremy Woodcock (2009, p. 29) goes so far as to describe the Oedipal myth as "a perfect bridge between the systemic and the psychoanalytic" if we can move beyond its contested role in Freud's foundational theorising on sexuality. Along similar lines, Carmel Flaskas (2012) urges a reappraisal of so-called 'first-order' theories of triads, linking them to the contemporary interest in reflection, conceptualised, as Britton (1989) does, as a triangular space.

Sibling Triads

Even though rivalry appears to be a feature of a sibling *pair* it is organised around a third—originally the primary caregiver—so is best considered triadic rather than dyadic. For Freud to be the "indisputable favourite of his mother" also implies, not just triumph over his father, but also over his siblings. He was the eldest of eight. The second-born, Julius, died in infancy and then, a year later, Anna arrived, the first of five sisters born annually, followed after a longer gap by a brother. A mutual antipathy between Freud and Anna lasted into adulthood. Freud (1933) writes:

> [The child] feels that it has been dethroned, despoiled, prejudiced in its rights; it casts a jealous hatred upon the new baby and develops a grievance against the faithless mother which often finds expression in a disagreeable change in its behaviour. (p. 123)

While the famous cases of Little Hans and the Wolf Man show the impact of siblings on development, it was Oedipal triangulation that dominated Freud's metapsychology. For his followers the sibling triad almost disappeared. A cross-referencing index of Freud's writing produced by the American Psychoanalytic Association, for example, contained no listing for 'sibling', 'brother', or 'sister' (Bank & Khan, 1980). This situation has been rectified in recent years by, among others, Prophecy Coles (2003) who helpfully puts sibling transference on the map. For example, a parental relationship may develop a rivalrous quality for one or both of the couple on the birth of a first child. A father may feel especially left out not just because of his experience of being an outsider to the intense mother-infant bond but because this reactivates painful, unresolved, unconscious experiences of feeling the less-favoured sibling in his family of origin (sibling transference). A second-order mapping of the causal tendencies of multiple interlocking triangles can be an important aspect of layered systemic formulation in individual and family therapy as we will see in the examples in this and the following two chapters.

Curiously, triads made up of a pair of siblings and one parent are less prominent in the family therapy literature than triangles of one child and two parents. This is despite the emotional intensity of rivalry in sibling triads as anyone who has been a sibling, or parent of siblings, can no doubt testify! De-identification, where each sibling finds their own niche through becoming different from the other, has always struck me as a prominent dynamic in families. This may be a factor in the surprising finding that the environment that shapes individual personalities is largely unique to each child; the environment that siblings share has little impact on personality development (Dunn & Plomin, 1991; Pocock, 1992). Summarising the extensive research on the non-shared environment, the behavioural geneticist, Sandra Scarr (1987), writes:

> [L]et us make explicit the implications of these findings: upper-middle class brothers who attend the same school and whose parents take them to the same plays, sporting events, music lessons, and therapists, and use similar child-rearing practices on them, are little more similar in personality measures than they are to working-class or farm boys, whose lives are totally different. (p. 38)

The Triangulated Child

Rather than describe each theorised triad in isolation, I plan to show the value of mapping multiple triangular tensions (as one of several layers of light theorising) through the use of case examples. But, first, a quick tour through the history of triangular theory in family therapy.

In 1960, John Weakland, one of the members of Bateson's schizophrenia research project, was the first to describe how the double-bind could be triadic. Up to that point the emphasis had been on an incongruent pair of communications from the same parent to a child (e.g. loving words said in a hostile tone). Weakland (1960) noted that two parents between them could supply the incongruent messages as well as denying the incongruency—denial and inability of the recipient to step away from the relationships being the final binding aspects. Hoffman (1981) notes that this move to the triadic heralded a major shift from communication to family structure as the matrix for symptoms.

Jay Haley (1977) identified *perverse triangles*. Two people who are on different hierarchical (e.g. generational) levels form a coalition against a third person. In families this may take the form of one parent and child in a hidden (i.e. denied) coalition against the other parent or another source of authority. Murray Bowen (1978) theorised that two-person emotional systems are always unstable and used the term *triangulation* to show how a third person enters—or is recruited—to create stability. Salvador Minuchin et al. (1978) in their book *Psychosomatic Families* identified three 'rigid triads' in their work with conflict avoidance. Along the same lines as Bowen, they called the first simply *triangulation* but defined it more specifically: "The child is put in such a position that she cannot express herself without siding with one parent against the other" (p. 33). The second was called a 'parent-child coalition', redescribed as a *cross-generational coalition* in Minuchin's later work (Minuchin & Fishman, 1981). This disrupts a clear boundary around the parental subsystem, undoing the capacity of parents to work together. For example, one parent 'enmeshed' with a child may covertly undermine the authority of the other parent who is relatively disengaged from both. We will explore this further in the next chapter.

We have already encountered the concept of 'detouring', Minuchin et al.'s (1978) third rigid triad, in my layered formulation in the case of Emma in Chapter One. In detouring, the parents submerge their conflict in either concern for their child—*detouring concern*—or in blaming (scapegoating) the symptom-bearing child, called *detouring attacking*, sometimes with shifts between the two detouring modes. John Byng-Hall (1995) described how the child can act as a *distance regulator* for his parents. Symptoms may unite the parents when there is anxiety about too much separation and divide them when there is too much feared intimacy. Ivan Boszormenyi-Nagy and Barbara Krasner (1986) described how children can be caught in *divided-loyalty conflicts,* for example in cases of separation and divorce. It was Boszormenyi-Nagy's (personal communication) view that severe situations of divided-loyalty conflict can be more damaging than the more recognised forms of child abuse.

Before moving onto case examples I need to add four caveats.

1. As an imperfect parent myself, I have probably been involved in all of these triangular arrangements from time-to-time! Disagreements between parents over how to handle a situation with their child are not in themselves problematic, even should a child experience these

directly. Such experiences may instead build confidence that differences can be resolved and allow the child to experience each parent as an individual with a mind of their own, as well as a couple. As Minuchin et al. (1978) explain, problems occur when these triangular arrangements become the main or sole means of managing conflict—hence *rigid* triads.

2. The language in which triads are described often includes terms like 'recruitment of a child' or the child 'offering themselves as a third' to help resolve conflict. I think this language of intentionality is unhelpful and generally misleading. Most parents, in my experience, are both trying to do their best and survive emotionally themselves. I think it is more helpful to speak of the *co-evolution* of triads. They emerge through non-conscious trial-and-error adaptations by all participants and become reinforced when they reduce anxiety; or at least when they exchange a lesser danger (a child being symptomatic) for a greater one (e.g. that a parent may break down or parents may separate). Understanding the development of triads in this way links them to unconscious co-evolved dyadic attachment strategies whose main purpose is to feel safer in relationships (Crittenden, 2008).
3. Locating these ideas in a critical realist frame, triads have causal powers which may or may not be actualised. A couple may manage their disagreements without recourse to triangulation until interaction with another causal power. For example, the financial and emotional disruption caused by sudden loss of employment may stress a couple which then actualises a conflict-reducing triad. Resolving the external stress (e.g. a new job) may then de-actualise the triangle which then remains as a real *potential* power but without current influence. The same is true in, the much better-known, dyadic attachment strategies, the more extreme forms of which (higher numbered C and A strategies in the DMM) may only come into play when family members are under high stress (Crittenden, 2008).
4. Finally, the constant reminder that all theories are socially constructed and therefore fallible maps of the territory in the mind of the therapist, not solely the territory itself. Experience—in this case of triangles—is made up of what is there, external to us, *and* what we make of it internally: the given and the made (Orange, 1995).

Triangulation in Practice

I once reviewed the thirty most intractable cases I had worked with in the child and family guidance service and 'found' a high proportion of situations in which the child's primary attachment seemed to be with a caregiver (alive or deceased) no longer living in the child's household. The lost parent can be frozen into an internal idealised image protected from reality and the possibility of mourning. Against this image, the real new caregiver falls short and the child's wish for a new attachment can create an irresolvable *divided-loyalty conflict*. Adoption life-story books showing happy smiling birth parents, while well-meaning, can inadvertently reinforce the problem, as can any enforced denigration of the birth parent. Frozen idealisation, whether conscious or non-conscious, may help to shed light on Crittenden and Spiker's (2023) sobering review of a century of research on evidence of harm to children being separated from their parents into foster care and adoption. In around 250 studies separation was found to be unequivocally harmful with not a single study reporting positive effects. The following case shows the complexity of triadic formations and incomplete mourning in both the adoptive mother and daughter. I have noted the hypothesised triads in brackets in order not to interrupt the flow.

Yvonne

I met with Yvonne, a white British adopted child, aged thirteen, together with her white British parents, Bethany and Mike. Yvonnes's relationship with Mike had always been closer since there seemed to be a situation-vacant for a father that he could occupy. This sense of exclusion from the apparent closeness of Yvonne and Mike was painful for Bethany and seemed to make Yvonne a rival in her relationship with her husband (*triangulation*). Mike found himself increasingly taking Yvonne's side against Bethany (*perverse triangle/cross-generational coalition*) as he experienced his wife as too punitive. This had led to many destructive rows which threatened the marriage, and in recent months Mike had increasingly allied with his wife against Yvonne. This stabilised the couple (*detouring-attacking*) but Mike's withdrawal from Yvonne led to an escalation of rows with Yvonne which became her only point of intense connection with her parents. Yvonne's increasing non-compliance led to threats that she would have to leave the family to return into care, hence the referral.

Bethany and Mike had never seen Yvonne cry and they described her as "very hard" emotionally, complaining rather harshly to me, in the presence of Yvonne, that she had "not even shed a tear" over the death of her birth mother four year previously. This brought the loss into the room. Yvonne then began to talk about the death of her birth mother and shared that whenever she allowed herself to be close to her adoptive parents she felt she was letting her birth mother down (*divided-loyalty conflict*). At that point Yvonne began to cry, and Bethany leapt out of her chair and across the room wrapping her arms around Yvonne who then stopped crying. I felt confused and uneasy about what had just happened, sensing that the grieving was being smothered rather than emotionally supported.

Bethany had initially told me that her own childhood was "fantastic" but what emerged was that her mother had left the family when Bethany was (*also*) thirteen. She had become a carer for her younger siblings and continued her caregiving role into fostering, with adoption being a natural extension. In a later session with the Bethany alone, it emerged that seeing Yvonne cry reminded her of seeing her father in tears when her mother left the family. Bethany's grief seemed to have been adaptively set aside to ensure the survival of the remaining family. She seemed to desperately wish to be the good mother to Yvonne that both of them had lost. Neither had been able to mourn the disappointing loss of their mothers, who seemed to remain idealised; all negativity being relocated into their relationship with each other. Grief for lost mothers, rather than behaviour, became an agreed new focus for the work and provided a theme that both mother and daughter could share.

Misha

As said, triangles can be developmentally progressive in facilitating individuation and the working-through of rivalry and fear of exclusion. However, this can get derailed. I have written previously (Pocock, 2009) about Misha, aged thirteen, the only child of Black-Caribbean British parents. She feared getting an illness that might make her vomit and compulsively cleaned kitchen surfaces and utensils with a bacterial spray. She was especially worried about school assembly in case she caught cold or flu viruses and had begun to try to avoid school. She often drew her mother into her sterilising rituals, but this hadn't helped to reduce them.

Her parents had separated when Misha was six and she saw her father rarely and "only when he wanted". He would turn up at the door every couple of years and demand to see her. Misha and her mother joked, nervously, that he was not a man who would easily take 'no' for an answer. It soon emerged that Misha's mother was terrified of him since, although not physically violent, he had "put me down" throughout their relationship. She lived in fear of him returning although she hadn't talked about that openly with Misha. The mother said that she felt denigrated throughout her life and that her parents had not allowed her to stand up for herself. There seemed to be a generalised anxiety about what might happen if she ever stood up to anyone.

Misha herself seemed quite unconcerned about seeing her father but had no answer to the question of whether she wanted to see him or not. The idea of her having any choice in the matter seemed unthinkable. She seemed quite emotionless on the subject, but that was possibly the result of a *divided-loyalty conflict* as it might have been difficult for her to reveal positive feelings about her father in the presence of her mother.

I had recently read Deborah Luepnitz's (2009) work with dreams in couples' therapy. Luepnitz had found this a helpful approach, since emotion that does not reach consciousness seems often to be processed through dreams. So I asked Misha whether she dreamed, and she rather dismissively told me about recurring dreams of Viking raids. In some of these dreams everyone was killed apart from her. While the imagery was terrifying, the dreams, for Misha, did not include fear, in contrast to her deep fear of viruses. I pointed out that the Vikings were a frightening force that unpredictably invaded every couple of years. This was a force that no one could stand up to, just like how she and her mother had described her father. I asked her if she ever feared her father would take her away from her mother against her will. She confirmed that she did fear this which seemed to me a small breakthrough in understanding.

However, I was rather taken aback when she then told me that my idea of a connection between the dreams and her father was simply wrong. She wasn't obviously angry—just very clear on the matter!

I met with them both over several sessions and Misha continued to deny any link with her father if I tentatively suggested one. For example, the first time she feared she would be sick was when both mother and daughter were in the car with their father who was angry about something and drove very fast, refusing to heed the desperate pleas from them both that he should slow down. I liked Misha and noticed how much she seemed to enjoy disagreeing with me and how I enjoyed her entitlement to do so. Misha's symptoms improved during the therapy because, as she said, "I decided to change them myself". Misha's mother agreed to be referred for individual counselling to help with her fear of standing up for herself. This was also a problem for her at work where she was experiencing some bullying.

As usual, it isn't possible to know why Misha was able to change; other hidden factors in an open system are always in play, but these are my unprovable speculations. The triangle of her and her parents had become unavailable to support her developmental progression into safe relational autonomy. This was not just because of the separation, but also she had become enmeshed with her mother's deep anxiety about her father. (Misha's mother had little emotional support from anyone other than her daughter.) It felt to me that Misha's unconscious solution was to attempt to take omnipotent control over this threatening aspect of their world, split off and represented as viruses. Ritualised cleaning was an attempt at mastering the threat while keeping her father out of mind. She had enjoyed the freedom to (ostensibly) refuse to accept my linking of her symptoms to her father and instead pursued her own solution. It may be that this new experience of successfully standing up to me, as a stand-in for her father in our temporary therapeutic triangle, had helped to modify the feared disaster (Bentovim & Kinston, 1991), shared by her and her mother, of standing up to her father. The prospect of new adult support for her mother through individual counselling may also have helped to de-actualise Misha's parentified role.

Conny

After several years working as a child and adolescent family therapist I began to notice a three-generational triangular pattern that I have not previously seen described in the literature. The involvement of loving grandparents or other close family members can enrich the lives of everyone, but what happens if a grandmother becomes the primary attachment figure for a grandchild, even though the child lives with her birth parents?

Chloë Madanes (1980) describes the disturbing nature of 'incongruous hierarchies', one form of which is where a person has both hierarchically less power than another but, through a simultaneous hidden coalition with someone even further up the hierarchy, has more or equal power. For example, an employee who is unhappy with his immediate boss but goes out drinking with a senior manager and complains to her. Layering Madanes' theory with Bowlby's (1988) distinction between primary and secondary attachments together with Minuchin/Haley theories of cross-generational coalitions/perverse triads allows the construction of a composite model that can, I think, help explain the causal power. *A girl who is more securely attached to her grandmother than to her mother is a biological daughter of her mother but simultaneously a psychological younger sister in rivalry with her (big sister) mother over the grandmother.* It is, of course, well established that men can be primary caregivers, but I have intentionally used the example of females, first, because in most cultures women are still more likely than men to actually be primary caregivers and, second, because the rivalry seems more intense when the child is the same gender as the mother. (However, in the next chapter I describe this triad in relation to a boy.)

Let me give a specific example of how the underlying causal tendency may become actualised. Suppose that the granddaughter in this triad does exceptionally well in a school exam and excitedly rushes home to tell her mother. But let's assume the mother had not done well at school and/or had received little praise from her mother. Will the mother be able to enjoy her daughter's success, or envy it, or both? I now call these configurations in their most tricky form *mother/sister—daughter/sister triads*. The grandmother is intentionally not included in the term in order to represent the hidden nature of the 'sibling rivalry' around her.

Conny was a training patient in twice-weekly psychotherapy with me. This formed part of her psychoanalytic training. She was the only child of white parents living in Germany where she remained until her late teens. In the year before starting therapy her mother had died. Conny had sat alone with her in the hospital for many agonising days awaiting her death, often holding her hand to comfort her. Conny's father couldn't bear to visit his wife and soon after her death had begun a new relationship which understandably infuriated Conny, not least because of the disloyalty to her mother. He had thoughtlessly sold some of Conny's treasured childhood possessions and bought gifts for his new partner. Her sense of her father's betrayal of her mother and her painful exclusion in the triangle of her, her father, and father's new partner had led Conny to consider cutting him out of her life.

Shortly after Conny was born her mother returned to work and Conny was cared for by her maternal grandmother who, together with her chronically sick maternal grandfather, lived nearby. It was never entirely clear why this decision was made but it seems likely that Conny's mother was depressed and overwhelmed by the responsibility of a baby and was eager to return to her old life. It later emerged that Conny's mother had also spent lengthy and happy periods cared for by *her* grandmother suggesting this causal tendency was something of a family script on the maternal side (Byng-Hall, 1995). Conny's entry into her grandmother's life seems to have been a source of great joy to the grandmother, bringing relief from the difficult relationship with her sick and frequently aggressive husband (*triangulation*). More speculatively, the relationship with Conny may have helped provide her with a second chance at a maternal role which had been compromised for various reasons with her own daughter.

Conny had vivid memories of every aspect of her grandmother's house and could describe it in detail. In contrast she had almost no memory of her parents' home, as if her senses were awakened, and she was only truly present with her grandmother. She resisted being returned to her mother and father when they came to collect her, but soon realised that this upset her mother. She learned to conceal her reluctance through passive forms of resistance such as pretending to be asleep so that waking her up to bring her home seemed unreasonable and unnecessary. Her grandmother was also sensitive to how her daughter might feel excluded, and encouraged Conny to ensure she spent time with her parents. I think this lack of *overt* rivalry between the grandmother and her daughter helped to mitigate the stress in this mother/sister–daughter/sister triad. Nevertheless, it was impactful, confusing, and in some ways developmentally inhibiting for Conny as we will come to shortly.

Conny felt that the only reason that her parents got married was because of the pregnancy. They seemed very different, with her father being larger than life, quick to argue and, in her view at the start of therapy, very selfish. Her mother was much less self-assured, suggested by her preoccupation with her appearance. She always had to have perfect hair, make-up, and immaculate nails.

The strain of the three-generational triangle on the maternal side seems to have been experienced most strongly in Conny's relationship with her mother, rather than between her mother and grandmother (or at least there seemed to be no conscious memory of the latter). Conny felt pressure to look and behave like her mother (we assumed, to try to strengthen their sense of connection). Her bitten nails and lack of enthusiasm for a girly appearance were a source of continuous regret to her mother and there was always some level of pressure on Conny to conform to her mother's ideal. There were trips for the two of them to a local café, which Conny valued, but they came with an expectation that they should be "two well-behaved ladies taking tea".

Conny's intelligence, and eagerness to please her teachers, made her a good pupil but Conny's mother's seeming lack of interest in her daughter's progress and school successes (because, as we came to realise, of the hidden sibling rivalry between them) was confusing and hurtful to Conny. This contrasted to the great enthusiasm from her grandmother to even the smallest of Conny's successes, reinforcing the triangle. Another solution to strengthen their togetherness, proposed by Conny's mother, was that they should learn English together, but this motivation was lost when Conny progressed rapidly.

As we will discuss in the next chapter, limit-setting for caregivers who are anxious about how much their child loves them is often compromised and this may have been a factor in Conny's mother quickly giving in when faced with Conny's fury and upset. A place in preschool and much-needed dental treatment were soon abandoned in the face of her tantrums. The former make it harder for Conny to manage peer relationships at school (hence the need to please and get close to teachers), the latter resulted in life-long dental issues.

Conny was terrified that her parents would have another baby—something they occasionally talked about. Her great fear was not in relation to her parents, but solely that she would then have to share her grandmother. She anxiously confessed in therapy that she used to make secret stick drawings of babies being stabbed: something that seemed understandable, indeed creative, given her precarious attachments and the absence of opportunity to adjust within a real sibling triad.

Conny's power in the triangle made her determined and assertive—qualities that were much needed later as we will see. As she matured into adolescence, this brought her into increasing conflict with her father. She felt her mother did not stand up to her father, so this seemed to become Conny's role, with her mother attempting to be the peacemaker. This second form of triangulation was a strong feature well into her late teens.

Parental conflict reached its most intense point on the father's discovery of an affair between her mother and a work colleague. Conny had vivid memories of her mother fleeing down the stairs with Conny in her mother's arms and her father hurling an alarm clock at them. Conny was later to learn that this was not her mother's first affair: a sign of considerable unhappiness between Conny's parents and a further form of triangulation.

As adolescence progressed Conny became more distant from her parents, easily deceiving them to travel to various cities with a friend to follow her favourite band. She began to secretly save money and hatched a plan to permanently leave for the UK. Matters came to a head when she was nineteen over an expensive telephone bill caused by Conny's many secret phone calls. In the course of a serious row she decided to leave immediately. Her parents strongly joined together (*detouring-attacking*) to oppose her leaving. Conny concluded from this that she was entirely unwanted by them. Later she could see that they were frightened and desperate not to lose her, but they could not reveal this. Instead there were threats that she would never be allowed to return if she left. They insisted that she pay the phone bill in full and could not use their luggage, so she had to take her possessions in plastic bags.

Conny then moved straight to the UK to stay with a friend in London. This was a vulnerable and often lonely period for her, but she was determined and resourceful. She soon found employment and began to establish a new life for herself. Her greatest regret and a source of (unreasonable) guilt was that her maternal grandmother, with whom she remained in contact, died from a long-standing medical condition a few months after Conny leaving.

Conny's adult relationships included several affairs with married men in which she seemed to need to triumph over another woman. She could, chameleon-like, adapt herself to be just what the man desired. However, before entering therapy, she had found a long-term partner, whom she eventually married, and this proved to be a successful, mutually supportive relationship.

Conny was a full collaborator in the psychotherapy, and we were able to form a strong and therapeutically productive relationship. Triadic forms of transference became available to work on in a number of ways. On one occasion Conny was passing my front door in her car, after a session, and had waved to me. I was engaged in a friendly conversation with a delivery-man and only belatedly noticed her wave. This was very painful for her. Later in the therapy she would occasionally message me to say that she was caught up in something enjoyable and would prefer to cancel the session. This seemed to revisit the requirement to comply with leaving her lovely grandmother to return to her parents, with me, in the transferential triangle, being the less desirable option. This also activated a real triadic tension in the present since, alongside my therapy agreement with her, I was simultaneously contracted with her training organisation to provide regular sessions. We worked through this, and she later explained that what seemed to help was me not being disappointed in her occasionally preferring to choose to be elsewhere, while at the same time being clear that we needed to honour the commitment to the training requirements. Significantly, there were no such cancellations in the year of therapy preceding her training or after completion of the course requirements: the relationship in those periods being dyadic.

Conny came to see that everyone in her childhood was so caught up in the various triangular dynamics that no one could see the bigger picture. Everyone was doing their best but simply reacting to the situation they were in, with little ability or opportunity to reflect. One major regret was she had no time to use her enlarged understanding to talk with her mother before her death. Nevertheless, their final days in hospital leading up to her death, with no third person to manage, were very meaningful to Conny. Although her mother could no longer speak, their closeness could be conveyed by Conny's constant presence and through their touching and squeezing of hands.

She became fully reconciled with her father before he died and, movingly, each was then able to say to the other how much their relationship had meant even though their love could never previously be openly declared. This put her in touch with all the times her father had stood up for her against anyone outside of the family—"Dad always had my back". She came to feel her relationship with him had been ultimately strengthening for her, since he too was a determined survivor of difficult childhood experiences.

* * *

There is a reason why theories of triangulation are common across systemic family therapy, attachment, and psychoanalysis. Namely, triangles have very significant causal powers. Destructive triangular adaptations can temporarily reduce tension but at the cost of moving individuals and families into developmental blind alleys in which one, or all, eventually suffer. Collaboratively mapping triangles and working towards detriangulation can provide a helpful direction for therapy. We continue to explore this in the next chapter.

References

Atwood, G., & Stolorow, R. (1993). *Faces in a cloud: Intersubjectivity in personality theory*. Aronson.

Bank, S, & Kahn, M. (1980). Freudian siblings. *Psychoanalytic Review, 67*, 493–504.

Bentovim, A., & Kinston, W. (1991). Focal family therapy: Joining systems theory with psychodynamic understanding. In A. Gurman & D. Kniskern (Eds.), *Handbook of family therapy, volume II* (pp. 284–324). Brunner/Mazel.

Boszormenyi-Nagy, I., & Krasner, B. (1986). *Between give and take: A clinical guide to contextual therapy: Conversations in theory and practice*. Basic Books.

Bowen, M. (1978). *Family therapy in clinical practice*. Jason Aronson.

Bowlby, J. (1988). *A secure base: Parent child attachment and healthy human development*. Basic Books.

Britton, R. (1989). The missing link; Parental sexuality in the Oedipus complex. In R. Britton, M. Feldman, & E. O'Shaughnessy (Eds.), *The Oedipus complex today: Clinical implications* (pp. 83–101). Karnac.

Byng-Hall, J. (1995). *Rewriting family scripts: Improvisation and systems change*. Guilford.

Coles, P. (2003). *The importance of sibling relationships in psychoanalysis*. Routledge.

Crittenden, P. (2008). *Raising parents: Attachment representation, and treatment*. Routledge.

Crittenden, P., & Spieker, S. (2023). The effects of separation from parents on children. In K. Cameron (Ed.), *Child abuse and neglect—Perspectives and research*. IntechOpen.

Dallos, R., & Vetere, A. (2012). Systems theory, family attachments and processes of triangulation: Does the concept of triangulation offer a useful bridge? *Journal of Family Therapy, 34*, 117–137.

Dunn, J., & Plomin, R. (1991). Why are siblings so different? The significance of differences in sibling experiences within the family. *Family Process, 30*, 271–283.

Flaskas, C. (2012). The space of reflection: Thirdness and triadic relationships in family therapy. *Journal of Family Therapy, 34*, 138–156.

Freud, S. (1933). Femininity. In *The standard edition of the complete psychological works of Sigmund Freud* (Vol. 22). Hogarth Press.

Freud, S. (1975). *The letters of Sigmund Freud*. Basic Books.

Haley, J. (1977). Toward a theory of pathological systems. In P. Watzlawick & J. Weakland (Eds.), *The interactional view* (pp. 31–48). Norton.

Hoffman, L. (1981). *Foundations of family therapy: A conceptual framework for systems change*. Basic Books.

Hoffman, L. (1990). Constructing realities: An art of lenses. *Family Process, 29*, 1–12.

Luepnitz, D. (2009). Interpreting dreams in psychotherapy with couples: Moving between the upper and lower worlds. In C. Flaskas & D. Pocock (Eds.), *Systems and psychoanalysis: Contemporary integrations in family therapy* (pp. 57–72). Karnac.

Madanes, C. (1980). Protection, paradox, and pretending. *Family Process, 19,* 73–85.

Marks, M. (2002). Letting fathers in. In J. Trowell & A. Etchegoyen (Eds.), *The importance of fathers: A psychoanalytic re-evaluation* (pp. 93–106). Brunner Routledge.

Minuchin, S., & Fishman, H. (1981). *Family therapy techniques.* Harvard University Press.

Minuchin, S., Rosman, B., & Baker, L. (1978). *Psychosomatic families: Anorexia nervosa in context.* Harvard.

Orange, D. (1995). *Emotional understanding: Studies in psychoanalytic epistemology.* Guilford.

Pocock, D. (1992). Parental perceptions of sibling differences: Towards a theory of sibling differentiation. *Journal of Family Therapy, 14,* 123–144.

Pocock, D. (2009). Working with emotional systems: Four new maps. In C. Flaskas & D. Pocock (Eds.), *Systems and psychoanalysis: Contemporary integrations in family therapy* (pp. 93–109). Karnac.

Pocock, D. (2018). You, me, and us. In S. Lord (Ed.), *Moments of meeting in psychotherapy* (pp. 199–208). Routledge.

Scarr, S. (1987). Distinctive environments depend on genotypes. *Behavioural and Brain Sciences, 10,* 38–39.

Weakland, J. (1960). The double bind hypothesis of schizophrenia and three-party interaction. In D. Jackson (Ed.), *The etiology of schizophrenia.* Basic Books.

Woodcock, J. (2009). Love and hate and the oedipal myth: The perfect bridge between the systemic and the psychoanalytic. In C. Flaskas & D. Pocock (Eds.), *Systems and psychoanalysis: Contemporary integrations in family therapy* (pp. 129–146). Karnac.

11

Aggressive, Out-of-Control Behaviour

> If you have never been hated by your child, you have never been a parent.
> Bette Davis.

In this, and the next chapter, the focus turns to the presenting problems of aggression against others and against the self which, through a combination of chance and choice, I have worked with a good deal. Through these challenging clinical themes I hope to draw together the elements we have covered so far in the book. In particular, to convey how theoretical pluralism—the layering of maps—within a critical realist frame can help guide the therapist in a collaborative second-order therapeutic approach.

Working with violence and aggressive non-compliance has been something of a constant in my professional life. As a probation officer I worked with violent offenders, including murderers in prison and on after-care licence. In the child and adolescent service I worked with a large number of children and adolescents and their families referred for 'conduct' problems. And, for two years prior to retiring from the NHS, I was employed in a specialist family assessment and safeguarding service working with high-risk child protection cases.

D. Pocock, *Expanding the Limits of Individual and Family Therapies*, Palgrave Texts in Counselling and Psychotherapy, https://doi.org/10.1007/978-3-031-76309-0_11

Human aggression is never far away. Each news bulletin brings graphic details of the latest wars, shootings, and stabbings. For entertainment we have massively popular TV series such as *The Sopranos*, *Breaking Bad*, and *Game of Thrones*, alongside a vast array of shoot-'em-up video games. We have learned to live with the threat of mutually assured destruction by atomic weaponry. Violence and aggression seem entirely woven into the human condition. David Buss and Todd Shackleford (1997) take an evolutionary perspective, arguing that aggression represents a "context-sensitive solution" to various adaptive problems of social living: defending against attack, co-opting the resources of others, negotiating status and power hierarchies, inflicting costs on same-sex rivals, and so on. They outline the "evolutionary logic" of why men are cross-culturally more violent than women within these contexts.

I don't recall much from my years in the probation service, but one event stands out. A colleague and I—to help escape the daily tedium of 'casework' with reluctant clients—organised a disco (this was the early 1980s when disco was still at its height) on one of the poorer estates. This was officially justified by some reductive reasoning that absence of enjoyable activities was a direct cause of youth offending. It was quite a lame affair until late into the evening when an ultra-tough group of our probation clients and their mates turned up. Every eye in the room turned admiringly towards them (or so it seemed to us). Boys and young men who were low down on the ladders of education and social advantage by conventional measures and were awkward and sullen in their weekly reporting to us were young gods in that setting. In school, a willingness to fight and a propensity to bully is a significant form of social capital and power, eclipsed only when higher education allows the rise of the nerds—a running theme in the hugely popular (and relatable!) US comedy TV series *The Big Bang Theory*.

Aggression has its uses. Indeed the capacity to *feel* anger (as opposed to enacting violence) seems to strengthen the self. Harnessed constructively, aggression allows people to stand up for themselves and others, to recognise and counter injustice, and demand respect. In *A Letter to My Daughter*, Maya Angelou (2008) writes:

> I am never proud to participate in violence, yet I know that each of us must care enough for ourselves that we can be ready and able to come to our own defence when and whenever needed. (p. 47)

Understanding Enacted and Mentalised Aggression

As we will see in the remainder of this chapter and the next, facilitating growth in capacity to think about feelings of aggression (mentalise) rather than enacting violence through attacks on others or attacks to the body is, I argue, a key aspect of therapeutic work. But how are we to understand the developmental fork in the road at which aggression tends either to be enacted through violence or contained and mentalised to strengthen the self?

I will shortly outline the theory lenses which I have found useful in mapping the causal tendencies but, first, a caveat. As mentioned, my work has been with a predominantly white British population which includes a range of parenting approaches now very familiar to me. All the families described in this chapter are white British. While many similarities in parenting are found across cultures, largely because they are universally adaptive to child and adolescent development, I am less qualified to write about wider cultural differences in parenting and further variations *within* other cultures. Nevertheless, I recognise that cultural and social contexts are always influential causal powers. Isabel Wilkerson (2010), for example, describing the Black American experience in 1930s Florida writes:

> [P]arents, forced to train their children in the ways of subservience, treated their children in the way that white people running things treated them. It was preparation for the lower-caste role children were expected to have mastered by puberty. (p. 50)

Keep in mind, however, the limiting assumption of intracultural homogeny in cultures—there is, for example, no single British way of raising children. I recommend a recent review of research on cross-cultural similarities and differences in parenting by Jennifer Lansford (2022).

As ever, a reminder that the following theories are fallible, socially constructed maps of the territory—not the territory itself.

Let us first return to Crittenden's Dynamic Maturational Model of Attachment and Adaptation (Crittenden, 2008; Crittenden et al., 2014). The DMM is built upon the idea that there are two basic transformations of sensory stimulation—cognition and affect. *Cognition* is defined in the DMM as arising from consistency of outcome. An event followed by a desirable outcome is repeated; an event followed by an undesirable outcome is not repeated. This is straightforward social learning theory. Cognition is, therefore, information transformed on the basis of temporal order. An infant who discovers that caregivers consistently reject her when she cries or is angry soon feels safer when she inhibits this affect. This is the A (avoidant) strategy.

Affect is information based on emotional arousal (especially anxiety) in the face of perceived threat. If an infant experiencing danger is reliably and predictably attended to by the caregiver *and* that attention is emotionally attuned such that the infant feels safe and comforted, then this combination of temporal reliability and affective attunement will favour the continued use of the B (secure) strategy. This uses a balance of cognitive *and* affective information. With the exception of societies in the midst of extreme social or economic turmoil, around 50–70% of children worldwide are classified as securely attached (Strand et al., 2019).

But now let us look at a situation where the parenting is unpredictable and the cognitive information can, therefore, no longer be relied on for the child to feel safe. *Under these circumstances the infant may come to rely on the intensity of affect (crying, raging) to activate parental responsiveness.* For example, a child may respond to even a minor separation with a high level of distress as if it was a catastrophic abandonment. This gives the infant a measure of safe control over what might otherwise be unpredictable parental responsiveness. This is the C (ambivalent) strategy. Older children may split off anxiety from aggression, alternating displays of coy helpless behaviour (C4 on the DMM) with aggressive-coercive behaviour (C3). With maturity to adolescence, higher C strategies (punitive C5 and seductive C6) become available, seen for example in bullies and their victims. In the lower strategies cognition is omitted but becomes increasingly distorted in the rising C strategies. This takes the form of the individual blaming others and dismissing every viewpoint but their own. Instead, either exaggerated anger or distress is used coercively in order to feel safe.

To summarise the C strategies: in the absence of parental consistency, cognition as a source of information is ignored or progressively distorted into blame of others. Instead, *some measure of safety is achieved by intensifying or falsifying affect to activate the caregiver who attends through guilt or exasperation.*

Triangulation and the 'Soft/Hard Split'

In her recent article on what she refers to as the 'soft/hard split' in parenting, Jenny Brown (2023) reviews the extensive evidence on the effect of particular parenting styles on children's well-being. She concludes:

> There is consistent agreement that *an authoritative style, which balances warm connection and firm limits, is optimal*; and harsh or dismissive parenting is most detrimental to children's development of healthy functioning. (p. 226 [My emphasis])

Leaving the technical term 'authoritative' to one side for the moment, it is worth reflecting that there seems to be no *single* common-or-garden word that encapsulates the balance of warmth *and* firmness in parenting. (I use the term 'firmness' to stand for an ideal of calm, clear, age-appropriate messaging, consistent limit-setting, and a willingness to enforce those limits without resorting to harsh punishments driven by anger.) As far as I have been able to establish, only the Japanese word *shitsuke* comes close and that has a variety of meanings. We tend to have single words for what is known in philosophy as 'natural kinds'—things that occur regularly and reliably in the world—dogs, houses, anger, kindness, etc. Language, as discussed in Chap. 2, helps to carry culture, and my tentative conclusion is that combining warmth and firmness is not a given, but something that has to be worked at, which can easily split apart under stress. Curiously, therefore, language / culture, on the whole, seems to offer no easy support for integration of warmth and firmness.

There is a link here to be made here with Klein's (1946) 'paranoid-schizoid position'. In the infant, love and hate are first separated followed, with the help of an emotionally containing caregiver, by integration to the more developmentally mature 'depressive position'. Here the parent can be related to with concern as a separate person. Under stress, the theory goes, the individual may revert to the paranoid-schizoid split. Integration is precarious—not a life-long achievement.

Wherever there is violence, the soft/hard split seems to be implicated. Rory Stewart was one of the most liberal UK Prisons' Ministers of recent years. In *Politics on the Edge* (Stewart, 2023) he describes his attempt to reduce the appalling levels of violence in prisons, encountering the same strong split between those prison governors who insisted that love and understanding was the answer and those who wanted ever more punitive sanctions. He called his approach 'loving-strict' and pledged to resign if his methods were not measurably successful. In nine months, despite only a limited increase in budget, there was a marked reduction in violence.

> We had focussed on making life better for prisoners, but we had also set more demanding standards of behaviour. We had held opposing [loving and strict] principles in tension. (p. 306)

In my work with children and adolescents who were referred for aggressive, out-of-control behaviour, I 'found' that *at least one split between indulgence and firmness was always present between—or within—those caring for the child.* Commonly, this came between two parents in the form of a cross-generational coalition / perverse triad. Each parent typically calibrates their response to the child to compensate for their perception of the other parent's 'error' in being too hard or too soft.

Elisabeth Depeursinge and Nicolas Favez (2006) show how infants as young as twelve weeks have the ability to relate triadically, alternating their gaze and whole range of affect signals between parents. In optimal conditions the infant then sees herself reflected in their responses. Under stress—for example, if the father is intrusive—the infant will turn to the mother to register her distress. There is then a variety of outcomes depending on the qualities of the parental alliance.

> [T]he mother may find ways to support the infant by validating her signal without interfering with the father nor withdrawing. This attitude is part of a functional family alliance in which coparenting is cooperative. In this context, the infant experiences empathic support and learns to handle the father's intrusion by herself. Thus, the infant's triangular capacities are mostly recruited in the service of her own development despite the limitations imposed by the intrusion-avoidance dyadic pattern. But the mother may fail to validate the infant's signal and exclude herself from the threesome. By the same token, the mother excludes the infant, who thus experiences rejection by both parents, or she may engage with the baby and thus interfere with the father. The infant is not rejected but will learn to align with mother against father. (Fivaz-Depeursinge & Favez, 2006)

In the latter case, chronic differences between the parents may provide a grounding pathway for other unresolved tensions between a couple. Over time, this over-compensating complementarity (Minuchin, 1974) can intensify, driving the parents apart until a crisis point is reached when the parents may either separate or join together against the child (detouring attacking) to protect their relationship, as described in the case of Yvonne in the last chapter.

There may be complex causal tendencies underpinning the separate positions for each parent. A separated father, anxious about losing contact with his child, may try to be an indulgent fun dad, avoiding ordinary limit setting. This seemed to be the case with a father and ten-year-old son who stayed up until the early-hours watching horror movies that the child's mother would never have approved. Taken further, indulgence by the non-resident parent can be used to attack and undermine the resident parent whose ordinary limits then become positioned in the child's eyes as mean and hateful. This kind of undermining was 'seen' in the cases most likely to reach our service. A stepfather may try to take over control when he sees a child 'disrespecting' his new partner. Underpinning this may be a causal tendency to rivalry with the birth father (identifying a boy with his father) and/or jealousy about the closeness of the children with their mother. A boy who has lost contact with a violent father may compensate for not being with him by being like him (non-conscious identification) creating a perverse triangle, even though the father is no longer on the scene (Goldner et al., 1990).

The soft/hard split may also occur *within* a caregiver. A parent who has experienced a lack of love and / or harsh parenting in childhood may over-compensate in order that the child never feels deprived as he did. John Byng-Hall (1995) refers to this as a 'corrective script'. However, the old (replicative) script remains unactualised in the memory of the parent. Under stress there can be a sudden reversal and the old script emerges. One mother I worked with, a child-care professional, was opposed to the idea of any kind of consistent sanctions for limit-setting which she perceived as "punishments". Instead she relied solely on persuasion and reasoning, up until the point when she "lost it" and would scream at her children as she herself had been screamed at. She would then collapse into apologies and self-loathing and try once again to get on the side of her increasingly non-compliant children.

Splits between the authority of parents and school are also very common in children enacting aggression at school. Cognitive distortion of the C (ambivalent attachment) strategies can lead the child to continuously blame others—peers and / or teachers—so convincingly that a parent or parents may side with the child against the school. Such scenarios in the present can reactivate memories for parents of perceived unfairness in their school life, providing an unconscious opportunity to re-fight old battles with school authority. Parents and child can lower tensions at home by a detouring-attacking triangulation of the school. In such cases, I always included joint meetings of parents with school staff to try to establish the facts around aggressive incidents (as far as that is possible) and to build a new working adult coalition.

The Experience of the Triangulated Child

Many family therapists are familiar with external relational descriptions of triangulation but what might be the internal, subjective experience of the child caught in a soft/hard split? Contemporary psychoanalytic views have moved beyond Freud's (1957) concept of primary narcissism to locate infant development within an intersubjective relationship with the caregiver(s). However, while intersubjectivity implies mutual influence, it is not symmetrical influence. A sensitive caregiver relates to her baby as an independent subject long before the infant has the capacity to see others or himself as having minds and subjectivities of their own. Infants are born with a remarkable range of abilities to relate and adapt to their caregivers (Beebe & Lachmann, 2002) but do not see themselves as separate beings until approximately eighteen months and their minds as separate until around age four. Transitional forms of object-relating predominate in the interim (Auerbach & Blatt, 2001).

Returning to the work of the feminist and relational psychoanalyst, Jessica Benjamin (1999), discussed in Chap. 6, the infant is seen as initially having an illusory sense of omnipotent control of the mother (or other primary caregiver). Ordinary psychologically healthy development allows a gradual breakdown of the omnipotent illusion as the mother stands firm (without collapsing or retaliating) in the face of aggression. As the illusion is destroyed in the mind of the infant it becomes incrementally replaced with an emerging sense of the mother as a subject—a person in her own right with whom there can be delight in love and mutual recognition. However, if the child is supported by another parent *against* the mother the gradual loss of the illusion is derailed. *From the child's perspective the caregiver supporting the aggression is 'with me / part of me' whereas the caregiver standing firm is 'against me / alien to me'. There is more at stake than the resulting non-compliance: the capacity for loving, accurate empathy is also compromised.* Anyone seeking to set limits becomes an enemy to be overthrown. For boys and men, in particular, mothers and women can remain objects to control rather than become subjects to relate to.

Triangulation, I suggest, therefore creates a simultaneous experience of excessive closeness and excessive distance. For Peter Fonagy and colleagues:

> Excessive closeness like excessive distance undermines the psychological self. In vain does the infant try to find representations corresponding to his internal state in the expression of the caregiver. The self remains incom-

pletely organised and internal reality continues to be experienced in the 'psychic equivalence' [omnipotent] mode. (Fonagy et al., 2002, p. 327)

The capacity to mentalise—to understand both one's own and other people's behaviour in terms of mental states, such as, for example, desires, feelings, and beliefs—is inhibited in the confusion of triangulation. (Recall, that absence—in this case, of mentalising capacity—also has causal power.) This has consequences for the ability of the developing child to participate in healthy self-and-interactive emotional regulation (Beebe & Lachmann, 2002) and to appreciate the usually benign motives of those setting limits.

Healing the Split

The main therapeutic strategy is to de-triangulate the child by re-establishing a parental coalition. With parents or parent figures working well-enough together, mindful warmth and firmness can recombine allowing the child to gradually experience himself and parents as subjects, each with a mind of their own. Sessions with all family members of a household can help initially to get a sense of the splits and triangular patterns, but thereafter sessions with parents and other caregivers (where relevant) without children present can begin to establish a clear boundary around the parental subsystem (Minuchin, 1974). The therapist needs to be careful to not take sides (unless there are child protection issues) but, instead, to offer support to all in rebuilding the parental team.

A couple may struggle to come together because of disagreement fed by other unresolved tensions (causal tendencies) which may need to be worked on, although I often found that parenting work can provide a new experience of togetherness that allows other marital tensions to be de-actualised. Working with exceptions—e.g. recalling and appreciatively dwelling on times when a couple has worked well together—and emphasising strengths, helps to build new confidence for embattled and exhausted parents. Caregivers who have become authoritarian and distant in the complementary split are encouraged to set aside regular time to play with their children. Flexibility in negotiating with an older child from a position of strength over age-appropriate freedom—rather than submitting when ground down—is encouraged.

I always warn parents that the child is likely to intensify the aggression initially to try to return to familiar safe patterns. A key factor is whether the new parental coalition can weather the initial storms. Much support may be needed during the first weeks. Work is generally needed on helping parents to stay calm and mindful, to review incidents together, and to think with the child about feelings. Occasional sessions including children are helpful to get a sense of how things are changing and to help children understand these initially painful changes. However, parental work is the main crucible of change.

Through the provision of an integrated parental experience the child is given a new developmental opportunity to move from enacted violence to self-strengthening mentalised aggression which facilitates empathy and love.

Paul

Paul, aged nine, was overwhelmed with anger when he couldn't have his own way. In his original family he was the younger of two boys. His parents separated and he lost contact with his father. His mother formed a new relationship and four further boys followed, aged from seven to four at the point of referral. I met the whole household—mother, stepfather, and the six boys—for a first session. Paul seemed out-of-place, not interacting, other than aggressively and dismissively, with his younger half-siblings and barely with his quiet older brother. Using my wooden figs. I asked each member of the family, in turn, to first show who they thought was close and distant from whom and, second, how they would prefer things to be. When Paul took his turn to show how he saw things in the present he placed himself next to a grandmother figure and apart from everyone else. This was the maternal grandmother who lived a few miles away. Paul was sent to her whenever he was "naughty", sometime spending several days there. He had turned to her after the loss of his father and the arrival of four more children. Paul struggled with the wooden figures to show how he would prefer things to be, putting himself as close as possible to his mother *and* grandmother, with his stepfather nearby. He then got frustrated when he couldn't simultaneously show them both close to him because of their separate houses. His mother was surprised and pleased that Paul wanted to be closer to her. She told me that she felt jealous of Paul's relationship with her mother and felt her mother was critical about her parenting of Paul, blaming her and her partner for his behavioural problems which were now spilling out at school in the form of bullying and non-compliance with teachers.

The parents agreed to invite the maternal grandmother to our next meeting without the children being present. They warned me that the grandmother was quite outspoken. This certainly proved to be the case and the grandmother pointedly made clear that *she* didn't experience *any* behaviour problems with Paul. There had been discussions in the family as to whether it would be better for Paul to live permanently with her, but she confirmed that this would not be possible. She could see, however, that Paul rarely needed to share her with anyone else and agreed that that this probably contributed to his better behaviour with her. She was a widow and Paul's older brother never wanted to stay overnight, so mostly it was just her and Paul.

Having talked through the issues and, with an emerging new systemic narrative around the difficulties, the adults agreed to work together with a focus on "helping Paul to be able to share and not accidentally rewarding bad behaviour with a stay with nanny". They agreed to plan Paul's contact with her in advance to make it predictable for everyone and no longer conditional on his bad behaviour. The grandmother conceded that Paul complained about his mother and step-father to her, and she agreed to try not to let herself get drawn into that. She also generously offered to have some of Paul's half-brothers stay on occasions with Paul. This new shared story of Paul's position within this three-generational pattern (see also the case of Conny in the last chapter) seemed to ease the mother's self-blame that she had been the cause of his problems. This helped to warm up her relationship with her son. The mother and step-father agreed to further parent-work to explore other ways of improving their relationship with Paul, to help him to recognise and think about his feelings, and to devise other clear, brief, non-retaliatory sanctions as an alternative to sending him away to his grandmother.

Jon

Jon, aged nine, was the youngest by several years in a white British Catholic family of six children. When I met him and his family in the waiting room, he said at the top of his voice "I really like you!" Within ten minutes this love at first sight came to a rapid end when I wouldn't let him bang my plastic dinosaurs very loudly on a metal filing cabinet while I was talking to his parents. He yelled "I hate you ... you fucking cunt!" and proceeded to try to fight with his parents to get out of the room, after which his father blocked the door. His mother was partially disabled, seemed worn out with caring for the children, resigned in the face of Jon's behaviour, and unsupported by her husband. After trying to stand her ground she readily acknowledged that she would soon tell him "Oh—just do what you like!" The father was clearly retaliatory and said, disturbingly, "I've found with Jon that the only way to get through to him is to threaten violence". Father could get very angry indeed and I suspected there were occasions when he had physically hurt Jon.

As I got to know Jon and his family a variety of causal tendencies emerged. As the mother had become more disabled and worn out, the caregiving had been shared increasingly with his older siblings The father, although not working, had over the last five years, become more withdrawn, spending hours alone working on his collection of model planes. Jon's twenty-year-old brother had not left home and had become Jon's main caregiver. Six months prior to the referral the brother had got a girlfriend. She had been made homeless and moved in with Jon's family. Jon instantly hated her in the way a child might hate a younger sibling (because she had taken his caregiver) and this further alienated his brother. In the absence of understanding, Jon's anger was mostly met with retaliatory anger. With this information, the functional and adaptive nature of Jon's behaviour began to make more sense. Jon was in danger of feeling lost and cut off from any caregiver. Since no one seemed able to find Jon's feelings understandable or containable, being loud, in everyone's face—the special problem child—seemed much more like a meaningful, systemically organised (although non-conscious) strategy. It seemed to allow an intensity of connection not otherwise available.

In this difficult first meeting, I asked them if they would agree to experiment with something different. I asked them not to respond to Jon's outrageous behaviour (the older children, in particular, had found his swearing at me very amusing) but to respond immediately, warmly, and consistently to any appropriate behaviour. I also modelled this and within fifteen minutes Jon became completely calm and co-cooperative and, indeed, anxious to continue to receive warm praise. At the end of the session Jon scrupulously tidied everything away. I felt this would probably be short-lived on returning home, but it helped the parents to experience that establishing clear behavioural contingencies and changing the emotional environment around Jon could be a great influence. It also showed how much Jon wanted the opportunity to please them. Up to this point they had been pressing for an ADHD diagnosis to be made.

During the next session I worked on clarifying who should hold a parental role. I encouraged this parental group to use clear predictable methods of control, working together, keeping themselves calm, helping Jon to understand his feelings, and using consistent warm praise. Importantly, his elder brother began to understand how his sudden unavailability had affected Jon and began to spend more time with him. Both parents also agreed to each experiment with thirty minutes of play with Jon three times per week, allowing him to take the lead, to warm up their relationship. No case ever goes smoothly, of course, but within two weeks both parents and school began to report encouraging changes in Jon's behaviour.

Mark

Individual work with a parent can also help when, for reasons that are unclear, the provision of warm firmness seems to make a parent uncomfortable. Mark aged twelve was referred by the school for major control problems at home and at school. He was the only child of Sarah, his unsupported lone-parent mother. He had limited contact with his father who had left the family several years previously. Sarah had found Mark's aggression intimidating and for years had backed away from confrontation. He had become increasingly demanding and powerful. She recognised that he was in danger of getting completely beyond her control as he moved into adolescence.

In a first 'parent only' session I talked with her about various strategies, but she told me that she became so "jittery" when she felt Mark might become angry with her that she doubted she could put any of them in place. As we explored this she said that she thought that the jittery feeling had begun with Mark's father. He had never hit her, but she had felt "unable to function" when she feared he might get angry.

We agreed to work on this traumatic memory with EMDR. For those unfamiliar with the method, traumatic memory is first brought to mind and then desensitised through bilateral stimulation of various kinds (e.g. eye movements or alternate tapping on hands). Despite the clear protocol, the method does facilitate free association, and during the desensitising process Sarah spontaneously returned to a powerful earlier memory of the same jittery feeling. She was six years old and a man had come to the home. She glimpsed him only briefly but somehow knew that he was her real father. She was quickly ushered away but was aware of shouting from downstairs and emotional upheaval that lasted for weeks. She never saw her father again and the incident was never spoken of. Sarah recognised through the work that anger of others had become associated with this profound unresolved loss. This causal tendency was specifically linked to an anxiety that she would lose Mark if he got angry with her.

The Smiths

Since her husband left eighteen months previously, Jane Smith had been the sole provider for her and her three sons, aged fifteen, twelve, and eight. Her husband had for many years carried the main authority in this working-class household and Jane had been happy to defer to him. "I'll tell your father when he gets home" being her main threatened sanction. His affair, departure from the family, and failure to support them financially or maintain regular contact with the children had been devastating and caused a crisis in the parenting. At our first meeting, the children were rude, demanding, and non-compliant with their mother and aggressive to each other.

In the first of our 'parent only' meetings, Jane talked openly about her despair at being the sole parent. This was especially stressful around issues of parental authority now that her husband was no longer able to carry that role. Her understanding was that the children didn't like her or care about her and she was quite convinced that, if she walked out (which she often fantasised about and sometimes threatened to do), the children would not miss her at all. Jane's sense of having little value to the children had been present throughout her parenting—a causal factor in her wish not to carry parental authority during the marriage. Even when the children were little, she could never bear them to be angry with her if she had to be "hard" on them by saying "no". She had no idea why this was other than the idea that "all mothers feel that way". Her perception seemed to have led to her protecting herself from further assumed rejection by distancing herself from them. This emotional withdrawal seemed to be a further causal factor in the escalation of arguments from the children, which at least offered them some intensity of connection.

How are we to understand this Jane's perception? Crittenden (2008) writes that, for all persons:

> The only information we have is information about the past, whereas the only information we need is information about the future. … Without understanding how each individual transforms information and derives self-relevant meanings we cannot understand why parents do what they do. (p. 90)

Using some questions from early in the Adult Attachment Interview protocol (Main, 1993), I asked Jane to provide five adjectives that described her relationship with her parents. This explores the semantic memory which encodes the overall meaning of past experiences. Immediately afterwards, I asked for specific (episodic) memories from as early in childhood as possible that illustrated why she had chosen those particular adjectives. She seemed surprised and initially chose normalising but vague semantic descriptions: "just normal", "nothing unusual" to support her more general schema that "everyone feels the same as I do". When I asked her for specific memories in support of her 'normal' relationship with her mother, she was unable to do this immediately but, in thinking about this, gave a new description of her mother as "distant". This was immediately followed by worry at sounding so critical—"it makes me sound horrible". She was not able to follow this up with an episodic memory and seemed uncomfortable when I gently encouraged her to do so. On asking about memories of her father to support her semantic description of "just normal", she was again unable to supply an episode but gave a further semantic account: "I didn't bother much with my father".

The value of this simple approach, if used with compassion and an absence of blame, is that it highlights discrepancy between memory systems, creating the opportunity for discussion, reflection, and integration. This allows the beginning of a more coherent representation of childhood and other life experiences to be narrated which, crucially for parents, may give a more accurate perception of their children's needs in the present.

As the work developed, it became apparent that for Jane, 'distance' from her parents had been normalised and, therefore, first her needs and then the needs of her own children were misperceived. She said she had never really played with them: she didn't seem to have the knack or the patience and, after a while, they didn't seem to want to. However, the emotional pain at her own neglectful experiences, while not integrated into a coherent self-narrative and therefore something she could correct with her own children, had not been forgotten. The pain seemed to be intensely re-actualised, first, by the breakdown of her marriage and, second, by the children not listening to her, strengthening the misperception that *they* did not care about her. Her solution of withdrawing further (the causal power of absence) increased the children's anxiety, which they seemed to manage by an escalation of their ambivalent attachment (hypothesised C3/4) strategies, which demanded her involvement.

I think that normalising neglectful experiences had been adaptive for Jane as a child. Even as an adult, she was at pains not to feel critical of her parents despite her experience that they showed little interest in her and her children. Even the neutral sounding term 'distant' in describing her mother (who she experienced as very preoccupied with her difficult older brother) left Jane feeling that she was horrible for daring to think this. The distance from her father was framed in a self-blaming manner as entirely her choice: she "didn't bother" much with him rather than the other way round.

As we discussed this in a subsequent session, a specific memory spontaneously cropped up.

Jane had been chosen for a small role in the school play and her father had promised to come (she knew her mother would not attend). She vividly recalled looking around for him among all the other parents and then her upset on realising that he had not come. She later found that he had stayed down the pub drinking as he did most evenings. "It's silly really to feel upset about that after all these years", she said, trying to shake off the memory of the painful feelings. I reassured her that her feelings were not silly but understandable and important.

I think the danger that Jane faced in the relationship with her parents was reduced through the use of an avoidant attachment strategy. Being a good, uncomplaining, and undemanding girl (hypothesised 'compulsive compliant'—A4 on the DMM) may have earned her some credit for not being aggressive like her older brother. She had also seen him sent away to a boarding school for behaviourally challenging children, which would, presumably, have engendered further anxiety and intensified her perceived need to be good. Anything bad in the relationship with her parents was split off and became her fault, hence her self-definition as 'horrible' at daring to describe the relationship with her mother as "distant". For the children to be angry with her, before her husband left, was therefore entirely contrary to her attachment strategy and threatened deep discomfort. Hence her partly conscious agreement for her husband to take the authority role when he lived with the family and the crisis for Jane at having to assume this role alone when he left.

Explosive Rage

So far we have discussed the aggressive non-compliance of the coercive C strategies. However, this has a different quality to very sudden outbursts of rage that can occur, seemingly out of character.

Prior to my probation and social work training I worked for a year as a nursing assistant in a psychiatric hospital, most of that time on an acute-admissions ward. Jenny, a patient in her mid-twenties, was a quiet—even meek—person, always very polite, keeping to herself as much as possible, closing down attempts at conversation, and especially avoiding more outgoing patients or members of staff. One lunchtime, with no warning, she suddenly screamed in rage to no-one in particular "I've had enough!" She turned over the lunch table spilling food and drink everywhere. This was shocking, but she hadn't hurt anyone (or seemingly intended to) and quickly collapsed into sobbing and apologies but, in line with ward policy on violence, was discharged from the ward that afternoon. This retaliatory action by the hospital seemed cruel but, sadly, not unusual when organisations become mindless (Ashforth & Fried, 1988).

In the A (avoidant) strategies of the DMM, a child with caregivers who reliably dismiss the child's emotional expressions of fear, upset, and anger finds safety in first inhibiting true affect and later, with maturity, in the use of false-positive affect: smiling for example in the face of danger. Readers from the UK may be familiar with the case of Peter Connelly (Baby P), a child subject to extreme physical abuse who, before his death, was known to his extended family by the nickname, Smiler. Alongside the repudiation of true feelings is cognitive distortion in the form of self-blame. (Note the difference from the C-strategy where the self is exonerated and the *other* is blamed.) However the A-strategy can suddenly break down with an outburst of upset and rage, although this then tends to be seen as a meaningless aberration. This is described in the DMM as 'intrusion of negative affect'.

Cathy, for example, grew up a quiet girl, always trying to please her mother whom she experienced as cold, critical, and more interested in Cathy's younger half-sister from her mother's second relationship. Cathy had no contact with her father. Her relationship with her partner broke down shortly after she gave birth to her son, Shaun. She hoped the new grandchild would draw her mother in but that proved not to be the case. She rejected all professional help other than a health visitor, stating that she just wanted to be left to enjoy her son and that his love would be enough. I met with her after she was referred to our service when Shaun was found to have bruises and fractures consistent, according to a paediatrician, with having been thrown or heavily dropped.

Cathy vehemently denied that she had caused the injuries, a position strongly supported by her health visitor who insisted that Cathy was incapable of violence, on one occasion bursting into my room without knocking to confront me about these "cruel accusations". I secured an agreement with the police that they would not prosecute Cathy if she disclosed the truth, using the argument that, if she was not free to speak without incriminating herself, then it would be impossible to assess future risk to the infant. She then told me that for days she had been unable to comfort Shaun and stop him crying. It felt to her that her son was now also rejecting her, and, in a sudden explosion of rage, she threw him against a wall. She agreed to continue working with me beyond the assessment and we had eighteen months of weekly psychotherapy which validated her anger and painful feelings of rejection by both parents through childhood.

She eventually gave up trying to please her mother and broke off all contact. She had met a new supportive partner and was strongly welcomed by his family, especially his mother. She had another son and with these supportive relationships, as far as I could tell up to the end of my work with her, was able to be a successful mother. Regrettably, she did not feel able to return to parenting Shaun who, by then, had spent a year in foster care. She did not oppose care proceedings and he was later adopted.

In this case, as with all examples in this chapter, there is a shift in focus away from the aggressive behaviour that powerfully first draws the eye, and towards mentalising: thinking about the thoughts and feelings behind the behaviours and helping to change the causal tendencies of the triangulating relational patterns. These patterns confuse the process of coming to experience self and other as persons in their own right capable of providing and receiving love and respect.

The theme of moving from violence—this time enacted against the self—towards an understanding of thoughts and feelings within relational contexts continues in the next chapter.

References

Angelou, M. (2008). *Letter to my daughter*. Random House.

Ashforth, B., & Fried, Y. (1988). The mindlessness of organizational behaviours. *Human Relations, 41*, 305–329.

Auerbach, J., & Blatt, S. (2001). Self-reflexivity, intersubjectivity, and therapeutic change. *Psychoanalytic Psychology, 18*, 427–450.

Beebe, B., & Lachmann, F. (2002). *Infant research and adult treatment: Co-constructing interactions*. The Analytic Press.

Benjamin, J. (1999). Recognition and destruction: An outline of intersubjectivity. In S. Mitchell & L. Aron (Eds.), *Relational psychoanalysis: The emergence of a tradition* (pp. 181–210). Analytic Press.

Brown, J. (2023). Making sense of the parenting 'soft/hard split'. *Australian and New Zealand of Family Therapy, 44*, 225–236.

Buss, D., & Shackleford, T. (1997). Human aggression in evolutionary psychological perspective. *Clinical Psychology Review, 17*, 605–619.

Byng-Hall, J. (1995). *Rewriting family scripts: Improvisation and systems change*. Guilford.

Crittenden, P. (2008). *Raising parents: Attachment representation, and treatment*. Routledge.

Crittenden, P., Dallos, R., Landini, A., & Kozlowska, K. (2014). *Attachment and family therapy*. Open University Press.

Fivaz-Depeursinge, E., & Favez, N. (2006). Exploring triangulation in infancy: Two contrasted cases. *Family Process, 45*, 3–18.

Fonagy, P., Gergeley, G., Jurist, E., & Target, M. (2002). *Affect regulation, mentalization, and the development of the self*. Other Press.

Freud, S. (1957). On narcissism: An introduction. In *The standard edition of the complete psychological works of Sigmund Freud, volume XIV (1914–1916): On the history of the psycho-analytic movement, papers on metapsychology and other works* (pp. 67–102). Hogarth Press.

Goldner, V., Penn, P., Sheinberg, M., & Walker, G. (1990). Love and violence: Gender paradoxes in volatile attachments. *Family Process, 29*, 343–364.

Klein, M. (1946). Notes on some schizoid mechanisms. In *The writings of Melanie Klein* (Vol. 3, pp. 1–24). Free Press.

Lansford, J. (2022). Cross-cultural similarities and differences in parenting. *Journal of Clinical Child Psychology and Psychiatry, 63*, 466–479.

Main, M. (1993). *Attachment across the life cycle*. Routledge.
Minuchin. (1974). *Families and family therapy*. Harvard University Press.
Stewart, R. (2023). *Politics on the edge*. Random House.
Strand, P., Vossen, J., & Savage, S. (2019). Culture and child attachment patterns: A behavioural systems synthesis. *Perspectives on Behavioural Science, 42*, 835–850.
Wilkerson, I. (2010). *The warmth of other suns: The epic story of America's great migration*. Penguin Books.

12

Self-Harm and Suicidality

> The blade sings to me. Faintly, so soft against my ears, its voice calms my worries and tells me that one touch will take it all away. Amanda Steele (*The Cliff*)

I don't usually ask people why they hurt themselves. I think if they knew how to fully answer that question they wouldn't need to do it. But, for some reason, I did ask sixteen-year-old Jerry, perhaps because in this therapy session he had his sleeves rolled up showing a latticework of scars, over-scored by fresh cuts in various stages of healing and, somehow, I felt he wanted me to ask. "I hurt myself" he replied without hesitation "so I don't hurt other people. When people piss me off I want to kill them, so when I cut myself it calms me down and they stay alive. It's quite a good deal, don't you think?" he said, staring at me and daring me to disagree. I might have told Jerry—as I do with some people frightened of their aggression—that, in my opinion, there is nothing wrong with *feeling* like killing people since there can be a big difference between feeling like doing something and actually doing it. But I didn't say that to him—not then anyway. As a ten-year-old, he had helplessly and repeatedly witnessed his mother so badly beaten by his step-father that on several

D. Pocock, *Expanding the Limits of Individual and Family Therapies*, Palgrave Texts in Counselling and Psychotherapy, https://doi.org/10.1007/978-3-031-76309-0_12

occasions he thought she would die. There was little difference between feeling and doing in his experience.

In fact, Jerry, over six feet tall and strongly built, was proud of his aggression and not averse to giving men "a good kicking" if he felt they deserved it. He had twice attacked strangers in the street: men whom he had observed "behaving like knobs" with their girlfriends. He felt good about this, he eventually told me, because he had not been able to do anything to stop his stepfather hurting his mother. Beating up those men lessened his burden of guilt, at least for a time. So, we worked out, hurting himself was reserved for occasions when those he cared about angered him—his mother, of whom he was enormously protective, his girlfriend, and his mates.

Jerry sometimes frightened me, but I assumed his intimidation of me and others (especially male teachers) helped him to disown, through projective identification, his own terrified feelings. He could then be fearless and turn his back on the despised weak child he felt he had been, who so pathetically, in his mind, had failed to protect his mother. I could add other hypothesised causal tendencies to this picture: an unreliable birth father whom Jerry idealised as "hard"; a white working-class youth peer culture in which status was proportionate to toughness; and an enactment of the violent alien stepfather object in his mind in what Ferenczi (1988) calls 'identification with the aggressor'. But the more general point I want to make is this: that self-harm which, especially in its more secretive forms can seem entirely individualistic, can be systemically understood as an unconscious attempt to regulate and preserve crucial relationships. Jerry knew that he hurt himself so that he would not hurt others who were important to him, but this was not an act of altruism. The possibility of hurting those close to him was, I think, experienced as more of a danger (since he might damage those essential relationships) than attacking his body. On the balance of risk, given the limited strategies available to Jerry, self-harm was safer.

Mapping Self-Harm

The idea of self-harm as causally preservative of important relationships may seem a strange concept. The UK National Institute of Health and Care Excellence (NICE) defines self-harm as "intentional self-poisoning or injury, irrespective of the apparent purpose" so this covers the spectrum from mild self-injury right through to the most serious suicide attempts. Can a determined suicide attempt be in any way preservative? Psychiatrists and psychotherapists Donald Campbell and Rob Hale (1991) describe the manner in which the hated other in a current or historical close relationship becomes identified with the body of the self. Murderous feelings towards the needed other are diverted by the self, instead, wishing to kill its own body. Perhaps the preservative aspect of this makes more sense in the light of the common fantasy, reported by Campbell and Hale that, even in the most serious suicide attempts, part of the self will survive beyond death. They described an assessment with one man who survived the ingestion of 199 aspirin from a bottle of 200. One tablet had dropped on the floor. He feared it had picked up germs and would make him ill if he swallowed it.

Although, I suggest, that for many of those referred to psychological services, turning anger against the self has become systemically adaptive and stabilising of relationships, the solution of self-harm may be non-consciously preferred to being in touch with other unbearable feelings including sadness, shame, guilt, envy, and despair and their cultural variants. Peter Fonagy and Mary Target (1995) describe how violence directed against the self may be closely linked to failures of mentalisation: that difficulties in tolerating and thinking about painful *mental* states may compel individuals to manage powerful emotions in the *bodily* realm. This itself is complex. For some people hurting the body seems to take away emotional pain. For others, physical pain allows them to feel something other than numbness (Horne & Csipke, 2008). As discussed in Chap. 6, mentalising (Fonagy et al., 2002) is only understandable in the context of relational processes. The capacity to reflect upon oneself and others depends on experiences of being thought about in an emotionally attuned manner in caregiving relationships.

After working with a number of children, adolescents, and their family referred for self-harm over the years, I sketched two contrasting patterns which I call '*communicative / other-regulatory*' and '*secretive / self-regulatory*', with some cases a mixture of both (Pocock, 2011). The reader is urged to take a cautious reflexive (second-order) position on these sketches: nothing as complex as human behaviour can be reliably divided into two parts. Like all categories these are over-simplified constructions for the purposes of assisting thought. In particular they should not be used in assessing risk. For this I recommend the book *Self-harm In Young People: A Therapeutic Assessment Manual* (Ougrin et al., 2010).

Communicative/Other-Regulatory

I wasn't the only person to have seen Jerry's scars and wounds. Nearly everyone who knew him had seen them. Showing them was, I suggest, a pragmatic aspect of his communication (Watzlawick et al., 1967), the functional effects of which depended on the particular relational context. For his mother and girlfriend they invited great concern and care; for his teachers, they seemed to organise an avoidance of confrontation for fear of what he might do; and with his mates they helped to pattern a response of heroising awe—they referred to him admiringly by the nickname 'Mad Dog'. Such behaviour easily attracts the tag 'manipulative', but in a childhood consistently lacking mindfully attuned care, his emotionally driven behaviour, in the absence of mentalising, gave him some means of regulating the behaviour of others. I assume this reduced the anxiety and guilt associated with the traumatic experiences of helpless unpredictability in the face of his step-father's violence towards his mother.

Katie, aged seventeen and white British, swallowed twelve paracetamol the day after she discovered that her boyfriend had cheated on her with one of her friends. The previous year her mother had begun a new relationship and was pregnant. A month before the overdose she learned, by accident, that her father planned to move abroad with his girlfriend. I think that her heightened sense of doubt about her value to each of her parents seemed not to have been processed and the double betrayal by her boyfriend and best friend was then the actualising last straw, triggering overwhelming emotion. I think that overt anger with boyfriend, friend, and parents was not sustainable because of the danger to the viability of those relationships. She already perceived these as fragile, since all those close to her seemed to be moving away. Instead, anger was turned destructively against herself.

She must be no good, she reasoned, otherwise why did people let her down? The psychiatrist and psychoanalyst Ronald Fairbairn (1952) describes this causal tendency as the 'moral defence'. As a thought experiment he asks, "Is it better to be a saint in hell or a sinner in heaven?" Children, he says, will choose the latter: making themselves wrong to make the other right to preserve the relationships. It also provides an unconscious strategy—to correct their own badness to become good—or, preferably, perfect—rather than feel anger with the other. Pursuing perfectionism—an unachievable solution—becomes a new risk since one inevitably fails. This tendency is also seen in some eating disorders in pursuit of an idealised body shape. I think, for that reason, self-harm and eating disorders are commonly found together. In a recent UK study, around two thirds of females who were self-harming also reported some form of disordered eating (Warne et al., 2021).

Katie soon regretted the overdose and told her mother who took her immediately to the hospital accident and emergency department and then telephoned her father. When I saw Katie the following day in the hospital for an assessment I asked her if there was anything in the whole experience that was important to her in a positive way. She explained that it was seeing both her parents in tears at her bedside. She then knew that she still mattered to them. This helped to de-actualise her wish to kill herself.

To summarise, in the absence of mentalisation, I suggest Jerry and Katie used a non-conscious pragmatic strategy of regulating others in order to increase their control and safety. Using the lens of attachment, these may be seen as ambivalent attachment strategies (C3-coercive / C4-feigned helpless on the DMM). I realise this sounds like an overly cool and technical-sounding description for a desperate state of mind. I need to emphasise again that I am not suggesting that a *deliberate* choice is being made. In such cases, I see self-harm as an emotionally driven event to attempt to feel better and safer without damaging vital relationships. However, such behaviour is not just risky to the body, but can fail to achieve a safer outcome. What if, as sometimes happens, Katie's parents had been furious and rejecting of her following the overdose?

For example, Michael, who I have written about previously (Pocock, 2009), first risked overt anger when he experienced his father dramatically letting him down and had smashed the DVDs that his father had lent him. This did not organise concern but instead led to his father calling to the house and, in front of him, retaliating by crushing under his foot the mobile phone he had bought for Michael's birthday. That evening Michael made, what appeared to his mother, a serious attempt to hang himself. Very fortunately this high-risk behaviour ended the symmetrical escalation (Bateson, 1972) of destruction and shocked his father back into a position of parental concern.

Secretive/Self-Regulatory

The cases described so far are those most likely to appear in hospital accident and emergency departments and later in child and adolescent mental health services. Distress is pragmatically communicated through 'loud' unignorable violence against the body, and important others are prompted to care. In contrast, the world of secretive / self-regulatory self-harm is insular, dark, and mostly invisible to public agencies (unless discovered by accident) or even to the family. Community-based (Euro-American) studies show around ten per cent of young people harm themselves (McMahon et al., 2022) at some point, but only a tiny proportion of these ever come to the attention of mental health services. I suggest this second pattern is strongly represented in the silent majority who do not reach professionals. Ten years ago, the easiest way to access that world was to search on YouTube for 'self-harm stories'. There were hundreds, but fewer currently, now that social media have been forced through a number of publicised teenage suicides to be more careful about content. Young people who self-harm in this more hidden way want others to bear witness to their distress as long as those others are not family members, especially parents.

While the press frequently mentions *adolescent* self-harm, this more secretive form seems to be spread well into the adult population, at least in Euro-American culture. In an anonymous web survey conducted by the UK mental health charity SANE (Horne & Csipke, 2008), just under a thousand people who had self-harmed, or were currently self-harming, responded. *Of these 84% (ranging from 12–59 years, average 22 years) sought to hide their harming from their family and 66% hid it from their friends.* This is not a world of occasional impulsive acts. Of the 532 who were still self-harming at the time of the survey almost half had been harming for more than five years and a quarter for eleven years or more. Twenty per cent were hurting themselves daily and thirty per cent weekly. Only one person in eight said that their first act of self-harm was motivated by the wish for others to take notice and care. This figure dropped to one in twelve for subsequent acts of self-harm. Only twelve per cent who hid their self-harm expected family and friends to recognise that they were hurting themselves as a response to their emotional distress.

Horne and Csipke capture the sense of a 'secret self' which has to be kept hidden at any cost, leading to a great discrepancy between the self as presented to the world and the self as perceived within. As one adolescent girl put it:

> When others find me attractive or pretty or socially appealing I harm myself a lot more, because I know that they are wrong, and I am right. (Quoted in Horne & Csipke, 2008, p. 7)

Jody, aged fourteen, who I began to discuss in Chap. 7, from a professional middle-class, white British family, had been harming herself, often daily from the age of eleven. It started when she hurt herself by accident and discovered that it made her feel less stressed. (The discovery of the de-stressing effect of self-injury through an accidental wound is an account I have heard several times.) She told no one for three years. When her mother discovered the self-harm she shamed Jody saying, "You have destroyed me as a parent" and the mother then withdrew to bed for three days. Jody's father was furious with Jody. She had been the good child who seemingly was doing really well, and her apparent trouble-free progress was a considerable compensation to the self-esteem of her parents since they had a tough time through adolescence with their older daughter, involving regular screaming rows. Jody was highly attuned to her mother's fragility as her mother had experienced two major breakdowns requiring hospitalisation during the first six years of Jody's life. There was also a good deal of marital conflict and Jody felt responsible for smoothing things between her parents (triangulation) by being as helpful and caring as possible when tensions were high. We will return to Jody and her family shortly.

I suggest that, in the secretive / self-regulatory pattern, the self-harmer gains some sense of control and safety, not by communicating the distress to activate the other, as in the communicative / other-regulatory pattern, but by taking over responsibility for the wellbeing of the other(s) through inhibiting anger and distress in the self—especially anger with the caregiver. Instead, these feelings are managed by hidden and destructive forms of emotional self-regulation including routine and often ritualised cutting, burning, bruising, and abrading, or a combination of these. This allows a pleasing, compliant or caregiving (but false) self to be presented to the caregiver to preserve the relationship.

The layered theoretical vantage points that I am using here to lightly construct a composite model of this pattern are mostly those already discussed, especially in Chap. 6: parentification (Boszormenyi-Nagy & Krasner, 1986); destructive forms of emotional self-regulation (Beebe & Lachmann, 2002); Fairbairn's (1952) moral defence; Winnicott's (1986) 'false-self'; Crittenden's (2008) DMM strategies of compulsive caregiving (A3) and compulsive compliance (A4); and the non-availability of mentalising or a relationship in which mentalising may be developed (Fonagy et al., 2002).

The inhibition of anger, as a causal mechanism, alongside other negative affect to avoid upsetting a fragile or retaliatory caregiver usually leaves the child unassertive and therefore vulnerable to bullying, further compounding the need to hurt the body to manage the feelings arising from this. This routinised pattern of self-harm is likely to be reinforced by a further causal tendency: namely, the addictive nature of physiological and psychological release from emotional pain (Blasco-Fontecilla et al., 2016).

Peer and Cultural Factors

Put more simply, I am suggesting that self-harm in both presentations (but more evidently in the secretive / self-regulatory pattern) is in line with the more general requirement to make the other right by having the self be wrong to preserve an unsatisfactory relationship or relationships. The corresponding lack of self-worth, authenticity, and failure in any bid to be perfect also makes individuals especially susceptible to the causal tendency of certain cultural pressures. The failure to live up to the assumed standards of peers or—especially for girls, but increasingly for boys—the failure to conform to the impossible (for most) ideals of attractiveness, may additionally motivate the self to punish the body for not measuring up.

Daniel, aged fifteen, white British, was a promising rugby player but chose not to take up the offer of a trial for a leading professional rugby club. His father, an ex-professional sportsman, was massively disappointed. Daniel's parents separated some years previously and rugby seemed the only meaningful point of connection between father and son. However, Daniel found it hard to cope with the constant pressure from his father to succeed but could never address this with him, or even sustain any anger about the pressure, for fear of losing him. Daniel's mother loathed his father, so he found it impossible to turn to her for help with his feelings. After turning down the trial he entered a lengthy period where he felt depressed and useless (hypothesised self-denigration to avoid fury with his father), but it was the failure of his friends to invite him to a party because (so he believed) they didn't think he was cool enough which was the last straw, actualising self-harm. He kept this hidden for months until his mother eventually discovered cuts on this leg.

I am not able to provide examples to illustrate a wider cultural variation in self-harm but, in a recent wide review of around 2600 papers, significant differences were found in the rates of self-harm between ethnic groups, with Asian males being least likely and black females most likely to self-harm. Black and South Asian people were less likely to repeat self-harm (Al-Sharifi et al., 2015).

Therapeutic Strategies

There are several techniques for distress management, distraction, and 'first-aid' forms of constructive emotional regulation. These may be useful, especially in the early stages of therapy, but are primarily aimed at temporary state changes rather than more lasting relational change. *However, if we accept that self-harm is a strategy for managing endangered relationships then taking away the solution of self-harm may not succeed long-term unless a better relational solution is provided.*

By 'endangered relationships' I am referring both to relationships as they exist in the present between self and external others, and important relationships as represented internally within the self. Sophie's mother was murdered by her step-father when Sophie was staying with friends. She felt profoundly guilty that she was not present to prevent the murder—she was then ten years old. Sophie believed she had failed her mother to the extent that she no longer deserved to live. Only as she began to feel her forbidden anger with her mother, because she had not protected Sophie from years of her step-father's violence, did she begin to recover. It was the internal relationship with her deceased mother that needed to change.

In Chap. 9 I discussed individual therapy with Mary who had a history of serious attacks on her body. For child and adolescent self-harm, while a systemic perspective is always helpful, I found a meeting with the whole family is generally not the best starting point. In the secretive / self-regulatory pattern it is not safe for the young person to speak openly of (or in some cases to even think about) authentic feelings. I generally start with an appointment with the young person and the caregiver with whom they feel safest (relatively speaking, since I assume nothing is safe). I later include other family members or see other sub-groups of the family as needed.

Safety in the therapeutic alliance is paramount if the young person is to begin the highly risky business of thinking and communicating emotionally in words. In a first session I usually spend the first half with the young person and parent together exploring the limits of what can be spoken about in that context and getting a sense of how much feelings can be thought about. If it feels sufficiently safe, I offer a new frame about the protective nature of self-harm. I might say "In my experience, parents of teenagers are pretty annoying—I'm quite an annoying parent myself—but I'm always struck by how little anger is expressed by young people who hurt themselves. Very often they have told me that they hurt themselves because they are afraid of upsetting other people, including their parents". Almost always, the response from the parent is that they would much prefer to cope with anger and upset than to have to worry about the self-harm. If this reframing is not made prior to seeing the young person alone, it is much harder to make later, since it then feels to the young person that their unique secret has been betrayed.

Young people are usually much more forthcoming in the second half of the session when seen alone, once the appropriate limits of confidentiality are negotiated. I explain that I will not communicate with anyone else about what we speak about unless I have the young person's permission, or unless I think there is serious imminent risk to the young person's life, in which case I would tell the young person first. (It is rare to have to breach confidentiality since, in the secretive pattern, the self-harm tends to be routinised cutting, bruising, or abrading rather than life-threatening, although this needs to be assessed.) The primary task is to begin to emotionally understand the child or adolescent and to help them to think about their emotional states. In the secretive pattern the affect may be minimised or falsified so the therapist may need to use themselves (countertransference) as an affect-amplifier. For example, if an upsetting-sounding event is described flatly and unemotionally but stirs up anger in the therapist, the therapist might ask "I wonder where your anger is about that?"

The difference in what the young person reveals of themselves between the two parts of the session can be considerable. An appreciation of both parts by the therapist constitutes the beginning of a bridge between the inner and outer self (as shown to the parent and others). The task then is to negotiate whether and how much that bridge can be relocated between the young person and the parent. In the work with Jo and her mother (Chap. 9) Jo, having rehearsed speaking about the anger with her mother, when seen alone in the second part of the session, was then, in the third part of the session, willing to allow her mother to guess the reasons for

Jo's anger, which she did with remarkable accuracy, opening up a new emotionally meaningful dialogue and the beginning of healthier self and interactive emotional regulation (Beebe & Lachmann, 2002).

Bridging across to the caregiver needs to be managed with considerable care. Seventeen-year-old Michelle, a girl with a learning disability, was seen in our service for a long history of cutting. She attended with her parents and was clumsily invited to immediately disclose to her mother her unhappiness that her mother seemed not to love her. (This had been mentioned in the referral letter.) The mother heard her out politely in the session but verbally attacked her daughter thereafter for "saying all those nasty things about me". She and her husband refused to attend any further sessions and Michelle withdrew from them, instead assembling a 'family' of professionals upon whom she made great demands.

Jody

In the case of Jody, who I began to discuss in Chap. 7 and above, her fear of upsetting her parents was so great that she would only be seen individually. Her parents were seen in parallel by a separate therapist. However, Jody and her parents were willing for the therapists to talk regularly to each other allowing some indirect bridging. I undertook the individual work with Jody, whom I saw for around six months of mostly weekly sessions.

To recap, in the second session Jody had, after telling me that everything was 'really fine', acknowledged that she had hurt herself on all but three of the days in the last week. I asked her what she thought had been different about the non-hurting days in order to try to track protective causal tendencies. She told me that she had been busy with friends and had spent hardly any time at home. I felt she was indirectly beginning to allow focus on her home relationships. She went on to tell me that she had harmed herself more on one particular day and this followed her father shouting at her mother. Jody had simply assumed this was her fault (A-strategy cognitive distortion into self-blame), and she harmed herself to manage the guilt. She had linked her feeling of bodily tension to the guilt and this first mentalised moment that she shared with me seemed a hopeful indication that she could make use of the therapy, despite her great ambivalence about attending. I'll pick up the session from that point and, in the right-hand column, try to reconstruct my inner conversation.

Outer dialogue	My inner conversation
DP. What had you done to harm yourself?	*I'm not sure why I asked this? How is this relevant? I think I just want to encourage her to find words for things unspoken. But it feels risky.*
J. [she seems to go blank.]	*I think I've pushed too hard. I'll offer her a possible answer, so she only has to agree or disagree.*
DP. I'm guessing you used the rough stone?	
J. [smiles uncomfortably.]	*This feels like a very uncomfortable 'yes'.*
DP. And when you say you did it more that day, I'm guessing you mean longer and harder?	
J. Probably a bit of both.	*I feel relieved at her acknowledgement of my 'guess' and there is some lowering of tension.*

Later, I asked her if there were any other reasons why she thought she had harmed herself more on that particular day. (Events are the combination of multiple causal tendencies.)

J. Yes, a friend told me she is not eating but wouldn't let me tell anyone, nor would she do anything about it herself.	*I'm feeling irritated with the friend which I think may be an identification with Jody's inhibited affect.*
DP. She left you feeling responsible?	
J. Yes.	
DP. It sounds like you've learned to care for everyone. Were you not a bit irritated with your friend?	*I offer her the beginnings of a new relational frame for her self-harm. That it allows parentification and other forms of one-way caregiving. I link this to my irritation with her friend, which I think may be resonant with that of Jody, although muted in her.*

(continued)

(continued)

J. Why should I be irritated?	*Jody sounds a little exasperated with me but there is a small reduction of tension.*
DP. She put you in a very difficult place by not doing anything about it or not allowing you to help her, so you end up feeling responsible.	
J. No. I know how she feels with not eating.	*Jody stands up to me and also tells me something new about herself. That she has struggled at times with eating. She feels a little more robust just now.*
DP. OK. Actually you sound a bit annoyed with me for not understanding.	*I say this lightly and warmly, to convey her entitlement to be annoyed with me and, by implication, others including friends and parents.*
J. No .... No.	*Said politely ... but not, I sense, a complete denial.*
DP. [lightly] I know I can be annoying!	*I let her know in a joke that if she was angry it wouldn't damage me.*
J. [smiles more naturally]	*Tensions feel eased.*
DP. Its nearly time to stop. Thank you for letting me know more about you. I don't think that's been easy for you.	*It doesn't feel OK, but easier than at the start.*
J. No, it's OK.	
DP. Do you feel you've told me too much?	*I try to anticipate—And hold—Anxieties that she has stepped outside her safe strategy of not thinking or speaking about her feelings.*
J. No, it's fine.	
J. Yes, bye.	

In a session a few weeks later, Jody spoke freely (and healthily) about her anger with one of her friends at school. I notice that she said little about what was happening at home and when I enquired about this she became silent. What slowly and painfully emerged was Jody's triangulated position. Her father frequently raged at her mother who sat quietly and didn't answer back but just sobbed. Jody would then put her arms around her mother to comfort her, again in complete silence. Once these incidents were over they were never spoken of, as if they hadn't really happened. When Jody speaks about them they become more real and frightening. There seemed to be a definite sense of progress, though, and a greater degree of trust as she discovered that her words to me are not leaking back to her parents as she feared.

A few weeks further on, Jody seemed lighter in mood and able to talk more freely. Her father had gone away for a weekend to do an anger-management course, and this seemed to give her hope. She was apprehensive about a forthcoming family holiday in Geneva since, although it is some time since her father raged at her mother, she is always waiting for it to happen again. She was able also to speak of her frustration with her mother whom she finds "confusing". On one occasion her mother told Jody that she deserved a better mother and hinted that Jody would be better off without her.

After the holiday Jody talked animatedly about issues with friends at school. She had not enjoyed the family holiday as her father had been "childish". She said she had no feelings for him but then changed this to the wish that he would die. I accepted this and she then went on to tell me how her father used to rage at her brother and sister. Eventually she gave an account of the parents' discovery of her self-harm. Her mother had started screaming and her father had beat her in fury, hitting her several times on the side of her body. She had been terrified.

After six months, Jody said she was ready to stop therapy. There were still occasions when she harmed herself with abrasions, but they were less frequent. She was more able to be in touch with—and convey—her authentic emotional self and had developed a supportive and confiding relationship with a member of the school staff. Her home life was still difficult, but school and friendships were a haven for her, and she was no longer a "one-person counselling service", as she put it, to her friends but was willing to also confide in them in a more reciprocally supportive manner.

The Future for Family Therapy with Self-Harm?

In 2018, David Cottrell and colleagues reported on the results of the SHIFT study—the largest ever UK study into the effectiveness of family therapy for self-harm (Cottrell et al., 2018). Disappointingly, no additional benefits were found for family therapy over treatment as usual as measured by repeat hospital attendance. Dennis Ougrin and Joan Asarnow (2018) commenting on the study in the same issue of *Lancet Psychiatry* note that, although self-harm of any type is a strong predictor of suicide attempts, it might be that different approaches are needed for suicidal and non-suicidal youths. 'Non-suicidal' corresponds to my suggested pattern of secretive / self-regulatory self-harm, rather fewer cases of which were likely to have been seen in the SHIFT trial which used the entry criterion of hospital admission. Most secretive self-harmers are not attempting suicide; indeed, I have several times been told by young people using this pattern that their self-harm helps them to stay alive.

As Ougrin and Asarnow also note, 'treatment as usual' allows a greater flexibility of approach and personalisation of treatment compared to the necessary manualisation of the SHIFT treatment. My view is that some individual time with the young person is *always* needed since, in my experience, the discrepancy between what can be spoken of confidentially with a trusted therapist compared to what can be spoken of in the direct hearing of other family members is often vast. I also agree with Sebastian Kraemer (2019) that—as with the case of Katie (above)—prompt intervention (the same or following day after a hospital admission) allows the emotionally raw crisis of, say, a self-poisoning, to be worked with directly before post-hoc defensive rationalisations set in. As one teenage boy told me, a month after a hospital admission, "I think I was just bored". SHIFT did not include rapid intervention after hospitalisation.

As I understand it, the SHIFT manual—in line with Post-Milan practice of that period—places emphasis on *beliefs* as context for behaviours. In my experience, self-blaming beliefs are commonly found but an equally important focus is the manner in which non-mentalised *emotion* is processed through attacks on the body, either consciously or non-consciously. This either activates a caregiver (communicative / other-regulatory) or takes responsibility for that caregiver (secretive / self-regulatory)—in both cases, to adaptively attempt to reduce danger in the relationships. Incorporating ideas of mentalisation into family therapy practice seems to be a promising way forward (Rossouw & Fonagy, 2012). It is one of the many ways that family therapy can learn from its neighbours.

Ougrin and Asarnow (2018) finish their commentary with a note of optimism that I fully support:

> As for family therapy for self-harm, the form described by Cottrell and colleagues might not be the way forward, but it certainly has not had its final word yet. Effective treatment of self-harm in young people without family involvement seems just as unlikely as effective treatment of anxiety without exposure. (p. 188)

References

Al-Sharifi, A., Krynicki, C. R., & Upthegrove, R. (2015). Self-harm and ethnicity: A systematic review. *International Journal of Social Psychiatry, 61*, 600–612.

Bateson, G. (1972). *Steps to an ecology of mind.* Balantine.

Beebe, B., & Lachmann, F. (2002). *Infant research and adult treatment: Co-constructing interactions.* The Analytic Press.

Blasco-Fontecilla, H., Fernández-Fernández, R., Colino, L., Fajardo, L., Perteguer-Barrio, R., & de Leon, J. (2016). The addictive model of self-harming (non-suicidal and suicidal) behaviour. *Frontiers of Psychiatry.* https://doi.org/10.3389/fpsyt.2016.00008

Boszormenyi-Nagy, I., & Krasner, B. (1986). *Between give and take: A clinical guide to contextual therapy: Conversations in theory and practice.* Basic Books.

Campbell, D., & Hale, R. (1991). Suicidal acts. In J. Holmes (Ed.), *Textbook of psychotherapy and psychiatric practice* (pp. 286–305). Churchill Livingstone.

Cottrell, D., Wright-Hughes, A., Collinson, M., Boston, P., Eisler, I., Fortune, S., Graham, E., Green, J., House, A., Kerfoot, M., Owens, D., Saloniki, E., Simic, M., Lambert, F., Rothwell, J., Tubeuf, S., & Farrin, A. (2018). Effectiveness of systemic family therapy versus treatment as usual for young people after self-harm: A pragmatic, phase 3, multicentre, randomised controlled trial. *Lancet Psychiatry, 5*, 203–216.

Crittenden, P. (2008). *Raising parents: Attachment representation, and treatment.* Routledge.

Fairbairn, R. (1952). *Psychoanalytic studies of the personality*. Tavistock and Routledge.

Ferenczi, S. (1988). *The Clinical diary of Sándor Ferenczi*. (J. Dupont, (Ed.); M. Balint & N. Jackson, Trans.). Harvard University Press.

Fonagy, P., & Target, M. (1995). Understanding the violent patient: The use of the body and the role of the father. *International Journal of Psychoanalysis, 76*, 487–502.

Fonagy, P., Gergeley, G., Jurist, E., & Target, M. (2002). *Affect regulation, mentalization, and the development of the self*. Other Press.

Horne, O., & Csipke, E. (2008). *Understanding self-harm*. SANE.

Kraemer, S. (2019). Deliberate self-poisoning by teenagers. *Archives of Disease in Childhood, 104*, 728–729.

McMahon, E., Hemming, L., Robinson, J., & Griffin, E. (2022). Editorial: Suicide and self-harm in young people. *Frontiers in Psychiatry, 13*, 1120396. https://doi.org/10.3389/fpsyt.2022.1120396

Ougrin, D., & Asarnow, J. (2018). The end of family therapy for self-harm, or a new beginning? *Lancet Psychiatry, 5*, 188–189.

Ougrin, D., Zundel, D., & Ng, A. (2010). *Self-harm in young people: A therapeutic assessment manual*. Hodder Arnold.

Pocock, D. (2009). Working with emotional systems: Four new maps. In C. Flaskas & D. Pocock (Eds.), *Systems and psychoanalysis: Contemporary integrations in family therapy* (pp. 93–109). Karnac.

Pocock, D. (2011). When anger endangers relationships: Self-harm as a systemic solution. *Context, 115*, 63–66.

Rossouw, T., & Fonagy, P. (2012). Mentalization-based treatment for self-harm in adolescents. *Journal of the American Academy of Child and Adolescent Psychiatry, 51*, 1304–1313.

Warne, N., Heron, J., Mars, B., Moran, P., Stewart, A., Munafò, M., Biddle, L., Skinner, A., Gunnell, D., & Bould, H. (2021). Comorbidity of self-harm and disordered eating in young people: Evidence from a UK population-based cohort. *Journal of Affective Disorders, 282*, 386–390.

Watzlawick, P., Bavelas, J., & Jackson, D. (1967). *Pragmatics of human communication: A study of interactional patterns, pathologies, and paradoxes and problem resolution*. Norton.

Winnicott, D. W. (1986). The concept of the false self. In C. Winnicott, R. Shepherd, & M. Davis (Eds.), *Home is where we start from: Essays by a psychoanalyst* (pp. 65–70). Norton.

13

Critical Realism: Why Bother?

> [C]ritical realism can certainly embrace adherents of other positions … In practice, my wager is that many will come to embrace critical realism, if only as a result of an appreciation of its greater inclusiveness. Roy Bhaskar (2016, p. 210)

In March 1972, Hiroo Onada, a second lieutenant in the Imperial Japanese Army, walked out of a Philippines' jungle and finally surrendered. He hadn't realised that World War II had been over for thirty-seven years. The world had simply moved on without him. This sobering tale came unbidden to my mind after a respected senior family therapy colleague, on hearing about this book, diplomatically raised the question about whether the new generation of systemic family therapists was any more interested in discussions of epistemological / philosophical issues which had burned brightest around thirty-five years ago. The world of family therapy had, he implied, also moved on. It's a fair question and perhaps one I should have thought more about nine months ago before starting to rake over those embers! He followed this up with an even harder question: did the apparent "infatuation" with those ideas, that

D. Pocock, *Expanding the Limits of Individual and Family Therapies*, Palgrave Texts in Counselling and Psychotherapy, https://doi.org/10.1007/978-3-031-76309-0_13

seemed so important at the time, make any real difference to the families we subsequently worked with? Hmm …

I am, of course, more than a little biased but I want to give a hard YES to the question of contemporary relevance. Critical realism is a progressive development for all psychotherapies precisely *because* it refuses to take sides in the old modern versus postmodern epistemology wars. It avoids the extremes to take a third position in which all theories of individuals and families and wider systems are welcomed, including those consigned to that back-room of family therapy misleadingly entitled 'First Order'. Postmodernism is returned to its valued role as a critic of the power of metanarratives (single dominating ideas subjugating other meanings) by deposing it from its paradoxical position in family therapy as *the replacement* metanarrative for modernism. Framing this as a dialectic process, if modernism was the thesis, and postmodernism the antithesis, then critical realism is the new synthesis.

I won't rehash all the arguments in favour; I hope these are explicit—or at least implicit—throughout the book, so in summing-up my case for relevance I'll make just six points.

First, as a philosophy of open systems, critical realism provides, in my view, a coherent basis for all forms of psychotherapy. It is finding influence in psychoanalysis (Collier, 1981; Will, 1986; Norrie, 2020), Gestalt therapy (Sternek, 2010), person-centred therapy (Hauser, 2023), as well as making inroads into psychology (Pilgrim, 2020). As with the nineteenth century standardisation of railway gauges in the UK, a shared epistemological and ontological foundation opens the intriguing prospect of a smoother passage for ideas to trundle across the borders of our psychotherapy neighbours. I hope this book has gone some way to demonstrate that possibility. To extend the metaphor, most of Europe uses the same track gauge as the UK. It is nationalist politics and protectionism (both mostly on the UK side) that currently inhibits free trade and travel. I don't think I need to spell-out the parallels with psychotherapy traditions.

Second, the dualisms that have dominated family therapy development, and to a lesser extent psychoanalysis, are shown to be no longer meaningful by critical realism. The distinctions modern / postmodern, structural / post-structural, lineal / circular, constructionism / realism, Family Therapy Part One / Part Two, autonomous / relational, and qualitative / quantitative forms of research all lose their causal power to divide the field. Even strong constructionists are necessarily covert realists. That isn't to say that tribalism within and between psychotherapies on epistemological and ontological grounds will not continue, only that it is no longer philosophically justified. This is why multi-positional or integrative therapeutic approaches float perfectly well in practice and do not founder on dualist rocks. There are now rational grounds to argue that we are all realists; it only remains to decide what kind we will be—naïve, covert, or critical. Similarly, critical realism shows that, in our production of knowledge, we are also moderate constructionists, whether acknowledged or not.

Third, while all theories are ultimately fallible, it is part of our everyday experience that some ideas about the world are less fallible than others. I can very reliably use my internal map of my house to find the front door when the postwoman knocks; I am at more of a loss to know how much the heavy rain is contributing to her looking unhappy today. Where we can, we try to test our ideas for object-adequacy much of the time. Both qualitative and quantitative research are formal ways of doing this, allowing greater confidence to be placed in some socially constructed maps than others, assisting us in making rational choices. In critical realism, science is no longer reduced to the production of just another story as in postmodernism, or valorised as the search for objective, value-free, context-free, and invariant knowledge as in positivism. Instead, science tells us about mechanisms, powers, or tendencies that may or may not combine in an open system to form an event. Science cannot meaningfully begin and end with fixed laws for the relationship between events, since such 'covering laws' only exist in the closed system of experimental conditions. Bateson's (1972) concern about science chopping-up the world to create positivist scientific laws is thereby addressed.

Fourth, how are we to respond to injustice when it shows up in the therapy room? Are sexual abuse, racism, and structural poverty real or just socially constructed experiences to be re-storied? Critical realism says they are always both. As Bhaskar (2016) puts it, "Homelessness is not only a conceptual question, it is also about not having a roof over one's head" (p. 12). Racism, for example, has real potential causal power beyond any storying of it. This is brute (intransitive) reality—the given half of experience (Orange, 1995). But the actualised effects of racism with an individual or family partly depend on what is made of it, individually and socially. It is in this transitive dimension that therapist can play their part, but step one is surely to acknowledge the given injustice as real. Not to do so is, at best, a missed opportunity and at worst—since absence also has causal power—an inadvertent reinforcement of the toxicity.

Fifth, the depth-realism of critical realism recognises that an event such as symptomatic behaviour is generated by multiple interacting causal tendencies, many of which are not immediately available to surface observation. Remembering the hand-torch analogy, only one of the constituent parts needed to be de-actualised to change the system and switch the light off. As with the serendipitous woodlouse incident in Chap. 7, the actualised change may not even be apparent to the participants. This provides hope that even small changes can prove transformational. Critical realism scaffolds transdisciplinary pluralism, providing plenty of vantage points for the therapist to help look for the differences that make a difference.

Sixth, the *critical* half of critical realism reminds us that our knowledge is socially constructed, with all the caution that should entail. This means holding theory lightly, and reflexively, in full awareness of the role of bias, and the seductions of language. As with my blind-man poem counterfactual, the more standpoints we have the less likely we are to be in thrall to any one, and the more resources we can bring to flexibly serve the dialogical therapeutic process.

Do Theory and Philosophy Matter?

Picking up the second question of my friendly colleague, and taking it back a step further, do we, in fact, need theory at all, and if so, how much, and what kind? In the opening chapter of his recent book, *Becoming an Effective Family Therapist*, Peter Rober (2024) summarises the emerging research evidence that some therapists are more effective than others:

> [E]ffective therapists succeed in building a good therapeutic relationship with many different clients, including challenging or difficult clients (Wampold et al., 2017). In other words the therapeutic relationship is the crucial concern of the effective therapist. (p. 19)

There is not a word in this, or in Rober's book as a whole, that I disagree with, but what is the role of theory in helping those relationships move in the direction of beneficial change? From the research, having a model of therapy matters, but which *particular model* barely seems significant and, by some margin, is less important than the strength of the alliance and of therapist factors such as warmth, empathy, presence, and sensitivity to client goals and feedback (Rober, 2024).

I was a serial modeller for my first decade as a family therapist. Structural, strategic, Milan, transgenerational, Post-Milan, brief solution-focussed: each held me in its power for a time, until they lost their shine and I moved on to the next. I didn't exactly decide to give up on models; after a while the constraints of model-fidelity just didn't seem to be worth the effort. Instead, the boundaries of the *models* gradually dissolved, freeing-up a *muddle* of ideas derived, as I've shown, from many sources (Pocock, 1999) including psychoanalysis and research. I found that some ideas, combination of ideas, and ways of expressing them, seemed to fit better with some people and their problems than others. Rather than pull information out of my observations to fit a specific model, I found this looser approach allowed me to find ideas, combinations of ideas, and ways of translating those ideas that might fit better with *that* relational moment with *that* client in *those* contexts. So, gradually, I adopted a relationship-first rather than a theory or model-first approach. The same is true for my individual therapy. From supervising individual and family therapists, I think a lot of people—maybe even the majority—work in this way. For Glenn Larner (2002, 2011), our ethical responsibility to the other means drawing on a wide range of approaches to find what helps. As said, the very fact that integrative and pluralistic approaches are possible in practice (see also Goldner et al., 1990) suggests that we should reappraise the philosophical and ideological splits that *appear* to hold them apart. This is a role for critical realism as under-labourer, clearing away untenable and divisive philosophical distinctions to create a new inclusive foundation.

If clinical theory matters, which I think it does, then what is the status of that knowledge? This takes us inevitably to philosophy. If we don't articulate a philosophical position, I think we can fall into the everyday invisible pull of naïve realism and, like Saxe's blind men, forget our role in the observation and come to quietly assume that we have in our minds is the objective truth. This risks a loss of flexibility in our thinking.

If we are using theories of individual, family, and wider systems (and how can we not?) then I think we should do so in full knowledge that we have made a choice (or choices) and become aware of the limitations of that choice. This, whether we like it or not, cannot be separated from our philosophies even—perhaps especially—if we don't think we have any. This is why I believe questions of epistemology and ontology must not be left in the past.

As things stand in family therapy, the dominance and wide acceptance of strong constructionism in many parts of the world stand on highly contestable arguments, but with little recognition or memory of just how insecure those foundations are. As I have argued, realism—overtly rejected under the sway of postmodernism—returns in disguise to all strong constructionists in practice. If we take seriously Foucault's (1977) argument that knowledge and power are the same, is it not better for our realism to be out in the open where we can keep an eye on it and hold ourselves and our power in check? This is the second-order position—holding theory lightly, reflexively, and with humility. I believe that has value for all psychotherapies and can help our maps of individual and family processes serve the relational process rather than attempt to drive it.

I should add (as I have written elsewhere) that I do welcome many of the methods that the postmodern turn has inspired. Dialogical therapy is the approach that I most identify with, and I can, for example, hardly think of a family or individual I have worked with in which narrative techniques ('thickening' new descriptions, externalising) or solution focussed ideas (searching for exceptions) have not played some part. I just don't buy the accompanying anti-realist philosophical rhetoric, so I can allow in other methods and ways of thinking to play alongside when I sense they might help.

Top Ten Limits

Turning back to the title of the book, what are the limits that critical realism, hosting a transdisciplinary approach, might help us to expand beyond? The following are best considered as risks rather than inevitable impediments. Some apply to specific psychotherapy modalities and some to all. In no particular order:

1. *The disappearance of power and all depth realism in shallow circular empiricism/positivism.*
   As we explored in Chap. 4, *apparently* powerless circular relationships between behavioural events are simply an artefact of superficial empirical / positivist surface observation. In the hypothetical example explored, the seemingly power-free observable relationship between male dominance and female submission is generated by combinations of deeper causal powers including historical violence, patriarchy / misogyny, limited housing, structural poverty, family scripts, and football team failure. Power is not, I believe, a myth as Bateson suggests, but its deep causes are not handed to us on an observational plate; they need to be collaboratively searched for.
2. *Assuming only language and discourse have real causal powers and rejecting all other theories of—and research into—individual and relational processes.*
   To accept the power of texts, narrative, and discourses, as strong constructionists do, is to commit to their very existence thereby confirming ontological realism. To repeat Pilgrim's (2020) question, why then "only isolate words as being real and nothing else? Why special plead for language, rather than other palpable and hidden forces in our lives?" p. 35. Our ethical responsibility to the individuals and families we work with surely means bringing as many reliable resources for understanding as we can to the therapeutic table.
3. *Assuming that science is empiricist-positivist or just another story, and / or has nothing to teach us.*
   Critical realist science invites us to create the best account of reality that we can. As illustrated in Chap. 1, the treatment of John Bowlby's

attachment theory within the main streams of psychoanalysis and family therapy exemplifies a regrettably dismissive attitude to the contributions of science by some psychotherapy approaches especially when it challenges the 'received wisdom' and practices of the big names and movements. But challenge is the entire point of good science, assisting us in using what Bhaskar calls 'judgemental rationality' in choosing between—and improving the object-adequacy of—our social constructed maps. Critical realism changes our *understanding* of science when it comes to open systems but does not reject it.

4. *Assuming that other therapy traditions have nothing to teach us.*
   Once we accept that the world is an open system made up of a myriad of structured, layered, and interacting causal tendencies then we encounter a complexity that cannot be encapsulated by a single psychotherapy tradition. All traditions have something important to say if we are willing to listen, together with allied fields such as psychology, anthropology, and sociology. Transdisciplinarity in critical realism is not an eccentricity, it is routine. Critical realism supports integrative developments in many psychotherapies—perhaps the biggest contemporary movement of all, but a quiet one without the usual accompanying fanfare of new models and movements.
5. *Inattention to non-conscious causal powers of the inner world of individuals in relationship.*
   The critical realist, Christian Smith (2010), offers this comprehensive definition of personhood which is then unpacked throughout his brilliant book.

   By *person* I mean a conscious, reflexive, embodied, self-transcending centre of subjective experience, durable identity, moral commitment who—as the efficient cause of his or her own responsible actions and interactions—exercises complex capacities for agency and intersubjectivity in order to develop and sustain his or her own incommunicable [unique, irreplaceable] self in loving relationships with other personal selves and with the non-personal world. (p. 61).

   At times in the history of family therapy, individual selves have been 'black boxes' in which only the circuitry between them was relevant. Later, for those under post-structural influence, individuals became grammatical fictions—'empty subjects'—outlines coloured in by discourses. Somewhat paradoxically, despite its post-structural affiliation, narrative therapy has promoted work with individuals in family therapy. Nevertheless, there is, I think, still considerable discomfort about the idea of the individual and relational unconscious. Smith, a sociologist, has no such qualms about including the unconscious "the depths of which in its influence on complex behaviour appears to be extensive among [and between] humans" (P. 44). We can and do exercise agency, but we don't always know why we make our choices. The depth realism of critical realism puts non-conscious internal causal powers of family scripts, myths, object-relations, internal working models, transgenerational trauma, schema, co-transference, and culture back on the agenda.

6. *Inattention to multiple systemic causal powers in the outer world (and body) of individuals.*

   Conversely, the psychoanalytic world can be reductively preoccupied with supposedly universal decontextualised unconscious internal processes of the individual. Patients, like therapists, live in a real systemic world only part of which is internal. What we make of our experiences is powerfully influenced by the unconscious domain but the multiple, ontologically real, brute, given aspects of experience in the complex system of the individual, including injustice, also find their way to the unconscious. Lynne Layton (2020), for example, reworking Bion's (1984) attacks on linking, traces the way that psychoanalytic practices that break the link between the psychic and the social "unconsciously re-create the very kind of decontextualised individual that sustains a dominant heterosexist, racist, classist, dominant [Euro-American] culture" (p. 2).

   The patient's transference is not just formed by their past; it gathers around and is shaped by the specific, ontologically real aspects of the therapist. The behaviour, thoughts, and non-conscious processes of the therapist are all context for those of the patient and vice versa. Neither is transference confined to the patient's relationship to the therapist. Like Saxe's blind men, we all process our world through the causal power of our presuppositions, all of the time.

7. *Assuming that change occurs primarily through patient insight via therapist interpretation.*
   Freud could not have known that meeting reliably with a patient and emotionally attuning to them mindfully, evenly, and non-judgementally over months or years creates the very conditions for the patient to gradually move towards attachment security. In psychoanalysis the role of consistent emotional support in good outcomes emerges strongly from research but is overshadowed by institutional assumptions that therapist interpretation is the cutting edge of change. As Donna Orange (1995, p. 98) notes, "Ideas, insights, interpretations, and other cognitive approaches may support emotional healing, but they do not provide it". Critical realism casts doubt on single causes for all events, including positive transformation.
8. *Forgetting that all successful therapy is relational and collaborative, regardless of therapist intention.*
   As above, clients are not usually passive recipients of therapists' thoughts. Any signs of this suggest worrying colonisation. The joys and struggles for new meaning and new experiences are both relational *and* autonomous. Critical realism recognises that the generation of knowledge (including knowledge of self and other) and experience is a social process. But what is understood together may not be understood in an identical way: that depends on the deep structure of each individual in their relational matrix. Critical realism does not split individual autonomy from relationality (Smith, 2010).
9. *Reification of theory through conflating map with territory.*
   A running theme throughout the book, from the Blind Men and the Elephant poem onwards, is that inattention to issues of epistemology and ontology call allow free reign to what Bhaskar (2016) calls 'the natural attitude': the everyday experience that what we see is straightforwardly outside ourselves. Those with strong single-model commitments are particularly at risk of succumbing to the naïve realist pull, but it is an ever-present risk for all therapists. Critical realism recognises that the view always includes the viewer.
10. *Forgetting that we are always part of the system.*
    The solution to the risk of reification is reflexivity—a second-order state of mind that what we see depends partly on where we stand. We

don't achieve second-order thinking by rejecting all ideas prior to the constructivist / constructionist turn as first-order. No theory can logically be first-order or second-order, that is entirely determined by how much we can responsibly own our part in the seeing. This does not mean we shall necessarily become lost in extreme relativism—there really are such ontological entities that we call 'elephants' which can be fruitfully assembled into a good-enough picture by taking up a variety of vantage points.

Summary of My Position

For those (like me) who appreciate a diagram, Fig. 13.1 summarises my take on the critical realist frame. Lower levels each, in turn, act as context for the level above. Starting at the bottom, critical realism reintroduces a realist ontology (1): an intransitive open system that can be spoken about, contra the 'ontological mutism' of some strong constructionists. The 'holy trinity' of layers of reality (2) is Bhaskar's (1977) outstanding contribution to understanding ontology. There are multiple and layered

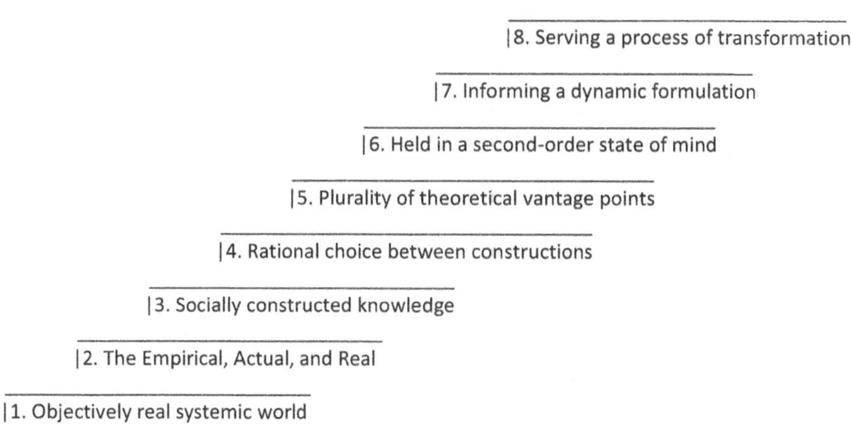

Fig. 13.1 Summary of my position

causal powers (The Real), which may or may not combine in an open system to generate an event (The Actual) which, in turn, may or may not be observable as a specific behaviour, set of behaviours, or symptoms (The Empirical). It is understood that knowledge of these causal powers is a fallible, transitive, social process (3). Nevertheless, the existence of an intransitive world, beyond all our ideas of it, enables us to exercise rational judgement (4) between constructions. We can and do make such choices all the time and science can assist us if we allow it.

We can speak meaningfully about the world only from a vantage point; there is no God's-eye view available to us, but a plurality of positions (5) enables us to engage with the complexity of open systems. For this we may need to transcend interdisciplinary boundaries. A full awareness that what we see depends on our viewpoints is the second-order state of mind (6). This allows us to be humble and flexible in our thinking and informs the lightly structured dynamic formulation in the therapist's conscious and unconscious mind (7) which continuously shifts and develops as new information arrives. This serves the collaborative therapeutic process in pursuit of positive transformation (8) for those who seek our help.

Finally ...

Let me now address you, the reader, directly. For all the strange new terms, does this approach seem oddly familiar? Is it roughly what you are already thinking and doing in practice but without necessarily articulating the underlying philosophical assumptions or exploring their full potential? That is the feedback I have received from many when I have explained basic critical realism in workshops and in other writing (Pocock, 2008, 2013). It is not for nothing that Bhaskar (2016) entitled his final summarising book *Enlightened Common Sense.*

At times this book this has necessarily involved thinking about, and reappraising, some complex intellectual concerns. I fear, looking back on what I've written, that I may not have adequately represented the deep satisfaction and, at times, the simple joy of working collaboratively with individuals and families. I want to end with that: there is really nothing more interesting than people. Martin Amis warns that, in writing, "one should avoid cliches like the plague" but, nearing the end of a long career, I can honestly say that I wouldn't have missed it for the world. If you've made it to the end of the book, congratulations, and thank you for your company.

References

Bateson, G. (1972). *Steps to an ecology of mind.* Balantine.

Bhaskar, R. (1977). *A realist philosophy of science.* Harvester.

Bhaskar, R. (2016). *Enlightened common sense: The philosophy of critical realism.* Routledge.

Bion, W. (1984). Attacks on linking. In W. Bion (Ed.), *Second thoughts* (pp. 93–109). Aronson.

Collier, A. (1981). Scientific realism and the human world: The case for psychoanalysis. *Radical Philosophy, 29*, 8–18.

Foucault, M. (1977). *Discipline and punish: The birth of the prison.* Pantheon Books.

Goldner, V., Penn, P., Sheinberg, M., & Walker, G. (1990). Love and violence: Gender paradoxes in volatile attachments. *Family Process, 29*, 343–364.

Hauser, H. (2023, December, 1–18). More than *my* experience: An argument for critical realism in person-centred psychotherapy. *Person-Centred and Experiential Psychotherapies.*

Larner, G. (2002). Towards a critical therapy. *The International Journal of Critical Psychology, 6*, 9–29.

Larner, G. (2011). Deconstructing theory: Towards an ethical therapy. *Theory and Psychology, 21*, 821–839.

Layton, L. (2020). *Towards a social psychoanalysis: Culture, character, and normative unconscious processes.* Routledge.

Norrie, A. (2020). The flesh made word: Critical realism, psychoanalysis, and the ontology of love. *Journal of Critical Realism, 19*, 341–361.

Orange, D. (1995). *Emotional understanding: Studies in psychoanalytic epistemology.* Guilford.

Pilgrim, D. (2020). *Critical realism for psychologists.* Routledge.

Pocock, D. (1999). Loose ends. *Journal of Family Therapy, 21*, 187–194.

Pocock, D. (2008). Be dragons here? Why family systems therapy needs a new operating system. *Context, 97*, 20–23.

Pocock, D. (2013). A philosophy of practice for systemic psychotherapy: The case for critical realism. *Journal of Family Therapy, 37*, 167–183.
Rober, P. (2024). *Becoming an effective family therapist: Research, practice, and case studies*. Routledge.
Smith, C. (2010). *What is a person? Rethinking humanity, social life, and the moral good from the person up*. University of Chicago Press.
Sternek, K. (2010). Critical realism, the epistemic position of Gestalt Theoretical Psychotherapy. *Gestalt Theory, 43*, 13–28.
Wampold, B., Baldwin, S., Holtforth, M., & Imel, Z. (2017). What characterises effective therapists? In L. Castonguay & C. Hill (Eds.), *How and why are some therapists better than others? Understanding therapist effects* (pp. 37–53). American Psychological Association.
Will, D. (1986). Psychoanalysis and the new philosophy of science. *The International Review of Psycho-Analysis, 13*, 163–173.

Index

D. Pocock, *Expanding the Limits of Individual and Family Therapies*, Palgrave Texts in Counselling and Psychotherapy, https://doi.org/10.1007/978-3-031-76309-0

C

The manufacturer's authorised representative in the EU is Springer
Nature Customer Service Centre GmbH, Europaplatz 3, 69115 Heidelberg,
Germany. If you have any concerns regarding our products, please
contact ProductSafety@springernature.com

Printed and bound by CPI Group (UK) Ltd, Croydon, CR0 4YY
22/07/2026
02174132-0001